BRIDGING CULTURAL CONFLICTS

BRIDGING CULTURAL CONFLICTS

A NEW APPROACH FOR a CHANGING WORLD

Michelle LeBaron

Foreword by Mohammed Abu-Nimer

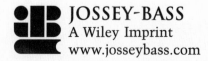

JOSSEY-BASS
A Wiley Imprint
www.josseybass.com

Published by Jossey-Bass
A Wiley Imprint
989 Market Street, San Francisco, CA 94103-1741   www.josseybass.com

Jossey-Bass books and products are available through most bookstores. To contact Jossey-Bass directly call our Customer Care Department within the U.S. at 800-956-7739, outside the U.S. at 317-572-3986 or fax 317-572-4002.

Jossey-Bass also publishes its books in a variety of electronic formats. Some content that appears in print may not be available in electronic books.

Library of Congress Cataloging-in-Publication Data

LeBaron, Michelle, 1956–
  Bridging cultural conflicts: a new approach for a changing world /
Michelle LeBaron.— 1st ed.
      p. cm.
Includes bibliographical references and index.
  ISBN 0-7879-6431-X (alk. paper)
  1. Culture conflict. 2. Conflict management. I. Title.
  BF698.9.C8L43 2004
  303.6'9—dc21   2002154427

FIRST EDITION
HB Printing 10 9 8 7 6 5 4 3 2 1

CONTENTS

❧ PART THREE

❧ PART FOUR

LIST OF FIGURES

To David

and

to all whose hearts belong to peace

FOREWORD

Conflict emerges when people have difficulties dealing with differences—differences related to race, ethnicity, language, class, gender, age, religion, and more. These differences influence the lenses through which people view each other, often leading to mismatched perceptions and expectations, resulting in conflict. How can we constructively deal with these differences so that conflict contributes to positive political and social change? For twenty years I have worked with thousands of culturally diverse people to find ways to answer this question. Through this work I have come to see that cultural and power differences are central to the global and local conflicts we face.

In *Bridging Cultural Conflicts,* Michelle LeBaron presents us with a timely guide for working with these complexities. This book is the first comprehensive road map connecting the fields of conflict resolution and intercultural communication. It shows readers how to actively handle cultural conflicts while also remaining authentic and true to their cultural identities.

Michelle describes a set of new tools to address cultural conflict, including cultural fluency, conflict fluency, and mindful awareness. These tools are flexible resources for addressing the multifaceted interplay between culture and conflict at personal and political levels. Mindful awareness is fundamental, because conflict is never just "out there" but is always relational and social. We are well served by learning how our personal and collective cultural lenses shape what we see, how we relate to others, and what we perceive as our choices. There can be no intercultural conflict resolution if we do not move beyond our ethnocentric views and blind spots.

Awareness of the multiple identities that each of us carries simultaneously (for example, one person may belong to many groups, including parents, soccer players, males, teachers, authors, Muslims, and so forth) is a basic tool for learning how to shift our perspectives and expand our behavioral choices. As we recognize our own and others' multifaceted identities, we are better able to see the "big pictures" of our conflicts and the contexts, both private and public, in which they take place. This awareness comes from being willing to see culture both within and among us and from developing cultural fluency.

With her concept of cultural fluency, Michelle reminds us of our need for a language and an approach that can deepen our understanding of cultural dynamics. Cultural fluency goes hand in hand with conflict fluency, allowing us to explore and trace the contours of conflict and the differences it surfaces, rather than frantically seeking similarities and unity as so many approaches to intercultural relations suggest.

The events of September 11, 2001, confronted us with the reality that it is essential to become aware of both our similarities and our differences, engaging in interfaith and intercultural dialogues to explore and understand our respective worldviews. Through dialogue we come to understand the nature and roles of culture in our changing worlds. Michelle uses the beautiful metaphor of an underground river to convey the influence of culture on our conflicts: "Cultures flow through our lives like underground rivers, powerfully nurturing, potently influencing, and sometimes dividing." This metaphor makes it clear that culture is an important influence, even when it seems, on the surface, that people are fighting over resources and culture has nothing to do with it. Everything around us is shaped and influenced by the underground, often unacknowledged, dynamics of culture. Because we do not see them, we often neglect the importance of cultural dynamics in our conflict resolution processes.

Through careful examination of real-life examples, Michelle demonstrates the importance of cultural differences and then provides a clear conceptual framework for working through them. She writes in a voice that is accessible, drawing from the intercultural communication and conflict resolution fields. She distills research and experience, offering practices from the use of metaphors to adventure learning for addressing interpersonal and intergroup conflicts. Readers with or without academic training will find themselves acquiring creative tools for expanding their understanding of others as long as they are willing to try.

The stories and examples used in this book are an enormous resource for learning, teaching, and training. Using her life experiences in intercultural training and teaching, Michelle tells stories from indigenous, urban industrial, and rural communities around the world. These stories and examples capture the need not only to pay extra attention to the role of culture but to integrate cultural awareness into every aspect of our lives.

On a foundation of mindful awareness and fluency with both culture and conflict, Michelle introduces an approach called dynamic engagement. Dynamic engagement applied with a spirit of dialogue provides a way to change conflictual relationships to transformative ones. Learning, creativity, and individual and collective growth arise from the constructive shifts in relationships facilitated by dynamic engagement.

These two ideas—dynamic engagement and a spirit of dialogue—are exactly what is needed to address the growing schisms between Muslim and Western communities and policymakers. The last decade has seen an increasing gap between these groups, fed by cultural misunderstandings and stereotypical categorizations. Michelle's creative idea of a spirit of dialogue, in which we make space for another in our hearts and open our minds to receive what is said, would do much to deepen understanding among Muslims, Christians, and others in Western societies.

Above all, Michelle asks us to listen and to care on both the local and global levels. She asks us to share our pictures—those that are the same and those that are different. With attention not only to tools but to the spirit with which we use the tools, she gives us ways to apply the long list of creative practices this book suggests. Without the listening and caring this book promotes, we will continue to experience cultural misunderstandings and miscommunications, becoming further isolated in our economic, political, religious, and cultural enclaves. Given the danger and estrangement this picture evokes, we are well advised to avail ourselves of the wisdom in *Bridging Cultural Conflicts*.

Mohammed Abu-Nimer, Ph.D.
American University
School of International Service
International Peace and Conflict Resolution Program
Washington, D.C.

ACKNOWLEDGMENTS

Thanks are due to many people who contributed to the process of conceiving and writing this book. I am indebted to colleagues who contributed to these ideas, sharing their experience and exuding creativity. They include Amr Abdalla, Sharmin Ahmed, Ann Baker, Mary Clark, Craig Darling, Jo Golden, Kenneth Hawkins, Sara Looney, Mark McCrea, Chris Mitchell, Catherine Morris, George Renwick, and Lisa Schirch. For many hours shared, questions explored, and new ideas tried, my thanks.

I appreciate the inspiration and rich imagination of the faculty of the Summer Institute for Intercultural Communication, and especially Janet and Milton Bennett for inviting me to develop a course on conflict and culture over ten years ago.

My editor at Jossey-Bass, Alan Rinzler, caught the spark of the idea, provided me prompt and always helpful feedback, and supported the process of creating this book in multiple ways. My assistant Venashri Pillay helped immeasurably, always ready with insightful observations and generous suggestions.

Thanks are due to my students, from whom I constantly learn. Graduate students at the Institute for Conflict Analysis and Resolution at George Mason University have enriched my work in many ways, posing questions and proposing links that stretch my thinking. Participants in the Caux Scholars Program, sponsored by the visionary leaders at Initiatives of Change, have brought new perspectives, energy, and heart to conversations. Graduate students at York University, the University of Victoria, the University of British Columbia, American University, and Pepperdine University have contributed thoughtful applications and creative suggestions. I also very much appreciate the support of the directors of these programs, Mohammed Abu-Nimer, Sara Cobb, Paul Emond, Barry Hart, John Hogarth, Randy Lowry, Julie McFarlane, Maureen Maloney, and Peter Robinson. Maggie Little and Lois Pegg at the University of Victoria have been unfailingly supportive and have encouraged me to speak many of these ideas into the world.

Sincere thanks to the following students and colleagues who have generously allowed me to relate their stories and case examples: Tatsushi Arai, Karen Bhangoo, Eleftherios Michael, Ismael Muvingi, Venashri Pillay, Ibrahim Sharquieh, Katherine Slaney, and Zheng Wang.

Bouquets to the members of the culture working group at George Mason University: Tatsushi Arai, Karen Bhangoo, Nike Carstarphen, Al Fuertes, Pushpa Iyer, Venashri Pillay, Catalina Rojas, Ibrahim Sharquieh, and Cheryl Simmons. I look forward to your continuing work on this important topic.

Special thanks to the wise women: Fanchon for the irreplaceable lunches, Zena for visions of place and the place of Spirit, Jo for "getting it" early and often, Ann for hearing inside the words, Jessie for the sparks, Karen for unfailing support, Mary for the inspiration of her writing, Sara for believing, Elena for stories shared, Riki for chocolate and renewing conversations, Sheila for being creative—your listening hearts and wise ways stay with me always.

Boundless appreciation to David, without whose ideas, questions, clarity, and support this book would not be what it is.

Those nearest me were the most enveloped in the project yet showed patience and understanding beyond their years: Genevieve, Emily, Justin, and Daniel—may each of you continue in your commitment to creating a more just and free world.

The ideas in this book are cast now to the wind, to sprout wherever they will. For the errors within them, the responsibility is mine. For their fertility, the credit is shared.

M. L.

BRIDGING CULTURAL CONFLICTS

PART ONE

Capacities for Engaging Cultural Conflict

CHAPTER ONE

Bridging Cultures
Uncovering Paths
That Connect Us

Culture. Cultured pearls, cultured appearance, throat culture, cultural heritage, youth culture. *Culture* is one of the most common words in our vocabularies and one of the most challenging to understand. Culture breathes richness and vitality into our lives; it animates those things that make us human—meaning-making, identity, belonging. Just when we think we have a grasp on culture, it can slip between our fingers like water flowing to the sea.

Conflict. What comes to mind when this word appears? For many, the associations are negative. Few people welcome conflict as an intriguing opportunity for learning and change. Many prefer to avoid conflict when they can. Notice the negative tone that is often associated with *conflict:* conflict of interest, conflict prone, conflict torn, conflict ravaged. To suggest befriending conflict is like inviting cruise ship passengers on a storm-tossed sea to enjoy the seascape—it is hard to enjoy amid the fear, threatened destruction, and sick stomachs that so often accompany it.

Conflict and culture. When these two words come together, the associations are also largely negative: culture wars, culture of fear, culture clash, culture of conflict. This book is about the intersections of culture and conflict. It seeks to find—and invent where none can be found—constructive, hopeful connections between the two. The purpose is practical. It is to show ways of understanding and healing conflicts that recognize culture as an underground river: full of life, dynamic, and powerful in shaping the course of conflicts, yet often outside awareness.

Culture is integral to understanding conflict. It cannot be separated from conflict, but neither does it cause it. Like the cultural influences in our lives, underground rivers flow continuously, feeding and shaping the landscapes that sustain us. Though culture often goes unnamed and undetected, it is a vital influence in our lives. Culture is central to our identity and the ways we make meaning. Conflict occurs when identities and meanings feel threatened.

From cultures we learn the language of relationship that connects us to others, confirming our belonging and deepening our purpose. In conflict we react because we care. We care to protect our identities and the meanings we cherish. We care to preserve our ways of life, our views of the world. We care to safeguard those we love. Even across the chasm that divides us from an adversary, there is connection. If we had no connection and no interdependence, there would be no conflict. We could, and would, simply walk away. Negative as the relationship may be, relationship there is, sustained by feelings between and within us, whether positive or negative.

This book seeks to explore our relationships as we express culture and encounter conflict. The metaphor of culture as a life-source that both animates and heals conflict informs the capacities, practices, and tools presented in this book. Together, these capacities, practices, and tools show practical and creative ways to bridge cultural conflicts. They draw on multiple ways of knowing to inform creative means of shifting stuck situations. In the end, culture, an underground life source, and conflict, carrier of challenge and change, come together as partners in our unending quest for belonging to life.

This book will be most useful as it is applied. Can you think of a conflict where you wondered what culture had to do with it but did not have the answer? As you read this book, choose an experience you have had in which culture and conflict were part of the picture. Bring it vividly to mind. Then relate the ideas in this book to the experience as you go along. Notice what you might have done differently if you had had this book. Consider how the choices you made might have been expanded if you had thought of them in the light of the stories and examples in the book. Collect sparks that illuminate new strategies for use in the future.

The experience you choose may be something that only you are aware of, a difference that mattered to you but was not or could not be discussed. Or it may be something that surfaced between you and someone else. It may be something that happened between two groups of people when you were a member of one of the groups, or it could involve a conflict you tried to help with as an outsider. Here are some examples of situations that might help you bring an experience of your own to mind:

As a busy account executive, you set aside time at lunch to go to the bank to make a deposit. The transaction is difficult. The teller seems unfriendly and reserved. She puts a hold on your funds even though another teller deposited an identical check for you last week without placing the funds on hold. You have an impulse to argue with her, but decide against it, resigned. As you reflect on the experience, you wonder whether culture had anything to do with it. After all, the teller asked you to repeat some of the things you said, and you have had experiences like this before since English is your fourth language.

ᕫ

As a young woman of twenty-four, you have the world at your feet. You are in the middle of earning a master's degree and live in a community where lectures by cutting-edge scholars and modern art exhibits are part of your daily life. You also belong to several activist organizations on campus. You are in the middle of writing your thesis, supervised by a woman in her sixties. She has grown increasingly distant lately, commenting on your tired appearance (too many late nights), your behavior (too vocal and opinionated), and your lack of deference to a male colleague on the committee (unseemly for a woman). She once commented that women in their twenties should settle down rather than roaming around "with packs of tarts and cads" without direction or discipline. You suspect that her distant and judgmental behavior relates to generational differences between you and her. Because you share her ethnic background, you hadn't anticipated this kind of problem. Worse, the tension is playing out over your thesis. She wants a structured, by-the-book approach that conforms to research standards in your discipline. You are interested in exploratory, creative scholarship through which you can apply some of the new ideas that animate the art and social activism you love. You are too far into your work to change supervisors, but the tension is getting harder to navigate.

∿

You have finally graduated as a teacher and find yourself in front of your own class for the first time. As you look out over the faces, you realize that most of them do not look like you. They have come from different countries; they speak a dozen different languages in their various homes. You realize that whether you are teaching geography or history, mathematics or writing, you will be teaching cultural understandings that differ from theirs, and the responsibility seems huge. Early in the year, you notice with surprise and dismay that a historic event you portray as a humanitarian action by your country is received by a group of students as unjustified interference that escalated conflict and supported an unjust regime for political ends.

∿

You are a community mediator in a small town midway between the Pacific and Atlantic Oceans. You decided to become a mediator because you wanted to give something back to the community. You liked the idea of people's taking responsibility for their own neighborhoods rather than relying on outsiders or authority figures to take charge. As you mediated your first handful of cases, you became increasingly concerned that your lack of training about cultural differences was a liability. In one difficult conflict between people from cultures unfamiliar to you, you took decisive action to calm emotions and remind everyone to stick to the facts. The parties failed to reach agreement. Later you read in a magazine that people from these cultures are typically comfortable with high levels of expressiveness and emotionality. Perhaps you cut the mediation participants off from what might have been a productive direction. You wonder how to increase your effectiveness in working with those from different groups.

We all encounter cultural differences every day, in our communities, workplaces, classrooms, and homes. Yet often the workings of cultures remain mysterious to us. Many of us muster as much goodwill as we can when we face visible differences, and hope somehow that will get us through.

But keeping our heads above water when complex cultural dynamics surround us is not just a matter of good intentions. Developing constructive ways to work with conflict and cultural differences is a key requirement of participation and leadership in today's world. Although this is a lifelong project, never finished because it is undertaken in the midst of constant change, it is possible to make progress. This book is offered as a way for all those whose work or personal life brings them into contact with cultural differences to increase their understandings of culture as it plays out in their relationships both smooth and conflictual.

Bridging cultural conflict is more important now than ever before. We stand at a crossroads between two metaphors for our global future: on one side is the market, with its unending appetite for expansion, and on the other is the heart, with its inextinguishable hope for connection. In books, television programs, and public events, the sacred and the secular seem pitted against each other in dramatic and sometimes destructive ways. We encounter a seemingly binary and divided world in book titles like *Jihad Vs. McWorld* and *The Lexus and the Olive Tree*.[1] There are other ways to understand our differences, ways that acknowledge the multifaceted richness these differences lend to our lives. And there are ways to work through the differences to deepen relationships and prevent destructive conflict, ways both generative and hopeful.

If we are to realize our human potential for creativity; if we are to belong to shared pictures in our diversity, conflicts arising from our differences must be addressed respectfully and thoughtfully. We need new ways of moving through cultural conflicts, ways that associate them with learning, growth, and constructive social change. Engaging conflict in partnership with others, we imagine new futures instead of perpetuating old conflicts that wreak destruction in our neighborhoods, workplaces, and nations.

Culture and Conflict in Focus

For many Americans and Canadians, culture and conflict came screeching into focus on September 11, 2001. Cultural conflict was no longer something "over there," dividing Palestinians and

Israelis, Serbs and Croats, or English and Irish. The violence that ripped through a pristine September morning was apparently perpetrated by men who shared some cultural identities including religion, ethnicity, and political perspective, though not nationality. U.S. officials were quick to declare war on terrorism and the terrorist group Al Qaeda, while the alleged mastermind of the attacks, Osama bin Laden, reiterated his vow to counter American "occupation of the holy places," a reference to the Gulf War and U.S. bases in Saudi Arabia. Were we experiencing the clash of civilizations Samuel Huntington once predicted[2] or something not yet named?

News pundits everywhere scrambled for information to address the many questions that arose from the events of that tragic morning. As they wove stories together, religion, ethnicity, nationality, and gender were necessarily part of the mix. A language of difference marked these journalistic explorations—distinctions between them and us, goodness and evil, Muslims and Westerners. This language of difference arose naturally enough from pain, fear, and anger in the face of the horrific, unjustifiable acts.

In the days following September 11, pleas came from faith and community leaders to recognize that the great majority of Muslims decried the attacks. Even as people came together to mourn, others lashed out. A desire to strike back apparently motivated attacks against people based on their appearance, religion, and nonwhite identities.

> Worshippers at Idriss Mosque in north Seattle were threatened with a gun and fired upon, and cars outside the mosque were doused with gasoline. No one was injured because the gun misfired.
>
> ᘓ
>
> The Curry in a Hurry restaurant in Salt Lake City was set on fire. The restaurant was owned by a family who had moved to the United States from Pakistan fifteen years earlier. The accused arsonist said he "did this because of what happened" on September 11.
>
> ᘓ
>
> Balbir Singh Sodhi, a Sikh man, was shot to death outside his gas station by a man in a pickup truck in Mesa, Arizona. When

the man accused of the shooting was arrested, he reportedly shouted, "I stand for America all the way!" Police reported he also later said, "I'm an American. Arrest me. Let those terrorists run wild."[3]

Several other violent incidents with racial or religious overtones were investigated following September 11. Such violence is not new in America. Its surge was fueled by racism, strong emotions, and the impulse for revenge. Such violence only underlines the urgent need to deepen our understandings of cultural conflicts and to broaden our repertoire of ways to meet the challenges they pose.

The ripples of loss from September 11 will be with us forever, marking us with the brush well known around the world by those whose lives have been changed by terror. Even as we honor the lives lost on that day, we still must resist seeing the event as evidence of the clash of civilizations some say was heralded. This analysis is far too facile, too intertwined with stereotypes, and too blind to the constructive relationships that exist and continue to be nurtured across differences in our global village. To interpret this tragedy and others like it as evidence of a clash of civilizations is to accept and perpetuate a distorted view that only reinforces hopelessness and separation. It is to ignore the multiple differences and bonds that exist among us, aggregating them instead in categories so large that constructive engagement seems impossible. Multiple worldviews and cultural differences exist among us, as do creative ways to bridge them.

Escalating violence and divisive rhetoric are not new in human history, but the destructive tools accompanying them are more lethal than ever before. For this reason the quest for new approaches is pressing. Now, more than ever, we need capacities, practices, and tools to prevent and bridge cultural conflicts. To belong to shared pictures even as we celebrate our diversity requires a commitment to live into the answers of our most divisive questions. This book is about how this can be done. We begin our exploration here, realizing that understanding culture—our own and others'—is essential to meeting the challenges presented by conflict.

The Nature of Culture and Conflict

Although definitions of culture are often associated with customs like food and dress, cultures go far deeper. Cultures are shared by groups yet operate mostly beyond the awareness of group members. They are systems of shared understandings and symbols that connect people to each other, providing them with unwritten messages about how to express themselves and how to make meaning of their lives. Cultures gather people into belonging, tied by shared identities, histories, starting points, and currencies.

Cultural groups center around a wide variety of shared identities, including race, ethnicity, age, nationality, geographical setting, socioeconomic class, able-bodiedness or disability, sexual orientation, language, religion, profession or job role, and gender. It is thus inaccurate to ask which culture someone belongs to, because everyone belongs to multiple cultures. Cultures are living, changing systems that influence our interpretations of the past, starting points, and currencies or values. It is therefore inescapable that they also influence our conflicts.

Starting points are those places from which it seems natural to begin. Raised in the West, I find it natural to view myself first as an individual. For someone raised in China, it may seem equally natural to view the self primarily as a group member. These different starting points play out between people every day, without causing conflict or even drawing attention. It is often not the different starting points themselves that get in people's way but assumptions that the starting points are shared. One person acts autonomously and expects another to do the same; the other weighs actions as they affect a web of relations, expecting that these values are shared. Conflict flows from their different expectations about communication, behavior, and relationship as they try to accomplish tasks together.

To make things more complex, each person values different *currencies*, or ways of being and acting in the world. The individual-oriented person values independence, individual accomplishment, and straightforwardness. The group-oriented person values interdependence, group achievement, and face saving. Unless they develop awareness of their divergent cultural starting points and currencies, miscommunication and frustration may worsen their relationship.

Cultures exist within larger systems called *worldviews*. Worldviews contain three cultural dimensions: social and moral, practical and material, and transcendent or spiritual[4] (explored in more detail in Chapter Ten). Worldviews are deeply embedded in our consciousness, shaping and informing our identities and our meaning-making. They inform our big-picture ideas of the meanings of life and give us ways to learn as well as logic for ordering what we know. Cultural influences and personal habits of attention interact within worldviews, shaping what is visible and invisible, what is appreciated and ignored, and what is appropriate and unacceptable, including a whole realm of conflict behaviors and attitudes.

Worldviews, like cultures, are not the whole universe in which conflicts take place. A myriad of other influences—personal, political, and contextual—affect the course of conflicts. But worldviews—and the cultures that run through them—are important for their pivotal roles. Cultures operate out of conscious awareness most of the time, imparting rhythm, melody, and tone to actions. They function as invisible, shared codes, defining "common sense." The challenge is that everyone is singing a different song, drawing on his or her unique multicultural makeup. Common sense is not necessarily common. As our identities and ways of making meaning fail to harmonize, we look more closely at conflict.

Conflict, put simply, is a difference that matters. It may happen between two people, or between or among groups over any number of different ideas, goals, needs, or approaches. Some conflicts may be easily solved by correcting a miscommunication or finding a way to satisfy everyone. But many conflicts go deeper than this, eliciting strong emotions and sensations. Conflicts that touch us where we make meaning or that in some way threaten an aspect of our cultural identity are the subject of this book. Culture is a part of these conflicts because it is so intricately interwoven with who we see ourselves to be and how we perceive and engage others.

Capacities for Bridging Conflict

Since culture is inextricably entwined with conflict, it is essential to understand it—where it comes from, how it works, how it changes, and how it relates to identity and meaning-making. As our understanding of culture increases, our awareness of its pervasive influence on our lives increases. As we become aware of cultural starting points and currencies playing out in our relation-ships, we see others more clearly and have a wider range of choices for behavior and interpretation. This is *cultural fluency,* the subject of Chapters Two and Three.

Like a language, culture can be studied abstractly. But it really comes alive—fluency is achieved—when it is applied. We apply cul-tural fluency to ourselves through a process called *mindful awareness,* the subject of Chapter Four. To employ mindful awareness is to reflect on our own cultural ways of knowing and being, noticing how they are continually shaped by memories, experiences, and inter-pretations. Coming to know our inner contours, we see the effects of both blind spots and ways of paying attention on how we make meaning. Mindful awareness shows us how our naming, framing, and taming of conflict is always a set of choices, bound up with culture.

To effectively bridge differences, we need *conflict fluency,* the subject of Chapter Five. Conflict is a series of turning points. As we realize there is a difference that matters between us and another, we have many choices. Conflict fluency is the capacity to exercise those choices with awareness that all behavior and interpretation are cultural. The potential of conflict to generate learning, stimu-late creativity, and deepen relationships is realized when divergent starting points and currencies are recognized and respected.

The capacities of cultural fluency, mindful awareness, and con-flict fluency can be continually developed and deepened as we gather and reflect on new experiences. Capacities are broader than skills or tools—they are spaces carved within us by life experiences from which compassion, wisdom, intuition, and creativity spring. They are not formulaic but fluid. They help us adapt to complex-ities and shifting contexts with resilience and energy. Their impor-tance in preventing and bridging cultural conflicts comes from the awareness, sensitivity, and imagination with which they are applied.

Practices for Engaging Cultural Conflict

Recognizing that culture is integral to conflict, no one approach to resolving conflict can be used. Given multiple starting points and currencies, even the existence or absence of a conflict can be contentious. The process of *dynamic engagement,* a map through shifting territory, is presented in Chapter Six. This process highlights ways to engage across differences. Equally important, dynamic engagement includes attending to ways to be with conflict as well as to what to do, pairing each action with an accompanying attitude or spirit.

One of the keys to bridging cultural conflict is creativity. Creativity is enhanced when we draw on many ways of knowing, including emotions, sensations, intuition, imagination, and our sense of the big picture. In Chapters Seven, Eight, and Nine, twenty-four practices are presented that help people bridge cultural conflict. These practices draw on multiple ways of knowing, and work at three levels: *personal, interpersonal,* and *intergroup.* Personal practices are directed to our inner terrain, helping us focus, uncover limiting assumptions, and discern internal choices. Interpersonal practices address conflict in our relationships, helping us smooth differences and heal divisions. Intergroup practices help groups develop vital collective partnerships in the midst of negative images and painful histories.

In the end, bridging conflict is centered in relationships, with all the resilience and strength they offer us. As we bring our relationships into alignment with shared pictures of the future, we can change the collision course of cultural conflicts. Stories, myths, rituals, and metaphors are *symbolic, relational tools* that help us align with shared pictures. The use of these tools by intervenors—those standing in between—is the subject of Chapter Ten.

These practices and capacities come alive as they are used. They are specific and practical, inviting creativity in their application across cultures. They are invitations into conversations with self and others, since developing cultural fluency and conflict fluency is, first, an inside job, then a product of relationship. To know another, we must know something of ourselves. To understand an alternative cultural perspective, we compare it to our own. Deepening our awareness of our own cultural starting points, currencies, and boundaries, we understand and assimilate richer understandings of others.

Cultural Beginnings

We begin to understand culture and the boundaries it marks as we excavate our own experience. When working with elementary school children, I like to ask them about their cultures. What do

they call themselves? Are they African-American, Latino, multira-
cial, Arab-Canadian, Cree? Is there some other part of their identity they see as important to name? In a classroom of deaf children,
deafness is an important aspect of identity, relating to a set of
shared understandings about the world and how it works. In a
classroom where abundant wealth or pervasive poverty is the surrounding ecosystem, social class identifications are also present,
though far less likely to be named.

Once a number of identifiers have been named, I ask the children how they would describe their group to someone who had
never met anyone from that group. How does their geography,
region, language, religion, and so forth relate to who they are?
When did they start to notice differences between themselves and
others, and how do the differences matter? For many, thoughtful
answers to these questions develop only after they have traveled
some distance from home cultural groups. Culture, like a mountain, is more visible and comprehensible from a distance.

I like to get children thinking about these things because it is
important to counter stereotypes and biases with awareness. It
is often a stretch, but very useful, to enter into conversations with
ourselves and others that bring the invisible threads of who we are
into the light where we can see them, touch them, and come to
understand them. This journey is valuable for me each time I take
it, because I inevitably surface some part of my upbringing that had
been invisible to me even as it influenced me. Unpacking my early
experiences as a young girl in a prairie town has helped me understand how my cultural beginnings have influenced my view of others and my approaches to conflict. As I describe them, reflect on
your own beginnings, and how they affect your choices in relationships and in conflict.

My Cultural Beginnings

As a young, white, middle-class girl growing up in a small Canadian
city in the prairies, I remember well the treat of going downtown
to do an errand or peruse the records in the music department of
the local Woolworth's. The streets were dry and dusty, and tum-
bleweeds blew across them in gusts that nearly swept me off my
feet. The smells of the store were musty, with wafts of yesterday's

popcorn, and the aisles seemed to promise treasures, stuffed as they were with things from somewhere else. It hardly mattered whether the somewhere else was Akron, Ohio, or the factories of some far-off place like China. Somewhere else called me, promising the exotic and the mysterious, tantalizing my young mind with visions more felt than seen.

Thus I was introduced to culture, to its image as that which is far away, romantic, tinged with strangeness and difference. If someone had asked me to describe my own culture at that tender moment, I would have drawn a blank. My cozy, middle-class environment seemed devoid of the exotic, unfazed by the goings-on in the rest of the world, which surely harbored hidden secrets and combinations beyond my wildest dreams. So it is for many of us: cultural messages surround us unbidden and unnoticed, lodging themselves in our consciousness without any announcement or fanfare. Thinking culture is somewhere else, we fail to notice it at its closest, within us, gradually coming to see it immediately around us rather than imagining it as only distant. The first awareness we have of culture's ubiquitous presence is when we notice someone different among us.

Introduction to "the Other"

For I was not the only actor in this prairie scene. Doing business on these streets were Hutterites, men dressed in black, buttoned jackets with beard-edged chins and women in layers of skirts with polka-dotted head scarves covering all but the thinnest rolled strip of brown hair. There were also pale, round-faced women from Eastern Europe, bundled in browns and flowered scarves against the wind, and occasional Japanese women, looking thin and neat, somehow seeming to take less than the space allotted to them by the passersby. There were First Nations people, too, moving in small, retracted clusters through the inhospitable streets. In the postwar world of my childhood, sheltered and remote as it now seems, there were clear lines that demarcated difference, and I knew without anyone's saying that none of them were "us" and all of them were "other."

And it wasn't just dress or color that set them apart. I knew from watching my father that there were other lines of difference, invisible, yet as clear as the clock tower that dominated the horizon. There was the man in shabby clothes who ambled up to the lunch counter next to him one day and ate my father's food once it had arrived. My father watched him eat, paid for the food, and left. Later he explained to me that the man needed it more than he did, that the man just didn't have the money to pay for it. There were the people who waited at the back of our farmer's market at the end of the Saturday rush to gather the vegetables and fruit the shopkeepers thought not worth saving. There were the children in school whose clothes were well worn, who did not get a new coat with red buttons every spring as my girlfriends and I did. There were families who lived at the edge of the city on parcels of land looking out over the coulees, the ones who shopped for draperies and furniture in Europe. They maintained the country club and eventually formed the nucleus of a group who lobbied for a university.

There were the old people warehoused in the lodge down at the corner, the place with the shiny corridors that later I would polish in a first summer job, the place that smelt of bleach and a sickly medicinal medley. There was the Jewish family, solitary as far as I can recall, and the smattering of shops on the street we called Chinatown, full of wooden drawers, fireworks, and dried plant and animal remains hanging from strings. There was the teacher at the high school, unmarried in her fifties, reputed to have a female partner. There was the receptionist at the school who, due to a hearing loss in adulthood, learned American sign language and could be seen by those of us loitering in the halls practicing her fluid digital gymnastics. In the prairie town of my childhood, all of these people belonged to groups never named yet clearly understood by us and them, the groups called "other."

"Other" was not a value-neutral term. There were status and privilege differences that divided the various "others." Status was reasonably constant, but it could change. When the mayor came to his elementary schoolchild's classroom and sat in her low-to-the-ground chair, the teacher's power ascended. When the teacher came to protest a proposed bylaw and sat far beneath the mayor presiding from the stage, the mayor was in control. When First Nations people living outside the city blocked an irrigation channel, recognition of their power increased. Overall there was a remarkable clarity about social status and rank, and people played out their roles accordingly, absorbing them as I did from their earliest awareness. In obvious and subtle ways these differences acted as boundaries on relationships and factors in conflicts in my home community.

Like this one, every cultural context is rich with images, unwritten messages, and shortcuts known only to members. As you bring sensations, feelings, and pictures of your cultural origins to mind, be sure to look beyond the obvious categories of difference. What was named and what could not be named in your home cultures? Who was celebrated and who was not in your school, community, and area? and why? What stories were told about your group? About other groups? How did these stories relate to conflicts in the past or present? Chances are these stories are with you still. Can you identify some of their influences?

Formation of Cultural Identity

Early cultural experiences profoundly influence our identities. My prairie home was the crucible for the gendered, white, middle-class identity that gave me ready-made answers for how to be, what to see, and what constituted common sense. Anchored by smells, visions, and associations, this identity merged with the self I became, imperceptibly tracing itself into my values, ideas, and ways of seeing myself and others. It did not explain all my choices even then, but it gave me a series of starting points that became clear to me only as I put more and more distance between me and them. Cultures are multiple starting points that make it possible for us to function in the world without constantly having to invent "good sense" or make decisions starting from a blank slate.

Cultures are the sets of invisible rules that whisper prompts and frown at us in our mind's eye when we contemplate deviating from norms. They are sets of messages that swirl around us in overlapping circles, often outside our conscious awareness. In my family and religious culture, girls and women wore dresses or skirts to church. So clear was the unspoken message that it never occurred to me to question it. If I had, I would have received the explanation mothers give daughters when they have not considered alternatives: "It's just not *done* any other way." I was in my teens before I attended a service of another denomination and was shocked to see women in pants.

Cultures give our lives shape, definition, connection, and pleasure. Neither excavation nor aerial viewing reveals their full richness, for they are both within and without us, around and between us. They are glue and wedge; connective tissue and shared wounds. In my family, church membership and involvement was a tight bond, providing a language and a set of common views and goals. The sacrifices made by ancestors who left religious oppression in Europe for the freedom amid difficult conditions in America became family legends propelling us into obligation and loyalty. This same church membership was also a wedge, as members of the extended family who fell away from the church were mentioned in hushed voices with pained looks, now excluded from the inner circle.

Cultures are woven into the stories that greet us as preverbal infants and into the ways we will eventually prefer to die. So much more than apparel and food, they are the critical frame for the picture, without which it would be formless and undefined, fading into the woodwork or protruding invasively into the scene. They guide our vision; they soothe our bruises. Arising from an awareness of those we are unlike as well as those we are like, they offer paths both perceptual and physical and hide other paths from view.

Cultural messages are passed down in stories and by example, powerfully lodging themselves in our sense of self and our expectations of relationship, in language and our sense of what is valuable and defensible, surprising us years later when we think we have moved beyond them. These shared messages come from multiple identity groups, though we each have our unique personal collection.

If it were possible to map the cultural influences embedded in us, we still would have a poor tool for predicting human behavior. Cultures flow through our lives like underground rivers, powerfully nurturing, potently influencing, and sometimes dividing. How the rivers and their tributaries flow together and when they come close to the surface depends on many factors. Cultural identities and the messages that flow from them are salient in different contexts; we draw on different starting points at different times. We compose our behavior not just from messages from those with whom we are similar but also in response to those in relation to whom we experience ourselves as different or unique.

We do not accept all of the cultural messages we are given, discarding some out of discomfort or because they do not fit with other parts of ourselves. We act out our cultures differently depending on social context, time of life, external events, internal shifts, emotional states, baggage from the past, and countless other factors. Multicultural beings that we are, we are too complex to map yet so strongly guided by cultural messages that we cannot discount them.

Cultural Boundaries

Because we are aware of so little of our cultural makeup, we often act automatically, without inserting awareness and choice into the decision-making loop. Members of relatively privileged groups may spend little time trying to fathom their cultural influences. Residing in the comfortable understanding that their shared ways are "the norm," they label others' approaches different or alternative from "the way things are done." Those outside these circles of privilege find themselves all too acutely aware of not only the differences that exist but the difference the differences make.

Cultural Judgments

Whatever our level of privilege we engage in cultural judgments of others, often based on a quick appraisal of their apparent identities. We assign attributes, traits, and likely behaviors to others within seconds of setting eyes on them. Even when we are culturally sensitive we can catch ourselves in this act, finding that our training helps us more to interrupt the reflex than to prevent its use.

This happens in many different societies. Listen to the experience of a Chinese scholar:

> I was born in a divided society—in a small town. There were
> two groups of people—local indigenous people, most of
> them "Bai" people, a minority ethnic group in China, and out-
> siders. My parents, their colleagues and families were all "Han

Chinese," a majority group in China. Outsiders were sent to the small town by the government to build a hydro-power station. As a child, I knew that I was different from the local people. They were poor and dirty, they did not go to school and were ignorant. I knew I should not play with the local children. I do not remember that we had disputes with the local people, just not much communication.[5]

As this scholar reminds us, from early in our lives, we know who is "us" and who is "other." In each group there are standards of behavior and hygiene, and roles to be played. Parents around the world transmit ways of being and knowing to their children. Their "common sense" is derived from their parents and their parents' parents in a kind of osmotic transmission. In this way, cultures continue to evolve and change, giving our lives richness and challenges, meaning and boundaries.

Stereotypes and Cultural Assumptions

Just as cultural messages are potent shapers of our own behavior, they also organize themselves into templates that label and generalize about "others." They become expectations, based on stereotypes born of personal experience and the wide array of media and social messages we receive about specific groups. We resist them, yet they come unbidden into our consciousness, persistent as a recurrent dream and sometimes just as distorted. We harbor them about gender, race, ethnicity, class, disabled people; we assign them according to sexual orientation, education, linguistic and regional origin. Movies perpetuate them, and so do we in the ways that we structure our communities and our schools, our governments and our social lives.

Carlos Cortez, a multicultural educator, shares an example from the television program *The $25,000 Pyramid*. The show involves two-person teams of complete strangers. One player sees a series of words on a screen and must say things to get her partner to say as many of the words as possible in a short time. During one episode the word *gangs* appeared on the screen. Without hesitation the player shouted, "They have lots of these in East L.A." (a heavily Mexican-American section of Los Angeles). Cortez reports that the guest celebrity partner immediately responded with the right answer: "gangs!"[6]

Consider this example with the media's ubiquitous pairings of particular adjectives with identity groups: angry black rappers, shifty Gypsies, Palestinian terrorists, Muslim extremists, Christian fundamentalists, passive Asian women. Are there Chicano gangs in East Los Angeles? Yes, there are. But there are also schools, churches, charities, and many other groups and organizations. And are there gangs in many other places? Yes, there are, in all kinds of neighborhoods and among many different ethnicities. It is when one place or group gets linked automatically to a stereotype that problems occur, for we don't necessarily stop to think beyond these knee-jerk associations.

The stereotypes also fail us when we meet someone who does not match our image of a group. A South African colleague whose family has Indian roots relates how people she meets in the United States relate to her first as an Indian. They may ask where her family is from in India and how she likes the mild American food. When she says she was born and raised in South Africa, confusion and awkward silences often follow. People cannot decide how to relate to her when she does not fit their image of South Asian or South African.

When we know only a little about a group, or have had little actual experience, it may be difficult to find a starting point for connection. Milton Bennett tells the story of a group of African high school students who came to visit their counterparts in Oregon.[7] The U.S. students, anxious to be friendly, engaged the Africans by asking about large wild animals. Some of the Africans were amused; over time they became frustrated that so little was known about their home country. And that was the kernel of the problem. The U.S. students knew very little about the political, social, or geographical aspects of their counterparts' homes and lives, so they resorted to what they did know as a basis for their questions. What they did know was a stereotype, constructed from American movies and National Geographic specials.

This is an extreme example perhaps, but it highlights what we all do with cultural information: we store it for later use. When we meet someone apparently belonging to a group about which we think we have information, we pull that information out, often with the best of intentions. At best it may be an opening for conversation. At worst it will be a distortion, a set of assumptions that categorizes someone based on his apparent group affiliation; both the assignment and the assumptions may be entirely erroneous. Many cultural identities are not discernible from appearance. Because all of us belong to many different groups, choosing generalizations linked to one apparent identity as a basis for relating is presumptuous. We know that cultural influences are variously salient in different situations and that the influences themselves shift and change over time.

Since there is a great deal of variability within cultural groups, superimposing cultural characteristics onto someone without checking our assumptions may be not only inaccurate but offensive. Because the way we understand cultural characteristics is itself passed through cultural filters, there are likely to be gaps between expectations and understandings. My culturally influenced behavior of empathy and caring may translate in other contexts as patronizing or invasive. What is appreciated and seen as complimentary in one context may be insulting in another.

For example, my view of thoughtful conduct is sometimes quite different from that of my friend Natasha, an immigrant from Russia. Natasha recently contacted a friend living in the same Russian community as her parents, asking the friend to deliver something to them because they are old and cannot easily get around. She complained to me that the friend in Russia had responded to the request by sending her driver to deliver the package. Had my parents in Canada received a package delivered by a driver, it would have enhanced their status in the neighborhood. In Natasha's case, she interpreted her friend's failure to attend to the request personally as thoughtless and disrespectful.

Cultures also inform our ideas of how community and connection are properly balanced with privacy and distance. The first time I attended an African-American church service in Washington, D.C., my cultural assumptions were challenged. I found myself immediately greeted by warm hugs from strangers. Accustomed as I was to the restraint of mostly mimed, arm's-length hugs in a predominantly white congregation, I felt myself pulling back. This only elicited more warmth on the part of the congregants, who tried harder to help me feel a part of their community.

Reflecting later, I realized that the behavior of the African-Americans at church was a lot like the way my extended family behaves. Get near a LeBaron family reunion, and you will be hugged, ready or not. The congregants saw each other as family and responded accordingly. The familiarity and warmth they showed even to new attendees came from their drawing the family circle much wider than my cultural common sense had led me to expect.

How the circles around "us" and "other" are drawn varies from group to group. The circles may get smaller when a group feels threatened. They may be permeable in some contexts and impermeable in others. Stereotyping and cultural assumptions are shortcuts that we use to predict some boundaries and group rules and are probably inevitable given the number and complexity of our encounters across cultures. Surfacing stereotypes and cultural assumptions, at least to ourselves, reminds us that they are often wrong. Applying them in ways that frame others as "less than" imposes a ranking that turns difference to distrust and curiosity to conflict. One way to open up exploration rather than closing it prematurely with stereotypes is through examining metaphors.

Cultural Metaphors

Metaphors are windows into the terrain of a culture. They reveal how we see our relationships to each other and to ideas. Since metaphors map one set of ideas onto another, they direct our attention in particular ways. Countless metaphors are associated with culture and conflict. Conflict has been called a collision, a struggle, a doorway to learning. Culture has been called an underground river, an organic thing inside of us and between us, an iceberg almost fully submerged.

The metaphors we choose have images and feelings associated with them. Because these images and feelings are conveyed by familiar metaphors that are often unmarked and unquestioned, the embedded assumptions within them are also unexamined. When we accept a common metaphor for conflict, such as struggle or war, we may adopt the feelings of discouragement or resignation that go with it. We are less likely to see a whole range of constructive possibilities. With this in mind, we examine two common metaphors for cultural identity in the United States and Canada.

Common metaphors for cultural identity in the two countries are the melting pot and the salad bowl. The United States has often been described as a melting pot, meaning that immigrants subsume their home cultural identities, adopting an American identity as primary. Canada has been called a salad bowl, in which home identities are somehow mixed together with the Canadian one without loss of either.

Consider the sensations and feelings that accompany the two images—a melting pot and a salad bowl. It is interesting that both are culinary, evoking our ubiquitous identification with food as a symbol of cultural differences. A melting pot sounds warm, suggesting an iron vessel over a fire in which ingredients sacrifice their individual tastes and appearances for a delicious mélange. There is something cozy and comforting about this metaphor. The salad is composed of colorful elements that retain their individual flavor even in the presence of an encompassing dressing. It is crisp, clean, and cool—refreshing on a hot summer's day. If you had to be part of one of these images, which would it be?

While neither metaphor is adequate to convey the complex reality of Canadian or U.S. society, the metaphors direct our attention to differences in policies and values. Canadians tend to see themselves as part of a multicultural mosaic, while Americans are more likely to view their U.S. identity as primary and their ethnocultural heritage as secondary. A strong, primary American identity fits with the influence of the United States in the global community. Canada, geographically large but small in population, has more room for differences and came much later to articulate a set of principles to guide national policy. These differences are reflected in social policy and group relations in the two countries, influencing, for example, official language policies (Canada has two official languages; the United States has one), prevalence of bilingual education, and treatment of recent immigrants. These differences in turn affect intergroup relations and the course of conflicts in each national context.

The differences between the metaphors are not the whole story, however. Both the United States and Canada are home to people with hundreds of heritages, mother tongues, and cultural understandings. Neither country is homogeneous, nor are the immigrants who live in each country uniform in terms of assimilation and identity. In this sense the metaphors are limited, explaining the continuing formation of national and regional identities imperfectly. In both the United States and Canada, some people have submerged their ethnic and linguistic origins, choosing an American or Canadian identity as primary. Others have hyphenated, becoming for example Chinese-Canadian or Arab-American.

Generational differences explain some of the variations in retention of cultural traditions that sometimes exacerbate conflict within groups. But even when cultural traditions fade or are muted in a quest to blend in, cleavages surface related to identity and conflict. And this conflict need not be geographically bounded; it may involve people who share origins even though they are geographically dispersed. In 1984, attacks in India on the Golden Temple, an important site for Sikhs, ignited a divide between Sikhs and Hindus in British Columbia, Canada, where large numbers of South Asian immigrants live.

Because cultural identities continue to encircle us even after we leave a place or group where we first felt belonging, there are no definitive maps of culture. Metaphors show us starting points and reveal something about the images we hold of ourselves and others. As metaphors reveal complexity, paradox, and shades of difference, they deepen our understandings of the relationships among people who inhabit conflict. We will explore more of the way that metaphors bridge differences in Chapters Seven and Nine.

Tools like metaphor are important because cultures are complex and dynamic, transcending classifications based on terrain, food, dress, and language. They live within us, breathing energy, materializing meaning, and transforming our identities. Cultures change over time, influencing the course of conflicts. Conflicts change as well, influencing the dynamics in cultures. And so conflict and culture simultaneously touch our lives, each continually influencing the other.

The Relational Terrain of Conflict

Conflict happens in relationships; it emerges between two or more people. Conflict is not a disembodied event, nor can it ever be disconnected from the cultural dynamics at its heart. As evident as this sounds, much that is written about resolving conflict fails to acknowledge this simple truth. Since we are social (in relationship with each other) and since we are cultural (in relationship with many shared influences), conflict is a social and cultural phenomenon. It follows that culture and conflict cannot be separated into modules or manipulated like pieces on a chessboard. Capacities, practices, and tools for bridging cultural conflict must be flexible, adaptable, and creative. They must be centered in the relationships that spawned them—the same relationships through which they may be eventually transformed.

Conflict engages us, touches us where we know, where we define ourselves, and where we compose our ongoing identities. More than smooth or automatic interactions, it dredges up those visceral, primordial parts of us that hearken back to our childhood and beyond, to family, generational, and group patterns that form our heritage. Feeling threatened, we resort to the potency of what protects us, what seems natural and appropriate, and what makes sense. In our recourse to this completely reasonable reflex, we may engage and escalate conflict.

Conflict ensues when our starting points are different from others', our need for security infringes on another's territory, or the meanings we assign to behavior or events are different from others'. Sometimes we are aware of the way cultural influences weave their ways through our conflicts; often we are not. Sometimes we are taken by surprise by our own or others' responses when cultural meanings or boundaries seem threatened.

Naming Conflict

One of first boundaries we encounter as we venture into the world is the recognition and naming of conflict, itself a cultural act. I remember well conducting research in western Canada to learn how members of different immigrant groups experienced conflict. One of the interviewers was a bright Chinese-Canadian woman in her thirties, highly recommended by a community agency serving Chinese immigrants. She spoke both Mandarin and Cantonese; she had taken courses on conflict resolution. How surprised I was when she returned from her first pilot interview with nearly no data. It seems that when she asked her first interviewee, an elderly Chinese gentleman, to describe conflicts he had experienced in

Canada, he replied that he had experienced no conflicts since arriving in 1948. Alternative translations of the word *conflict* yielded no more answers, even when words meaning *trouble* and *disagreement* were substituted.

What my colleagues and I were learning from this experience was that conflict is personal, and revealing it to strangers can be uncomfortable. Conflict often involves discomfort, loss of face, struggle, and pain. It may have left scars or involved unpalatable choices. Conflict, when other than trivial, nibbles at who we are and what we value, and so we are wise to avoid it, as we do in many instances. It shakes up our internal order, jostling the pieces we have painstakingly put together, even breaking them apart when extreme. It disrupts relationships; it asks *why* questions of us when our attention has been directed more comfortably to *how* and *when*.

The tendency to divide our experiences into categories like "conflict" fits well within a Western, analytical tradition. It may fit less well for someone raised elsewhere, such as in a society influenced by Confucian thought. In that milieu, children's eyes were schooled to notice harmony, not its absence. From a holistic perspective, identifying and analyzing conflicts long past is more than unnecessary; it is an invitation to reframe a harmonious past into a fractured story. Who would want to spend his energy doing that? Who would want to take the risk of looking at the past that way, and then share it with a stranger, having lived through a series of experiences that taught him to distrust authorities and officials?

Not only were these factors at play but the young woman was asking these questions of an elderly Chinese man. His cultural expectations both generational and gendered led him to expect deference, not invasiveness. Filial piety, a strong value in his heritage, required that she should act respectfully, acknowledging but not probing, venerating but not contradicting, even implicitly.

Does this mean that there was no conflict in this man's fifty years as an immigrant in Canada? We cannot know the details of his experience nor how the scale of what he had experienced before leaving China may have made his time in Canada seem calm and peaceful. We cannot know the degree to which a cultural prohibition against airing dirty laundry was in operation. But we can reflect on one important learning he communicated: that conflict is a cultural event, questions about conflict are cultural questions, and identity is always connected to the asking of these questions.

As this project proceeded my colleagues and I learned about immigrants' experiences of conflict through the relationships we built across cultural boundaries, relationships of mutuality, inquiry, and generosity. One of the questions raised by this experience stayed with us: must conflict be acknowledged for it to exist? Who decides on the existence of conflict, someone involved or an outside observer?

Conflict need not be openly acknowledged or named to be real, but it must be felt and experienced before it takes on form. Those inside the experience are the experts: if none of them perceive conflict, then the label may not fit. Still, if conflict is denied but behavior involves violence or destruction, it may be time to take another look.

Conflict does not emerge from every difference; differences between two people next to each other in line at the grocery store do not normally register on conflict radar. Only when some aspect of our differences becomes salient and nudges the way we hold our identity or meaning does difference translate into conflict. Serbs, Croats, and Bosnians in the 1980s lived in the same apartment blocks in Sarajevo without seeing problems in each other's ethnic heritage or, indeed, even knowing that heritage. A colleague remembers that she came to know who was Bosnian, Croatian, or Serbian only by noticing who remained in her building as hostilities increased and who did not.

Conflict and Identity

Difference also fuels conflict when the difference itself interferes with some accomplishment, desire, or story that maintains our sense of identity, individually or collectively. As the only permanent female faculty member in my institution for the first five years of my tenure, I found myself increasingly focusing on my gender and how it influenced my opportunities. It was difficult to know how gender was a factor in course assignments and decision making. Although I did not know how gender was a factor, I became increasingly convinced of its salience. In a field where many practitioners were women and most academics were men, I wondered how could I bridge these boundaries and continue being both?

As a Canadian in a U.S. institution, I also became acutely aware of my distinctly Canadian ways as they contrasted with the ways of those around me. When I relied on my less direct style of communication, I found myself fading into the woodwork, unnoticed and unheard. I felt new kinship with European and Asian colleagues, whose style was also less confrontational. Keeping the Canadian aspect of my identity strong became increasingly important, and conflict arose when a colleague argued that there were no significant differences between the two national cultures.

Identity plays out in both symbolic and practical ways when diverse cultural groups are trying to bridge conflict. Events in a meeting between Canadian government representatives and Aboriginal people illustrate the multiple levels at which identity is expressed and experienced. Because the meeting was taking place on traditionally Aboriginal territory, it was convened by an elder and begun with a prayer. The prayer was a way of acknowledging the sacred in the meeting, inviting a spirit of respect and help from the Creator for the process. Uttered in the traditional language of this group, its meaning was unclear to government representatives. Beyond the literal words, and without denying its legitimacy as a sacred ritual, it could also be interpreted as an assertion of entitlements or rights, a tactic to emphasize a moral position, or a statement of power.

What did the government representatives do in response? Normally, they probably would just have waited without trying to actively engage the experience or understand the prayer, just as we wait for a red light to change before going forward. Instead, in this instance, a facilitator asked the elder to translate the prayer. The request had the effect of enhancing a sense of mutuality and respect, as the elder explained that the prayer was one of thanks and a request for a good spirit among those present and good outcome for the negotiations. A step had been taken toward developing a shared cultural frame through the simple step of having the prayer translated. Had the prayer not been translated, assumptions about it might have further widened the divide between the two parties.

As this example illustrates, cultural conflict is not easily analyzed. The quest to understand it takes us from the literal to the symbolic, from the obvious to the hidden. In cultural conflict there is much more under the surface than above it. Much more is sensed, felt, and intuited than can be named. Bridging conflict necessarily means cultivating comfort with change and ambiguity.

Engaging Change

Bridging conflict is messy business. It is to mix this and that, to experience spurts of progress and then find ourselves on a road that circles back; it is to have our buttons pushed and to be put out and thrown off and to have the determination to get up again, find our bearings, and continue. It is to lose our luggage and wear the same clothes for a few days, knowing that unexpected things always happen when we put ourselves outside our comfortable, habitual ways. It is to discover that others accept us anyway in our less-than-fresh, suboptimal state, that we cannot lose that which is most precious as long as we are alive: our creativity, our ability to choose, and our capacity to love.

Choosing to try seeing others from the inside out, to join with them in inventing new ways to relate, we gradually develop cultural fluency and its integral companion, conflict fluency. We work continuously to develop ways to situate ourselves that do not pretend to be value neutral but that respect ways of knowing, being, and doing different from our own. We proceed from a relational ethic, one that sees that everyone makes sense if we are willing to stand temporarily at his or her starting point. We will make better choices if we have the courage and the discipline to imagine standing where others have stood, even if their methods or goals are abhorrent to us. We also hold ourselves open to the idea that there are many ways to engage, that there is value in inquiry, that the cultural mazes that are part of each of us have not only trapdoors and secret chambers but hidden entrances and places of grace and beauty.

As we work together we recognize the gifts of the journey that does not follow a straight line but doubles back and zigzags around, catching everyone up in its momentum, with space for all those following different paces within it. Having faced the shadows and the demons that would deter or discourage us, we brush the touchstone of our shared purpose and shared humanity. We confirm our inklings that it is possible to bridge cultural gaps, in all of their labyrinthine complexity.

We are continually watchful for opportunities to redraw the lines around our pictures. Boundaries help us by giving definition and closure. They can also hinder us with visual and felt cues to stop when we need to find ways to keep going. Attuned to openings for changing our frames, expanding our boundaries, and releasing our limiting assumptions, we build strong relationships across difference.

Finding ways to dance with change—and conflict always begs change—is the subject of this book. Dancing gracefully means exploring the different ways we engage in both caring and conflict. It invites our minds to open to new information and possibilities rather than take refuge in the illusion that the world is static and predictable. Cultural fluency grows from open minds where learning continues, minds ready to improvise in response to the surprises that are an inevitable part of cultural conflict. Chapters Two and Three describes ways to develop and apply cultural fluency as an essential capacity for bridging cultural conflict.

CHAPTER TWO

❧

Cultural Fluency in Conflict
An Overview

It is a beautiful night and the moon is full. You are walking with someone you care about, taking in the perfumed air in silence. As friends and lovers have done for centuries, you take some moments to stare up at the moon. What do you see? Do you see the man in the moon, a feminine voice that whispers the tides into being, a piece of cheese, a place men landed, timeless beauty, or a rabbit pounding rice? A rabbit pounding rice? This is a popular image of the moon in Japan. Look at the next full moon and see whether you can see the rabbit too, adding that image to the others you hold, in a step toward cultural fluency.

To develop cultural fluency in conflict is to learn a language, to come to see cultural patterns much as we can learn to discern constellations when we see the night sky. We can be most effective in addressing conflict by developing fluency with culture: living culture; culture as a series of starting points; culture as a range of currencies; culture as pattern, form, and symbol; culture as ways we see, know, decide, and draw lines between ourselves and others; culture as an underground river that influences the course of conflict. As we become familiar with cultural dynamics, we learn ways to bridge differences that yield synergy not confusion.

Developing Cultural Fluency

As I prepared to write this chapter about cultural fluency, I remembered the sense of eternity I treasured as a child while looking at the starry night sky. The subject is so vast it eludes clear description. It is pervasive yet often missed in its significance. Daring to write about culture feels a bit like being in a room with an elephant that everyone is pretending is not there. You are the one who names it. Doing so, you face at least two dangers: either the people in the room turn their denial-cum-anger onto you, or the elephant, finally named, stirs into action and threatens to trample everyone. We are afraid of culture, afraid that our failure to understand its complex workings will trip us up, afraid of its potent capacity to disrupt the order we have grown accustomed to. It is safer and easier to ignore an elephant than to approach it; easier to photograph it and remark on its exotic distinctness than to understand and relate to it.

Carrying the metaphor of the elephant one step further, I am reminded too of John Saxe's poem about seven blind men.[1] Each felt a part of an elephant and described it differently. One man felt the trunk and said that the elephant is long and flexible with a soft, moist tip. Another felt the torso and said that the elephant is broad and thick and larger than life. And so on. None of them had a whole picture of it: its shape, its contours, its system, the way it moved, and the way it related to other elephants. So it is challenging to find starting places to describe the complexity of culture and the ways cultural fluency matters in understanding conflict.

Yet complexity is a reason to begin, not to withdraw. With the chutzpah of the little girl who looked at the stars and saw possibility, I invite you to walk with me as we sift through the richness of culture amid the sparkle of stories. I invite you to close your eyes at first, to dream that it is possible to develop a nuanced, textured understanding of culture that adapts to changing contexts and shines light on different times and lifescapes. With this foundation we learn more about our choices in resolving conflict and about the bridge building so critical to us in this new millennium.

Even as we strive to be aware of the ways our cultural lenses shape our seeing and to describe the things we see in a balanced way, we will skirt the edge of several *cultural traps:*

- The trap of believing the way we see things is natural and normal, called *automatic ethnocentricity*
- The trap of thinking that every kind of cultural information can be categorized, called the *taxonomy* trap

- The trap of assuming that cultural complexity and dynamism is so difficult to understand and track that intercultural effectiveness is impossible, called the *complexity* trap
- The trap of seeing only commonalities, minimizing or failing to notice important cultural differences, called the *universalism* trap
- The trap of seeing only differences and divisions, missing what we share with others across identity and worldview boundaries, called the *separation* trap[2]

Let's explore each of these as a way to inoculate ourselves against them.

Automatic Ethnocentricity

Automatic ethnocentricity means believing that the way we see things is the normal and natural way. It takes constant curiosity and willingness to interrupt our ideas of how things work and what is appropriate and to realize that we proceed from a series of cultural starting points rather than absolutes. One of my earliest memories of automatic ethnocentricity goes back to kindergarten.

My kindergarten teacher taught us in a suite of rooms in her home. One afternoon, when my father was late to pick me up, she taught me to eat with chopsticks. "This is a skill you will need," she predicted with confidence. The two sticks were awkward and very long in my small fingers, and the rice was very small. It took many years before I was able to manage chopsticks with any degree of gracefulness, and just as long before I understood that eating with chopsticks was a starting point as natural to someone from Japan or China as using a fork, knife, and spoon was to me. Through my child's eyes, cutlery was normal and chopsticks were exotic. Stepping back from the automatic ethnocentricity of my childhood, I realized that this cultural assumption situated my way of eating as "normal" and other ways as "alternative."

Automatic ethnocentricity is a trap because it lulls us into imagining that our ways of seeing things and being are central. Others are either imagined to share our ways of seeing more or less, or they are seen as alternative, peripheral. Much of the time, ethnocentricity goes unnamed, but it operates just the same. When a person talks about natural or normal ways of approaching conflict, for example, she is likely to be assuming that what is natural to her is at least somewhat shared by others.

It is worth noting that automatic ethnocentricity can also operate in reverse. This "Peace Corps syndrome" occurs when a person comes to denigrate his home culture and raise up his adopted one as central after a sojourn in another culture. Suddenly, home seems crass, ordinary, and uncultivated, while the new culture takes on a golden cast: refined, delicious, and sophisticated. The American sojourner joins Europeans in denigrating "loud Americans"; the Australian traveler adopts a view of her homeland as backward and undeveloped, opting to stay in London.[3]

This reversal is only the mirror opposite of automatic ethnocentricity. Even though the judgments are more explicit and deliberate, it employs the same degree of generalization. In both cases distortion follows, because whether we denigrate other cultures or simply see ours as the standard from which "normal and natural" flows, we miss opportunities to understand others in context. Cultural fluency means recognizing the validity of many cultural starting points. It does not mean abandoning our core identities but finding ways to try on others and appreciate them for what they reveal as well as noting what they may hide.

Taxonomies

Taxonomies are ways of organizing and categorizing information. Often, people learning about culture and conflict look for them as shortcuts to developing cultural fluency. They seek to know that "the Koreans are like this" or that "lesbians prefer that," so that they feel more comfortable navigating cultural differences. Although taxonomies may provide some useful guesses about this group or that, they can be equally deceptive and misleading. Any given cultural group has variation within it; none are uniform entities, just as any family does not share a closed set of cultural specifics. All cultures are in flux and dynamic. Each of us has multiple cultural identities, not just one, and they arrange themselves differently over time. We do not always act in accordance with any one of our identities but blend the cultural messages in a watercolor wash to which we respond differently depending on context, social dynamics, individual personality, mood, and a host of other factors.

While generalizations can be useful to illustrate broad differences and patterns, it is important to remember that they are general guides. A map is helpful in navigation, but it has its limitations. It does not show the newly completed road or the detour. It does not depict some of the beautiful or obstructing features of the landscape: trees, hills, curves in the road, flowers in the distance, impassable potholes, migrating birds.

I suppose that everyone who goes to another country for the first time wants some sort of taxonomy. I certainly did the first time I ventured to Japan. I knew there was a huge amount written about cultural miscommunication between Westerners and Japanese, and I was concerned not to commit any grievous errors. One of the things I learned in advance and shared with other North American colleagues who were also going to present at a conference in Japan was that Japanese people are less comfortable than North Americans in large-group discussions.

One of my colleagues later confided that she had taken this advice literally, not asking any questions or attempting any discussion in her session. She felt uncomfortable because she usually teaches more experientially. Only later did she realize that the Japanese participants would have been quite happy to talk amongst themselves in small groups, later reporting their findings to the large group. Because she had taken the generalization at face value, she did not get the opportunity to interact with the participants that she, and they, would have liked. Had she talked with a cultural informant, someone who understood Japanese and North American cultures better than I did, she might have found ways to meet both her interest in dialogue and the Japanese participants' preferences for small-group interaction.

Complexity

Complexity is a common cultural trap that everyone falls into at one time or another. Although we must acknowledge the complexity of cultural dynamics, we also should not be paralyzed by it. Paralysis can be a response to a growing awareness that culture is everywhere and it matters. We may feel overwhelmed with the many levels we ought to attend to if we are to be culturally competent and able to navigate effectively outside our familiar zones. The list of levels is endless: our multiple lenses; others' multiple lenses; worldviews that shape expectations, perceptions, and behavior; context; individual differences; and status and power dynamics.

While it is true that culture is multileveled and multilayered, there are ways to understand its patterns that can help us decode its symbols. Practice and experience, together with learning, awareness, and reflection, enhance cultural fluency. Examples of synergy among diverse groups and culturally sensitive ways of addressing conflict show us it is possible to make a friend of cultural differences. When we look at the alternatives to engaging complexity—denial, defensiveness, or resignation—we choose the more generative, hopeful possibility and move toward developing cultural fluency.

I remember the first group for whom I facilitated a dialogue on diversity. I felt as though I were in a minefield. The group was mixed racially and ethnically. One of the first things I said, in response to a question, was something like, "The answer is not black and white." Then I realized that this could be an offensive phrase to some people, because it drew a dichotomy between black and white and perhaps a ranking as well. Should I apologize or just move smoothly ahead as though it had not happened?

I stopped and addressed it, but later feedback was divided on the question of whether I should have taken the time to do this. I wondered whether I wanted to continue working in this area. Upon reflection I decided to substitute the word *mindfield* for *minefield* in my thinking. Rather than thinking of diverse audiences as volatile and frightening, I shifted to seeing the opportunity in the different minds in the room. Our collective opportunity was to open them, share them, and enjoy them, knowing that we would step on each other's toes from time to time, trusting that we could navigate our ways out of that. This idea of mindfields helped me see the possibilities as well as the dangers in talking about diversity and lessened my anxiety about the complexity of the task.

Universalism

Universalism means to see the commonalities among people and minimize differences. The statement, "We are all alike under the skin," is a universalist statement. It is true; it also problematic if we stop there. Even as we share humanness, we are also diverse. The wasteful, destructive potential of unchecked conflicts is a constant reminder of the importance of developing cultural and conflict fluency to navigate differences.

I remember the sinking feeling I had when my colleagues and I were nearing the end of Semester at Sea with 700 undergraduate students who had visited ten foreign ports while taking classes on a shipboard campus. As a faculty member I felt particularly responsible, close to them, and concerned to be sure their experiences were both productive and positive. As we gathered in community to reflect on our experiences, I felt my stomach tense when one or two of them made comments like, "I learned we are all more or less the same, all around the world." Without diminishing the importance of recognizing our common humanity, it is surely a desirable outcome of intercultural experiences to be mindful of our differences as well: those that delight us, those that confound us, and those that intrigue us. Only as we do this are we able to find ways to experience our commonalities more directly and reliably.

Separation

We fall into the separation trap when we imagine that there is no common ground between others and ourselves. This is particularly apt to happen when an aspect of our identity feels threatened. As the only permanently appointed woman on my faculty for five years, it was sometimes hard to remember that I shared a great deal with my male colleagues—concerns, ideas, and goals. Our ways of pursuing them seemed so different at times, I lost sight of what we shared.

In civil wars and large-scale struggles people on each side may have a hard time experiencing themselves as sharing anything with their adversaries. Indeed, these differences and their historical roots may be manipulated and amplified for political and strategic ends, so that the very possibility of seeing similarities is crowded out. If it were not so, fellow Yugoslavians might not have killed each other in large numbers, and the Rwandan slaughter might not have occurred on such a tragic scale. Closer to home, those on both sides of the abortion issue might have been spared violence had negative perceptions and rhetoric not framed them as enemies with nothing in common.

The antidote to the separation trap is to engage in what Adrienne Kaufmann calls connective thinking.[4] Connective thinking means to search for common threads, for shared meanings and overlaps in identities. In their work on abortion conflict, Adrienne and her colleague Mary Jacksteit found that advocates from both the prolife and the prochoice perspectives were surprised at how much they had in common: concern about the welfare of women and children, the desire to prevent unwanted pregnancies, and a commitment to social action. To uncover this common ground, people sat down and had conversations of a different kind and quality from the heated exchanges they were accustomed to. Thus they skirted the trap of separation.

Avoiding cultural traps takes intention and attention, as Kaufmann's work demonstrates. Given the many potential pitfalls, it is no wonder people tiptoe around cultural differences. Each of these cultural traps is like one-half of a piece of Velcro—the sticky side that may catch us as we develop our capacities to engage difference. Knowing that the traps are there, we don't allow doubt or fear to get us stuck. We keep ourselves supple and smooth, exploring the terrain of culture, communication, and conflict with confidence and awareness that this journey will always offer more learning than we can assimilate.

Culture, Communication, and Conflict

There are many ways to explore cultural differences. We explore them most powerfully through direct experience with others. We can also look through the eyes of poets, novelists, historians, artists, musicians, or philosophers. We can peer through the words of travelers or of scholars who have studied specific groups. We can study groups' ecology, technology, politics, or institutional structures.

While all of these are important, one of the most useful areas of study focuses on interpersonal communication patterns. These communication patterns relate not to the do's and don'ts for specific settings but to the codes that underlie norms, practices, and values in communication.

Communication theorists and anthropologists draw on cultural generalizations to give us insight into different groups' behaviors and meaning-making. Their work is useful in uncovering ways to develop cultural fluency, but it is not definitive. No one source can give us comprehensive insight into a culture—cultural fluency means to use as many sources as possible. And the more these sources of learning include actual cross-cultural experiences, the better.

Scholars' generalizations often sort groups according to place, identities, and meanings. Generalizations about place refer to national, local, or regional cultures (for example, Malaysian, Parisian, or Western). Some are related to identities like race or gender (for example, feminine, androgynous, or Asian), and others define groups organized around meaning systems such as religion or politics (for example, Buddhist, Communist, or Green). Generalizations must be broad enough to capture a group's ethos, yet specific enough to be clear. All generalizations break down if applied too literally since there are exceptions in every group. Because every individual has multiple cultural identities, no one person is a reliable exemplar of a group across situations. Since cultures are always changing, no one description holds true over time. Cultures adapt over time, just as the humans who embody cultures evolve, to meet environmental changes.

Exploring cultures is concentrated work and fascinating play. Developing cultural fluency is to experience from as many angles as possible the multiple levels of meaning, identity, and communication in cultures. In this chapter we examine cultural fluency as a core capacity for bridging conflict. Several dimensions of culture related to communication and language are considered, including large-scale cultural patterns that transcend national and regional borders. Throughout the exploration, stories, metaphors, rituals, and myths are examined for the rich contextual flavor they bring. This chapter helps build our vocabulary and understanding for relating across cultures—and enjoying the journey.

Cultural Fluency

Cultures, according to the insightful anthropologist Edward T. Hall,[5] are a complex series of shared, interrelated activities with origins deeply buried in the past. They define the boundaries of different groups, and shape communication. Tracy Novinger[6] gives us the image of a spiral, reminding us that cultures operate in a living, dynamic circle, governing complex communication even as communication creates, reinforces, and re-creates culture. Since culture is expressed through communication, culture and communication are indivisibly part of conflict. Although not all cultural differences yield conflict, effective communication across cultures is essential to its resolution. Since all communication is influenced by cultural factors—as present to our experience as the air around us—cultural fluency is important to effectiveness in bridging conflict.

What is cultural fluency? Cultural fluency means internalized familiarity with the workings of culture, the currents of the underground rivers inside us and the others around us. We usually think of fluency in relation to learning a language. To be fluent in a language is to be comfortable with it, so that accessing the words to express ideas is not a conscious chore but becomes automatic. At the same time, fluency allows conscious choice-making and versatility in understanding and interpreting behaviors and implicit rules. Fluency means knowing not only the vocabulary of a language but the grammar and the system of sounds underlying it, often intuitively. It comes from knowing the idioms, symbols, and something of the history, art, and experience of those who speak it. Fluency means befriending a language, coming to know what it is capable of revealing, appreciating its nuances and what it has trouble expressing. Fluency is best built by engaging those who are at home in the language we seek to acquire.

Fluency involves sense-making. Imagine a poem written in exquisite Spanish that you have been asked to translate into English. Can you substitute words with the same literal meaning and get a good result? Not likely. To translate a poem—carrier of images, feelings, sensations—you have to make sense of it, feel its tone, get inside the way the author made meaning. Only then can you make a translation that approaches the original in aesthetics and feelings. Achieving cultural fluency is the same. An analytical understanding of a culture can never be comprehensive, because cultures are sense-making systems. They are about feelings, aesthetics, sensations, and ways of seeing the world that do not easily translate. To understand them, our sensing, intuitive, emotional, and imaginative selves are needed. These aspects of ourselves are engaged as we form relationships across cultures.

Cultural fluency asks us to remember that culture is a set of internalized understandings and ways of interacting with the world. It draws our attention to the ways cultural messages influence identity and meaning-making. We can increase our cultural fluency in a variety of ways. One of the most productive is putting ourselves in situations that stretch us, where we encounter culturally unfamiliar people and situations, observe our responses, and develop resourcefulness and flexibility. As we learn to recognize cultures' influences and see their effects on perceptions and attitudes, behaviors and interpretations, we are better able to understand subtle nuances and relate well across differences.

When our cultural expectations are violated, it is hard to exercise cultural fluency. One of the most common challenges encountered relates to different senses of time. Time may be approached as *monochronic*—sequential, tangible, and schedule focused—or *polychronic*—fluid, cyclical, and unstructured.[7] Which sense of time fits better for you? Is punctuality important, do you like to get to the point quickly in conversation, do you plan events one after another, maximizing efficiency? If so, you may have a monochronic approach to time. Or do you like to do several things at once, do you not mind overlaps in conversation, and do you focus more on the activity and the people involved than the minutes elapsed? These perspectives are associated with a polychronic approach to time.

Different approaches to time can cause or escalate conflict, especially when they are outside conscious awareness. In negotiations, for example, monochronic approaches dictate prompt beginnings, scheduled breaks and closings, turn taking when speaking, and adherence to an agenda. Polychronic participants may arrive after the scheduled start, talk through breaks or adjournment times, interrupt each other to contribute to ideas, and freely deviate from an agenda. No one national culture is associated with either approach to time, though business cultures tend to be monochronic in North America and polychronic in Latin America.[8] Sense of time relates to context and relationship—polychronic time prevails in many U.S. and Canadian homes as different family members go in various directions throughout the day.

How have conflicts related to time surfaced in your life? Conflicts like this happen all the time, within and between cultural groups. For example, two Canadian women were in the early stages of developing a friendship when they decided to meet for lunch at a new restaurant. One of them arrived punctually, five minutes before the agreed time. The other came twenty-five minutes later, shocked to find her friend fuming. Realizing that they had different ideas about what "twelve o'clock" meant, they discussed how lateness meant disrespect to the first yet carried no negative message for the second. At the end of the meal the first woman had to leave promptly to get to an appointment. The other would have been glad to linger over a second cup of coffee. Their recognition that they had different ways of relating to time led them each to make adjustments to nurture their relationship.

Conflict Avoidance

The women's choice to talk through their conflict would be atypical in many cultural settings. Whether we come from a barrio in the Philippines or a Kansas town, many of us try to avoid conflicts. We pretend not to notice or imagine that something not named will fade away. Some conflicts, treated this way, do fade away. But these tend to be one of two types: either they are trivial, not reaching deeply into the way we hold ourselves inside and twisting us around, or they happen in a context where the costs of addressing them are too great. When there is a difference that matters to us, we avoid it at our peril, for it can act like a ball held under the water, even a slight shift in the pressures on it can make it pop up with great force, taking everyone by surprise.

When we cannot, or choose not to, avoid a conflict, there are many responses open to us, some more culturally fluent in a context than others. We can communicate directly or indirectly, naming the issue or asking a question that engages the other. We can choose to tell a story, share a metaphor, or find a ritual to help us surface and balance the swirling dynamics of the conflict. Sometimes silence or nonverbal messages are potent and expressive tools. We approach issues formally or informally, directly or indirectly depending on many factors including status, role, history of the relationship, power dynamics, and context. Whichever form of response we use, how we communicate will affect the course of our relationship and our conflict, serving to escalate, calm, or maintain differences that divide us.

Missed Signals

Two quite different forms of communication were chosen by the presidents of the United States and Mexico in 1977 speeches. The occasion was the end of a two-day meeting in Mexico City, in February of that year, when both President Jimmy Carter and President López Portillo gave short public addresses. Mexico had discovered significant reserves of oil and gas, and tensions had arisen between the countries relating to the discoveries and also to the ubiquitous issues of drugs and immigration. Here is an excerpt from President Portillo's remarks:

> It has now been two years since we met for the first time. Since then a great deal of water has flowed beneath the bridges of the Rio Grande. A great deal has also happened within our countries, as it has in the world and to the world. . . . Among permanent, not casual neighbors, surprise moves and sudden deceit or abuse are poisonous fruits that sooner or later have a reverse effect. Mexico has suddenly found itself the center of American attention—attention that is a surprising mixture of interest, disdain and fear, much like the recurring vague fears you yourselves inspire in certain areas of our national subconscious. Let us seek only lasting solutions— good and fair play—nothing that would make us lose the respect of our children.[9]

President Portillo spoke of conflict using metaphors rich with feeling and concern. He described his desire to engage with the United States in developing a relationship of trust and fairness. Perhaps he expected that President Carter would counter or at least acknowledge the conflicts he alluded to. Instead, President Carter's remarks took a different direction, as illustrated in this excerpt:

President López Portillo and I have, in the short time together on this visit, found that we have many things in common. We both represent great nations; we both have found an interest in archeology; we both must deal with difficult questions like energy and the control of inflation . . . we both have beautiful and interesting wives; we both run several kilometers every day. As a matter of fact, I told President López Portillo that I first acquired my habit of running here in Mexico City. My first running course was from the Palace of Fine Arts to the Majestic Hotel, where my family and I were staying. In the midst of the Folklórico performance, I discovered that I was afflicted with Montezuma's revenge.[10]

It is probable that these speeches had to do with politics and individual personalities as well as with cultures, but their cultural features are worth exploring. Carter, representing Mexico's powerful northern neighbor, emphasizes commonality, while Portillo, who has more to lose from such an emphasis, draws attention to differences. Carter focuses on their present-tense individual commonalities; Portillo speaks for Mexico and posterity, the collective. Carter takes a factual, almost recitative approach, while Portillo uses evocative, emotional language. Indeed, Carter's one evocative reference to diarrhea was taken as an insult by Mexicans, who heard it as a thinly veiled reference to inadequate sanitation. Perhaps Carter shared the story as a way of building rapport—it had the opposite effect.

It is important not to generalize from this example, feeding the stereotype of America's insensitivity to its southern neighbors. Indeed, Carter did many things right, including vowing that he would "go even further than is required through diplomatic courtesy to work closely with [Portillo] on a personal . . . basis."[11] Although increased awareness would be helpful among all the countries that share this continent, it is important to recognize how our expectations and assumptions collide, even when we intend goodwill. It is also useful to realize that cultural challenges to communication occur not only at the national level but in relation to other facets of cultural identity as well.

I remember a case involving an African-American mother receiving social assistance payments called to account for the ways she had spent her money. There was a requirement that the money be spent on "necessaries" and an allegation that she had failed to meet this duty. The mother was assigned a lawyer, a white woman. Together they went through her expenses in preparation for the hearing. One item in particular stood out from the list: a pair of new, red Sunday shoes. Since there were other shoes on the list, the lawyer suggested deleting the references to *red* and *Sunday,* as this description would surely raise questions. At the hearing the lawyer was surprised to find that the words *red* and *Sunday* had been added back in by the mother and were among the first things she mentioned when she was asked by the judge to talk about how she had spent her money. The lawyer wondered what had happened. Did the woman not understand the suggestion? Was she being obstinate and resistant? As the lawyer thought about it and replayed the woman's proud pronouncements back in her mind's ear, she realized that she was looking at the issue through her own worldview. To this mother, red Sunday shoes were just as necessary as eggs and milk. Emphasizing her choice was her way of speaking her values and maintaining her cultural voice and values in this adversarial process that squeezed, diminished, and second-guessed.

In these examples, the use of different cultural lenses caused people to miss signals. They did not intend to communicate in parallel lines rather than intersecting ones, but they did. Once this had happened they did not necessarily realize that a cultural miscommunication had occurred. Only later did this become clear. In both cases language issues contributed to the missed signals. President Portillo was using a language other than his birth language; the lawyer recommended a change in words to her client, for whom a special meaning was attached to the original words. Language can be a helpful tool and also a complicating factor when we communicate across cultures.

I Can't Say What I Mean

Mimosa was a Chinese woman who had grown up on Tahiti, born of immigrant parents. When she made the decision to leave her French husband to marry another man, she ran into difficulties trying to express her feelings to her father. Her intent was to let her father know that she did not love her first husband anymore and had fallen in love with her new fiancé. As she attempted to communicate with her father in his Chinese dialect, she found that there was no word that she could use that was equivalent to the word *love* in her Western language, French. The only words in his dialect that seemed to apply even roughly to her circumstances were words that translated as "esteem," "honor," "respect," or "duty." But if she told her father that she did not feel respect or duty toward her husband, this would only reinforce her father's negative view that she was not a good wife or daughter. Since there was no way to explain her feelings in Chinese, she despaired, concluding that it was simply not possible to communicate about the subject with her father.[12]

There are countless other examples of words and concepts that do not translate across linguistic boundaries. Inuit people can talk more specifically about snow than those speaking English. In Gaelic, there are no equivalents of *yes* and *no;* someone speaking Gaelic uses constructions like *I think not* and *this seems so* in place of *yes* and *no*.[13] Italian words for pacing and mood in music are used around the world: *andante, allegro, adagio*. We can say them in English—*slowly, quickly, very slowly*—but somehow they don't convey the same mood and nuance as their Italian counterparts.

Cultural fluency means recognizing that language shows us particular views of the world. Rather than being a direct representation of reality, language reflects our starting points, assumptions, and ideas about how the world works and our places in it. Remembering this, we keep an open mind to diverse starting points and assumptions. We also attend to the likelihood of miscommunication when different linguistic starting points are being used. When communicating across linguistic boundaries, it is helpful to use more than one phrase to convey intended meaning and to check for feedback often.

Beyond Words

We can make even more fine distinctions about communication if we focus on speech choices and styles. Depending on the cultural context, rate of speech varies. A "fast talker" may be perceived as glib and untrustworthy in one cultural context yet intelligent and engaging in another. The use of *uh-huh* and *mmh* may be encouraging in one setting and disrespectful in another. Native speakers of tonal languages, like Chinese, speaking English may sound agitated to native English speakers, who expect a flatter modulation. Because of different interpretations of pitch, volume, and tone, U.S. Americans may think that Latin Americans are arguing when they are just having a conversation.

Many other variables, verbal and nonverbal, lead to miscommunication. Tone, pitch, timing, and inflection mean different things in different contexts. Gestures too do not translate well across boundaries. The Canadian signal for *A-OK*, made by touching the thumb to the first finger, is an offensive insult in some African countries. Maintaining eye contact is a sign of respectful attention in U.S. dominant culture but disrespectful in Native American cultures. Donal Carbaugh tells the story of a Soviet colleague visiting his office during the 1980s who saw his display of family pictures as a sign that he devalued his family life because he had brought it into the public sphere.[14] Although for Carbaugh the display was a sign of endearment, its meaning was very different to his friend.

Pacing and degree of overlap are other variables that shift across cultures. Deborah Tannen reports that it is more common in most of the world for people talking together to overlap their speech than to take linear turns.[15] From Antigua to Hawaii, from Thailand to Israel, simultaneous conversations take place in ways considered both appropriate and normal. What might seem a rude interruption to an American or Canadian might be a comfortable way of showing involvement, participation, and connection to a native Hawaiian or Thai conversationalist.

We know from communication studies and our own intuitive experience that nonverbal communication is also hugely important in conflict. Moments may be pregnant with the unsaid; gestures may say volumes; eyes may communicate universes of feelings as they implore, criticize, or encourage, as they acknowledge or invade. Our body posture receives and invites or dismisses and protects. All these nonverbal signals are subject to a range of cultural expectations and interpretations.

The next time you are in a large gathering, watch the distance people stand from each other. There is often a kind of dance: those comfortable with a greater amount of personal space during a conversation back up as those accustomed to closer proximity move forward. The more one backs up, the more the other moves forward, until they have moved some distance from where they began. The dance is also influenced by context. When there is a high level of noise in the room, people may move toward their conversation partners. Uncomfortable with this proximity, the partner moves back. And so the dance continues, often outside our conscious awareness.

Of course all of these generalizations are situational. The distance from another that we find comfortable comes from a web of interconnected cultural messages in dynamic exchange within us and between us and the other person that is influenced by gender, age, relationship, context, time, setting, status, role, and many other factors. The interrelationship of these factors informs our behavior, often without thought. As we interact we perceive others' behavior and adjust our own in an unbroken multidirectional loop, creating a unique, culturally influenced thumbprint of our relationship at that moment in time. Later, that print may change as we change and the context shifts; yet it is also true that an aerial view may show us patterns that play out between us and others over time. We are often unaware of the patterns or the influences that shape them, until an expectation is not met or something in an interaction surprises us.

For example, whether conflict is best talked about or addressed indirectly varies considerably across cultures. A Canadian teaching English in Japan learned this the way we often come to cultural understandings: the hard way. He noticed that Japanese teachers on the staff where he was serving had become more distant. It was subtle, but there was less small talk and fewer contacts in general in the halls or the teacher's room. He wondered whether he had upset someone. So he asked. A perfectly appropriate and natural thing for him to do in Canada. The two teachers he asked seemed surprised. They assured him that nothing was amiss in their relations.

Yet still it seemed that things were not as they had been. As he continued to live in Japan, he learned that there were many things he did not understand and that asking about them directly often had counterproductive results. It was more effective to find someone who was not directly involved and who was willing to guess with him about what might be happening, or to ask the help of someone on the staff who was not directly related to those he felt the concern about. He was coming to see the streams and the tributaries where conflict flowed in his new national context and to learn to follow them to the river, rather than trying to name the places where they were dammed. This worked much better for him over time. He grew adept at reading nonverbal messages and at posing queries to those who might help, without ever surfacing a conflict directly. He also learned when not to act at all, recognizing that the hierarchy in place meant that certain things were not to be questioned but accepted.

European-Canadians may have similar experiences in First Nations contexts. Rupert Ross tells about his tendency, when he began spending time in First Nations settings, to ask directly for advice.[16] He was not refused directly, but he rarely got the advice he sought. Rather, people would answer his questions about whether to do something with words like "perhaps" or "you could." After a while he learned to cast his questions in a story that did not involve a direct request for an answer. He would review the factors he was considering out loud, as though for his own benefit. The problems were posed implicitly. He received verbal meditations and sometimes stories in return. As the characters in these stories made particular decisions, the storytellers' perspectives were communicated to him without interfering with his right to choose. Verbal communication was used to convey information, but what was not said was also very significant.

Just as Ross learned to adapt his style to a First Nations context, so we continually adapt our communication depending on a range of verbal and nonverbal cues. One of the important ways people's communication differs is in the norms for expression of emotions.

Communicating Emotions

There are many different cultural messages about emotions—how they are expressed or withheld, how they are experienced and used. Not only is there a range of possibilities across groups, ranging from dramatic expressiveness to completely "tucked in," but these expectations vary within groups, according to gender, age, status, and other identity and contextual factors. And it is not easy to predict or understand how these dynamics operate in groups, so dependent are they on time, place, setting, purpose of meeting, and the mix of individuals involved. As with any set of cultural norms and patterns, prescriptions won't do. They have as much capacity to confuse us as help us, depositing us at the door of the taxonomy trap before we know it.

For example, Tracy Novinger suggests that the rules about acceptable emotional displays for Arab males and females seem to be opposite of the rules for American men and women.[17] The U.S. American male, she tells us, is socialized to be stoic and undemonstrative or risk losing face, while women in the United States are given more latitude to express feelings. This male "stiff upper lip" tends to be seen as cold and unfeeling in the Middle East, where men can weep openly, she advises. Middle Eastern women, however, are said to be restrained in their emotional expression.

But American men should not take this at face value and head for the Middle East to freely express themselves. Like any cultural generalization, it is subject to contradiction. Mohammed Abu-Nimer, a Palestinian scholar living in the United States who has done many conflict resolution trainings in Arab countries, reports just the opposite of Arab men in his courses: "Men were uneasy about publicly revealing or sharing their feelings. Such a tendency, as the participants explained, is associated with the female domain and with weakness. They suggested using different methods to convey the hurt and damage done, for example, by utilizing community values such as honor and respect."[18]

Were the men in Abu-Nimer's courses atypical, or were the generalizations conveyed to Novinger inaccurate or applicable only to a small group of Arab men and women? We cannot know, short of a study investigating the question. But we can move toward the answer by looking at behaviors in settings close to us. Consider different cultural groups in the United States or Canada. Do members of these groups have different latitude for expressing emotion, and do these norms vary across settings?

I remember men in the church of my childhood witnessing to the truthfulness of the church and scriptures. Often they cried as they spoke of these things. This would be received by the congregation as a sign of strength and deep feeling, adding to the esteem in which the men were held. Yet there are also situations in which the display of public emotion by men is interpreted as a sign of weakness and undesirable susceptibility to the swampy realm of feelings when reason and determination are needed. Although the latitude extended to men in the United States for expressing feelings has broadened (President Bill Clinton was praised for his emotional expression), there are still limits on how much emotion is acceptable in the boardroom or a public speech.

Degrees of acceptable emotional expression vary not only with gender but with other aspects of culture. A highly emotional meeting takes place at a Jewish community center. People contend with each other, talking over and interrupting, raising their voices. Later, participants remember the meeting as constructive and satisfying. Someone from outside the group, however, unused to its communication norms, might have been uncomfortable with the level of emotional, overlapping talk, not recognizing that the group members' comfort with expressing strong emotions served them well. Whenever we feel concerned to contain the level of emotionality of a group, we should first ask ourselves whether group norms are in place that may be perfectly functional, even though different from our own.

Clearly, norms for emotional expression differ across cultural boundaries and settings, influenced by many factors. Cultural fluency increases as we come to understand cultural patterns of emotional expression that run through and across groups. Cultural fluency means recognizing that the person whose face displays no visible feelings and the one who jumps on a chair to make a loud point are both feeling beings; they just display their feelings very differently.

As we become aware of these differences, we are better able to tune conflict resolution processes to a range of emotional registers. Similarly, familiarity with nuances of nonverbal behavior and the ways language reveals and shapes cultural lenses improves our capacity for intervention in conflict. Cultural fluency and conflict fluency are thus intertwined and complementary capacities—each is dependent on the other for effectiveness. As we develop cultural fluency, we become increasingly attuned to the workings of culture within conflict and adept at responding with grace and flexibility. To further deepen our capacity for cultural fluency, we explore a series of cultural starting points and currencies in Chapter Three.

CHAPTER THREE

Cultural Fluency in Conflict
Currencies and Starting Points

In the first two chapters we have seen some of the ways that culture and communication are intertwined, leading, before we are aware of it, to conflict. Conflict is not just the product of generational tensions and warlike engagement. It happens when well-intentioned people get together to try to do something new. They each bring their perspectives and ideas about how to proceed and how to relate to each other. Inevitably there are differences in these understandings. Two problems flow from this. First, the differences themselves can confound communication, leading to misunderstandings and feelings of frustration, fear, or threat. Second, the people involved are often unaware that their assumptions and ways of making meaning are not shared. Because they are unaware of their divergent worldviews or cultural lenses, people expect others to behave in ways they see as appropriate or natural. When this does not happen, disappointment and resentment frequently follow, leading to an escalation of the conflict.

At a deeper level, conflict also arises when identities are not acknowledged or when negative assumptions are made about the threats posed by those with identities different from our own. When an aspect of ourselves that is precious is either unseen or denied, we become defensive and sometimes combative. The tendency at times like this may be to batten down the hatches, preserving what is precious rather than inquiring further to check assumptions and broaden our pictures. Cultural fluency asks us to suspend our defensiveness or urge to retaliate, replacing it with a spirit of inquiry.

With a spirit of inquiry, we explore the ways that cultural differences may be fueling our conflicts. Two ways to understand how cultures operate are by looking at what they value (*currencies*) and by understanding where they begin (*starting points*).

Cultures from a Bird's-Eye View

As I noted earlier, anthropologists and communication scholars tend to generalize about groups based on place, identity, and meaning systems. They identify broad cultural patterns that play out in different settings and identity groups as starting points, places that feel natural to members of groups as ways to see and be in the world. These patterns relate to values, or currencies, that play out in social relations and orientations to the surrounding world. These starting points and currencies help us get a sense of the lay of the land in particular groups, but they cannot function as complete maps because the territory shifts as cultures change and evolve.

There are many different ways of understanding starting points and currencies, involving numerous systems of categorization, labels, and definitions. I have chosen three patterns helpful in developing cultural fluency: high- and low-context communication, individualism and communitarianism, and specificity and diffuseness. The first two are frequently applied and are the basis of many studies and training materials for enhancing intercultural awareness and communication. Some fairly reliable cultural patterns related to communication and individual or group orientation seem to exist across groups.

The third pattern, specificity and diffuseness, is not as easy to match with particular places or groups. It provides an interesting contrast because it highlights the way shared differences can sometimes cut across group boundaries, connecting people in one group not necessarily to others in their region or affinity group but to people in other groups. Focusing on this dimension reminds us of two things: that all individuals are multicultural, sharing identities and meanings with people from a range of other groups, and that cultural generalizations are not manifested evenly within groups or across times but change with context, external influences, internal dynamics, and individual preferences.

We begin with high- and low-context communication, one of the most common ways of exploring cultural patterns.

High- and Low-Context Communication

Edward Hall introduced the concept of high- and low-context communication in 1976.[1] In high-context communication, most of the message is implicit in the context surrounding it, rather than being named explicitly in words. People rely on physical setting and shared beliefs, norms, and values to imbue communication with meaning. Interactions feature formalized and stylized rituals, the telegraphing of ideas without spelling them out. Nonverbal cues and signals are essential to comprehension of the message. The context is trusted to communicate in the absence of verbal expressions or sometimes in addition to them.

Cultures that emphasize low-context communication place more emphasis on asking for what you want and less reliance on the context as a way to communicate. Verbal communication tends to be specific and literal, with less attention to the symbolic meanings that may be communicated by setting. Generally, Western cultures tend to gravitate toward low-context starting points, while Eastern and Southern cultures tend to employ high-context communication. Within these huge categories there are important differences and many variations. Most people move along the continuum, tending toward a low-context approach in some settings and a high-context approach in others.

A classic example that shows the distinction between these two styles is the experience of the visitor from a low-context cultural background who asks directions in a high-context setting. Novinger tells the story of an American, Robert, doing business in the Costa Rican capital of San Juan.[2] Robert knew that only sixteen of the many streets in the center of the city had names and the others did not. Needing to get to a government office outside this core, he was told that it was two hundred meters west of the Coca-Cola plant. He searched in all directions around the plant but found no office. When he asked for directions again, he was given the same description. When he told his informant he had already looked all around the periphery of the plant, the man explained that it was two hundred meters from the old Coca-Cola plant, which was now a market. The San Juan residents had an internalized, historical, contextual understanding of the term *Coca-Cola plant* that Robert did not share. Their high-context directions operated quite differently from directions he would expect to receive in the United States, where all streets are named or numbered.

Of course, local residents will always have information not shared by outsiders. Visitors to the United States may be equally confused by high-context understandings that are implicit, not named. Understandings of how to use the subway or busses, find shared transportation to places not on bus routes, or determine where and when to walk or cycle are examples of high-context meanings shared by insiders that only gradually become known to outsiders. In close relationships or groups, shorthands are developed that all insiders know but outsiders do not know. People who tend to use high-context starting points may also employ explicit, low-context communication in some situations. Although broad generalizations about high- and low-context starting points can give clues about an individual's communication, they are not definitive.

Consider this situation to examine your affinity with high- and low-context approaches. It is late at night and you are out driving. There is no other traffic in sight. You come to a red light. Do you go through or wait for it to turn green? Novinger suggests that Americans tend to wait for the light while Mexicans go right through it.[3] Explaining this in terms of high- and low-context cultural influences, she says that Americans tend to respond to the direct, literal meaning (red means stop) and are less likely to consider the context (the lack of traffic, in this case), while Mexicans tend to respond to the context and so go through the light because it seems safe.

Of course, both high-context and low-context settings involve nonverbal communication. It is the proportion of verbal to nonverbal that differs. In high-context settings people tend to put more emphasis and content into the nonverbal domain, while in low-context settings they place more reliance on words. Miscommunication and conflict can happen when people trying to communicate use these different starting points. Consider the large number of popular books available in the United States on male-female communication. American men, we are told, are more direct, factual, and specific. American women tend toward indirectness, relying on the context to communicate their meaning. Linguist Deborah Tannen, in *You Just Don't Understand,* suggests for example that a woman who wanted her husband to go to the store might say, "Gee, I really need a few things from the store, but I'm so tired." A man who wanted his wife to go the store, she argues, would more likely ask directly, "Will you please go to the store?"[4]

Tannen rightly says that the couple needs to understand more about each other's style of communication. The woman is using a more high-context approach; his style is more low-context. If he listens between the lines for the meaning she is communicating and she recognizes that he is using a more direct and literal approach, they can prevent misunderstandings and conflicts. It may be tempting in this instance to evaluate the solution from one cultural perspective or another. From a low-context perspective, misunderstanding would be prevented if she simply asked explicitly for what she wanted. From a high-context perspective, miscommunication would be avoided if he heard her implicit invitation and responded with sensitivity. The challenge, however, is not to "fix" one person to fit better with the other's cultural perspective but to find an approach that expands both individuals' awareness, perhaps combining elements of each style in a comfortable way.

As helpful as the distinction between high- and low-context may be, it is important not to see it as explanatory across times and contexts. The tendency to directness varies not only by gender but by region, generation, and many other dimensions of difference. It is more helpful to use the distinction as a way of making educated guesses than as a means of assigning classifications. Although a low-context approach is often associated with the United States generally, high-context interactions abound. Walk into a meeting of an unfamiliar professional group, say health care practitioners, highway engineers, or corporate solicitors, and you will find yourself in a high-context environment in which you may not know how to recognize the cues. A great deal is unsaid because there is a shared language and many shared assumptions. Beyond jargon, there are shared understandings of how to dress, when to break, who can approach whom, and how conversations proceed. We recognize these understandings most painfully when we violate them, as when I wore one of my dark "lawyer" suits to an informal meeting and spent the day feeling out of place amid the men's open-necked shirts and women's casual sweaters.

Conversely, even a national culture typically considered high-context, like Japan's, will have situations in which explicit communication is expected. When I attended a conference there as a keynote speaker, I attended several receptions where I was expected to give formal, impromptu speeches thanking my hosts and expressing support for the activities of the sponsoring organization. In these cases, my low-context comfort with naming and celebrating successful features of the conference served me well.

Returning to the speeches of Presidents Portillo and Carter discussed earlier, while there are many cultural features in them, neither is purely high-context or low-context. In addition to explicit statements, each man was also speaking symbolically, using broad, general language to telegraph information to the other, to their national publics, and to broader audiences. Both relied on the context and implicit meanings in their words to communicate more than they said.

Although it may not always bear fruit, the distinction between high- and low-context starting points is an important part of cultural fluency. It helps us in our effort to get inside another's communication style and intended meaning, both of which are important to understand when conflict erupts. I found this especially true in family mediations. Families develop their own norms and signals for communicating, many of which are outside the radar of outsiders. Intimate partners become adept at reading each other's facial and body language and are often more aware of each other's nuances than someone from outside the family would be. When high-context cues cross cultural lines, many will be missed by outsiders.

A mediation took place between two Chinese-Canadian parents who were working on devising parenting arrangements for their son. Early in the discussion one of them suggested that he go to live with his grandmother in Hong Kong. Believing that he would do best if he were near his parents, the mediator listed this as one idea and went on to solicit others. The parents continued discussing their work schedules, lifestyles, and relationships with their son. Only circuitously did the wife and husband return to something they had both understood earlier, that sending their son to live with the grandmother was a workable and beneficial idea that appealed to both of them. Because they were respectful of the mediator as an authority figure, they did not insist on pursuing this option at the time it was first mentioned. But both of them were quite happy to settle on it. They had used a high-context style of communication, letting the suggestion and the context speak for itself. But the mediator, accustomed to a low-context, explicit style of communication, missed the signal. If she had been more attuned to nonverbal messages and more thoughtful about the way the parents' idea of "family" differed from her own, they might have arrived at the solution less circuitously.

These examples illustrate some ways that high- and low-context communication patterns help us understand and prevent cultural miscommunications and conflicts. Here are some ways understandings of these starting points can be applied:

Low-context communicators interacting with high-context communicators should be mindful that

- Nonverbal messages and gestures may be as important as what is said.
- Status and identity may be communicated nonverbally and require appropriate acknowledgment.
- Face saving and tact may be important and need to be balanced with the desire to communicate fully and frankly.
- Building a good relationship can contribute to effectiveness over time.
- Indirect routes and creative thinking are important alternatives to brainstorming or problem solving when blocks are encountered.

High-context communicators interacting with low-context communicators should be mindful that

- Things can be taken at face value rather than as representative of layers of meaning.
- Roles and functions may be decoupled from status and identity.
- Efficiency and effectiveness may be the goals of communicators focused on tasks.

- Direct questions and observations are not necessarily meant to offend but to clarify and advance shared goals.
- Indirect cues may not be enough to get the other's attention.

As we become culturally fluent we notice high- and low-context communication patterns and respond with sensitivity. We integrate elements of both, moving fluidly from one frame to another. Mediators and facilitators do this without thinking, explaining something unstated so that all parties understand it, telegraphing concern or emphasis through a gesture or a pause. We code-switch, trying different starting points when our favorites don't work, and attending to what is said and what is not. We are mindful that people see themselves and their relationships quite differently across cultural contexts. One way of looking at patterns of relationships is through the continuum of individualism and communitarianism.

Communitarianism and Individualism

Communitarianism and individualism are starting points that relate to the ways we think of ourselves and define our roles and relationships. Consider this example: a mediation service was set up to serve South Asian clients in a Canadian province. Workers were recruited who spoke Hindi and Punjabi, and outreach was done at temples and community centers. When marital disputes were mediated, the agreements seemed to break down; they did not last. Puzzled caseworkers came together to discuss the situation. What was it they were doing or not doing that was contributing to this pattern?

As they talked it became clear. In South Asian traditional cultures, marital disputes do not involve only husbands and wives, as envisioned by Canadian family law. They also involve other decision makers: mothers, fathers, grandparents, aunts, uncles, even siblings and cousins. When everyone was not at the table, agreements were made that were later discarded because everyone needed for the landing was not involved in the takeoff. In South Asian cultures, individuals are not the discrete, autonomous units they may be in dominant cultures of Canada or the United States. They are connected in a web of relations who are not only their supports and their guardians but actually extensions of themselves.

Decisions are not made individually but in concert with relations whose influence is fundamental and whose agreement is necessary.

Communitarian settings teach children that they are part of a unit, a circle of relations. They are rewarded for obedience, cooperation, deference to elders, and acting in harmony with family values. Wherever they go, their identity is connected to their father and mother and to their extended family. Their membership in their ethnic or racial group also goes out in front. It is not so much what they do that is featured as who they are. When conflict happens, they are expected to consult and act in accordance with familial and group norms and views.

Individualist patterns involve ideas of the self as independent, self-directed, and autonomous. Much of Western negotiation theory presupposes exactly this kind of person: someone able to make proposals and concessions and maximize gains in her self-interest. Children raised in this milieu are rewarded for initiative, personal achievement, and individual leadership. They may be just as close to their families as are children raised in a communitarian setting, but they draw the boundaries differently: in case of a conflict they feel more free to choose their own preference. Duty, honor, and deference to authority are less prominent than in a communitarian frame of thinking.

Individual and communal identities are two quite different ways of being in the world. They connect at some point, of course, because all groups are made up of individuals and all individuals find themselves in relationship with various groups. But the starting points are different. To discern the basic difference, ask yourself which is most in the foreground of your life: the welfare, development, security, prosperity, and well-being of individuals or the shared heritage, ecological resources, traditional stories, and combined accomplishments of your group? Generally, those who start with individualism as their orientation tend to be most comfortable with independence, personal achievement, and a competitive conflict style. Those who start with a communal orientation are more focused on social connections, service, and a cooperative conflict style.

We notice these patterns when we encounter surprises, when events differ from our habits and expectations. Recently, a friend told me the story of a twenty-five-year-old woman who wanted to move two thousand miles from her family to do an internship in her field of study. The woman was living at home in Canada with her South Asian parents, having just completed a graduate degree. Her family considered not only the career implications of the opportunity but how it would be perceived in the community and how it would relate to her marriageability. They declined permission.

I was not surprised that they were worried and concerned about how it might look for their daughter to live apart from them and how it might affect the course of her life. But I was surprised at her response. She simply complied, remaining at her parents' home and working in a local organization. By age twenty-five, I had traveled around the world, completed two academic degrees, and made an independent decision to marry. Her willingness to accept their refusal showed me how different were the ways she and I thought of ourselves: I as connected to my parents but the ultimate decision maker in my life; she as interconnected with her parents so they affected her relationships and decisions.

As we do with high- and low-context communication, we change these starting points depending on context and other factors. Few of us can claim to be exemplars of either an individualist or communitarian pattern. We all engage in webs of relationships, make some decisions collaboratively, and give others power and influence over our lives in some ways. We are all individuals, sometimes acting apart from those we feel most close to, relying on our own counsel as we make micro- and macro-decisions. We may be communitarian with those in our own group and more individualist with those outside. We change and shapeshift over time as conditions change and we transit different generations and contexts in our lives.

Still, how we see ourselves in relation to those closest to us does make a difference to our communication and conflict behavior. On one end of the continuum we ask how much of our identity is taken from group affiliation, traditions, and norms. On the other end we ask how much of our identity is forged in the fire of rugged individualism, inspired by the drive to be independent and the expectation to "make something of ourselves."

One way of discerning where people start on this continuum is by listening to how they introduce and present themselves. Many indigenous people introduce themselves by giving their lineage. This connected web is a representation of who they see themselves to be, someone joined to a group rather than a lone individual. Americans and Canadians who are part of the dominant culture are more likely to introduce themselves by listing accomplishments and roles than relationships. Consider these brief biographies as windows into cultural starting points:

- P. G. comes from seven lines of history rooted in three parts of the planet. As she imagines them all at the same dinner table, she is motivated to continue developing approaches to manage cultural conflict.
- T. P. is professor of sociology at Midlake College and director of the Center for the Study of Cultures. He has worked around the world in over thirty countries as a cultural specialist and has written several books on culture.
- S. P. is a professor in the Department of Human Studies, University of Althia. He has worked in Indonesia, Taiwan, and Hong Kong, and has authored 27 books and over 180 articles and chapters.
- T. B. graduated from a Japanese international university in Tokyo, where she wrote a thesis on cultural resilience. Since entering working life, she has worked for a major Japanese company conducting training, first in Tokyo and now in Malaysia.[5]

Two of these biographies were written by professors working in U.S. universities. Can you guess which ones? It is not hard to identify the middle two biographies as coming from an individualist starting point: they emphasize achievement, productivity, and quantity of work as ways to establish credibility. Now consider the first and last biographies. Both are more communitarian in tone and description. They emphasize group connections and downplay individual achievements. The first was adapted from the biography of an American professor teaching in Japan. The fourth was written by a Japanese consultant living in Malaysia.

Identifying starting points from their biographies does not give us a clear prescription of ways to communicate with each of these individuals, but it helps inform our guesses. Remembering that none of us inhabits one end or the other of the continuum under all conditions, here are some things to be aware of at each end:

From an *individualist* starting point:

- Achievement involves individual goal setting and action.
- People are ultimately accountable to themselves and must make decisions they can live with.
- Although people consult with others about choices, they are ultimately autonomous; they inhabit their own discrete circles.
- Equality is an important focus of attention, and others are seen as able to make their own personal choices.

From a *communitarian* starting point:

- Maintaining group harmony and cohesion is important, and an individual's decisions should not disrupt that.
- Choices are made in consultation with family and authority figures, and their input is weighted as heavily, or even more heavily, than the individual's. An individual is a permeable, overlapping circle amid other overlapping circles.
- People's decisions reflect on their group, and individuals are accountable to their group as members.
- People notice hierarchy and accept direction from those of higher status than themselves.

These patterns manifest in our lives in different ways at different times. They are starting points, not absolutes. But understanding them helps us see our conflicts with more perspective and more choices. Often we learn this best when the ways we try to proceed do not work well.

For example, a white American friend, Nora, is in a lesbian relationship with an American originally from Ecuador. Though Erika has lived in the United States for more than thirty years, she still travels to Ecuador at least twice a year, spending six to eight weeks at a time caring for her aging parents. When Erika returned from a recent trip, she brought one of her parents and two other family members with her to receive medical treatment in the United States.

Nora was anxious to see her partner and excited about their reunion after several weeks apart. She was shocked when Erika suggested that all of them go to a movie together. Nora started from an individualist starting point, expecting that Erika would extricate herself from her family so that she and Nora could see each other privately. Erika proceeded from a different place, seeing her family as extensions of herself who could not be excluded from any social plans.

Sensitive to her family's anticipated judgment about lesbian relationships, Erika had not told them about her sexual orientation or about the nature of her relationship with Nora. This was a source of tension for Erika, but she felt strong pressure to be a good daughter, not disrupting her parent's expectations any more than she already had by failing to marry and produce grandchildren. Nora, who had previously been married, had told her children and close friends about Erika and perceived Erika's choice of hiding the relationship as negative and worrisome.

Though both Nora and Erika were concerned to be sensitive to each other's cultural understandings, it was hard for them to make sense of each other. For Nora, Erika's behavior suggested that Erika did not value the relationship as much as Nora did. For Erika, Nora's actions raised questions about whether Nora accepted her and her family for who they were.

Nora and Erika did not go to the movies. They spent even longer apart as Erika tended to the needs of her family. Later they came together and talked. Even as they recognized their different individualist and communitarian orientations, Nora and Erika nursed hurt feelings. They continued as friends, choosing not to try to bridge some of the deeper differences that made an intimate relationship so complicated.

Specificity and Diffuseness

At first blush the terms *specificity* and *diffuseness* do not seem especially illuminating. Does it really matter if my starting point is specific and yours is more fuzzy? The answer is that it can actually matter a great deal. Look with me into a scene from the famous musical *Fiddler on the Roof.* Tevye, the impoverished Jewish father of five daughters, has to stretch his specific ideas of courtship and marriage as each of his two eldest daughters chooses her own spouse without the assistance of a matchmaker and, neither of them asks his permission before deciding. When his third daughter not only chooses her husband herself but chooses someone outside the faith, he can bend no more. Although she sees her identity as diffuse—a member of a community who finds someone with whom she shares a passion for literature and ideas—her father sees her much more specifically. To him she is a Jew first, and her identity as his daughter requires her to uphold those traditions central to this heritage. His tenacious hold on his specific (and threatened) identity as a Jewish patriarch leads to the severing of his relationship with his third daughter.

Charles Hampden-Turner and Fons Trompenaars trace the division between diffuse and specific starting points to Isaac Newton. The Newtonian worldview emphasized science and measurement over relationships, aesthetics, emotional bonds, and value systems. According to Hampden-Turner and Trompenaars, people in East Asia, South America, and Catholic Europe tend toward diffuse starting points, while those in the United States, Canada, the United Kingdom, The Netherlands, and Australia tend to be more pragmatic and specific in the ways they direct their attention.[6] Of course people within these national and regional groups vary tremendously along the specificity-diffuseness continuum. These different starting points are a frequent source of tension between groups and deserve attention as an element of conflict prevention.

For example, Novinger points out that the more diffuse French see U.S. Americans as too concerned with application at the expense of theory and abstraction. Mexicans, also with a diffuse heritage, see Americans as concerned with problem solving at the expense of associative thinking and emotions. Multiple misunderstandings and conflicts have arisen as a result of these different starting points. Some of the most well-known involve U.S. Americans with their get-down-to-business attitude meeting the more diffuse Japanese, who focus on relationship building before addressing specifics.

One of the founders of Sony Corporation, Akio Morita, likens the difference between specificity and diffuseness to the difference between bricklayers and stonemasons. A bricklayer uses a preplanned set of bricks to build a wall, each chosen for its specific size. Bricks may be whole, half, glazed, or plain, and they slot into their allocated places in an orderly, specific, and predictable way. A stonemason, in contrast, chooses stones that approximate the general size and appearance desired and then chisels them until they fit together perfectly, a more diffuse approach. Each approach yields a different aesthetic result, and each has its uses.[7]

Missed signals and miscommunications relating to specificity and diffuseness can be seen in many organizational conflicts. A new dean came into the Department of History at a university. She was hired because of her no-nonsense, get-down-to-business approach. One of her strengths was setting targets and reaching them. But she found herself blocked by the faculty whom she sought to lead. In one symptomatic interaction she sent out a memo requiring all faculty to set office hours and post those hours on their doors. These faculty members had never operated this way; students made appointments with them by phone or e-mail, and theses got written and advising completed. Faculty were attached to this more diffuse approach because it enabled them to tailor their schedules to the changing demands of each week and the needs of working students. It provided autonomy and flexibility, and besides, the system was not broken so they saw no need to fix it. Abashed, the dean realized that her specific fix did not fit with the diffuse culture of the workplace, and backed down.

Another example arises from a land dispute between the Hopi and the Navajo in Arizona. Tamra Pearson d'Estrée explains the Native Americans' diffuse starting point: "To the Hopi and the Navajo, the concept of land ownership is a recent one. With these tribes, as with many native peoples, the notion is reversed: they belong to the land."[8] D'Estrée goes on to explain the implications of this perspective, including people's need to maintain sacred sites, perform seasonal rituals, and perform the duties of a faithful steward. All of these roles are bound up with the ways members of these nations experience their identities and make meaning of their lives.

These diffuse roles and sets of relationships stand in stark contrast to the more specific focus of state, local, and national government officials on land ownership. It is not surprising, given these different starting points, that interventions by the U.S.

government to try to address disputes between these two native nations have fared poorly. Seeing the disputes as involving specific issues of land title and relocation, U.S. government representatives have failed to pay attention to the more diffuse cultural and identity needs of the Native Americans involved. Because of these different starting points, many issues are still unsettled, and no lasting process has worked to bring closure to the land-related conflicts in that area.

As we recognize the importance of specific and diffuse starting points, we add another facet to our cultural fluency. Here are some markers to watch for, always remembering that context and individual differences are also important influences on starting points:

Those beginning from a *specific* starting point tend to focus on

- Truth through analysis, by breaking things into parts and logically classifying them
- The "facts"
- Clarity and action planning
- Objectivity, detachment, and results

Those beginning from a *diffuse* starting point tend to focus on

- Quality infused into life experiences and job functions
- Multifaceted processes and holistic thinking
- Networks and systems thinking
- Aesthetics, harmony, and close relationships

Both specific and diffuse starting points are useful in any complex cultural conflict. To resolve conflict we need to concern ourselves with clarity and results as well as processes and systems thinking. From the diffuse starting point it is possible to see the complementary potential of apparently opposed values. From the specific starting point we find boundaries that guide our inquiry. This set of starting points, along with the others examined here, helps us deepen our analysis, broaden our understanding, and improve our interactions.

When we are facing a conflict, our cultural fluency nudges us to canvass the starting points of those involved. Are they individualist or communitarian, primarily oriented to self or group? Are they specific or diffuse, starting with practical steps or the big picture? Are they high- or low-context, indirect or direct?

These questions help us understand conflict dynamics whether in our own conflicts or others'. Next time you find yourself feeling stuck, take stock of the starting points you are using. If you are focused on specifics, try backing up to take in the whole picture. If you are mired in particular issues, consider whether there are some overarching principles that might help. If you are feeling personally trapped, try considering how group wisdom might assist. If your direct appeal is not working, try coming in a side window rather than the front door.

Many other starting points relating to communication, relationship, and ways of paying attention have been developed. As we increase our awareness of a range of starting points, we build insight into behavior and motivations. Each of these starting points relates to ways we compose our identities and make meaning. Identity and meaning-making are difficult to analyze or break into components. They are the embedded core of who we are and how we relate to others. We explore them using stories to reflect their holistic character. Understanding identity and meaning-making in context will increase our cultural fluency and so our abilities to decode and bridge cultural conflict.

Culture, Identity, and Meaning

Who is your hero or heroine? Do you choose a civil rights leader, a world figure, a movie star, a character from a novel, or someone from your family? A group's heroes or heroines are windows into their identity and what they find meaningful. Some years ago at a university in the Northeastern United States, the members of the incoming undergraduate class were asked to name their hero or heroine. Two people got the highest number of nominations: Nelson Mandela of South Africa and Oliver North, a conservative U.S. public figure. These two choices spoke of a diverse population with a range of values and experiences influencing their identities.

From our earliest days we internalize cultural messages about identity: who we are, who our people are, and the stories, trials, dreams, and ways of our people. We learn about battles, victories, losses, honor, and frontiers. Having learned these as children, we then live them into being. How else are generational disputes passed down except by being conveyed to the young as a legacy? We cannot conceive of ourselves independently of the cultural air that surrounds us. Even if we leave familiar places and go somewhere radically different, we carry still the songs we know, complete with time signature, key, and cadence. We can learn other songs, but we never completely lose those that rocked us in the cradle.

Our cultural messages are part of our worldviews, a whole logic about how to know and how to order what we know. Have you ever thought about how you know what is meaningful? I remember my father taking me on a trip to see religious sites of historical significance. For him it was an experience that built his faith immeasurably. For me it was a series of long car rides accompanied by incipient nausea, tedious films, and guided tours among dusty relics. I found far more satisfaction in reading sacred texts, thinking, and talking about their meaning. My faith grew as I walked on morning beaches or sat in quiet contemplation and prayer. We were two people from the same family with quite different routes to making meaning.

Integrating Starting Points with Identity and Meaning-Making

The relationships we experience in our cultural beginnings are not only person to person, they are our relationships to ideas, to what is important and why. These experiences shape our worldviews—the cultural and individual ways we pay attention, process information, and situate ourselves in the world. They offer us many messages as we compose our identities and assign meaning to events. We are culturally fluent when we are able to integrate and apply our understanding of starting points as bound up with identity and meaning-making. This is illustrated by the compelling story *The Spirit Catches You and You Fall Down.*[9]

> In this story, journalist Anne Fadiman describes multilayered worldview differences related to health, illness, and treatment. She recounts the story of the Lee family, Cambodian Hmong who settled in Merced, California, after years of refugee camps and harrowing experiences. Their baby daughter, Lia, devel-

oped seizures that proved difficult to control and impossible to predict. In their culture a child exhibiting these symptoms is on track for becoming a shaman because of her contact with other worlds. She is precious, to be nurtured and celebrated for her special calling.

Symbolic acts were performed to protect Lia and mark this gift from the gods, including the sacrifice of a live pig. Western medicine, designed to stop the seizures, did not have the same symbolic clout. If it was as useful as the doctors insisted, then perhaps doubling or tripling the dose would make it even better. This was the perspective of the family; to the physicians and nurses the family was noncompliant, irresponsible, inconsistent, and incapable of managing Lia's illness. For one period the baby was taken from the parents by child welfare workers as a result of this "neglect."

In the Western medical worldview of the staff at the Merced Hospital, Lia was to be medicated, controlled, carefully monitored, and tested. She was a patient with a serious problem, and the problem became the focus of her treatment and her identity for the staff. Through a combination of mounting frustration, lack of cultural awareness (Lia was once referred to as "Mongoloid" rather than "Hmong" in emergency room notes), and concern about her escalating symptoms, conflicts between the family and the hospital staff escalated.

Saddest of all is that the physicians and the medical staff involved in this case had the best intentions to work constructively with the family to manage Lia's symptoms. They were skilled and dedicated practitioners. Yet there were so many miscommunications and parallel communications that never intersected that the relationship deteriorated along with Lia's condition. Lia lived, but unable to walk, talk, or feed herself. As a school-age child she was still being carried around on her mother's back and fed pureed food. To her physicians she had experienced catastrophic brain damage as a result of septic shock. To Anne Fadiman, who wrote about her life, Lia's life had been ruined by cross-cultural misunderstanding. Only years later did the physicians and other medical staff realize the extent of the worldview differences involved and how these differences had complicated even the most routine communication.

Lia's case shows us that cultural meaning-making affects every part of our lives. It informs what we see as health or illness, how we nurture and care for ourselves and others, what we see as adversity, and how we manage it. Our cultures inform who we believe ourselves to be and how we see others. In Lia's case there were clear communication differences between the low-context, direct expectations of the medical staff and the high-context, indirect approach of the Lee family. There were miscommunications about medication traceable to diffuse and specific starting points: the doctors saw it as vital that the proper amount of medication be given at prescribed intervals (specific), while the family saw the situation as more diffuse, requiring a number of interventions on physical and spiritual levels.

The individualist perspective of the medical staff led to their focus on accountability and management of Lia's case; the communitarian view of Lia's family saw Lia as a part of an unbroken circle, a part that could not and should not be extracted for "treatment" and reinserted back into the circle once managed or cured. This communitarian starting point was metaphorically communicated by the way Lia's mother, Foua, carried Lia constantly on her back, even at the ages of five and six. While the doctors began to equate Lia with a smaller and smaller focus—her symptoms—Foua and Lia's father, Nao Kao, continued to see her as part of their larger family and culture, treating her by sacrificing pigs and chickens and recognizing her seizures as evidence of soul loss and her shamanistic potential.

When asked about Lia's very difficult case, her physician, Neil Ernst, said, "Lia taught me that there is a very dense cultural barrier, you do the best you can, and if something happens despite that, you have to be satisfied with little successes instead of total successes. You have to give up total control. . . . Lia made me a less rigid person."[10] Perhaps this is the most important part of cultural fluency: releasing our hold on what we believe the world to be and cultivating flexibility.

The field of cross-cultural health care has grown tremendously in recent years as the need for cultural fluency becomes more clear. Physicians, nurses, social workers, and community workers are receiving cultural training, recognizing that understanding identity—conceptions of self and group—and meaning-making—ways of valuing and interpreting—are essential to effective service delivery.

Fatalism and Free Will

Another set of cultural factors relating to identity arises from the degree to which we see ourselves able to change and maneuver, to choose the course of our lives and relationships. Consider the U.S. and Canadian landscapes. They are vast, full of space and possibility, from sea to shining sea in the American mind and from sea to sea to sea for Canadians. Is it any wonder that people from the United States and Canada are prolific inventors with a sense that dreams can come true? Children grow up with an epic sense of life where ideas are big and hope springs eternal. When they experience setbacks, they are encouraged to redouble their efforts, to "try, try again." Action, efficacy, and achievement are emphasized and expected. Free will is enshrined in laws and enforced by courts.

Now consider places in the world with much smaller territories whose histories reflect repeated conquests and harsh struggles: Northern Ireland, Mexico, Israel, Palestine. In these places we see more emphasis on destiny's role in human life. In Mexico there is a legacy of poverty, invasion, and territorial mutilation. Mexicans are more likely than other North Americans to see struggles as inevitable or unavoidable. Their fatalistic attitude is expressed in their way of responding to failure or accident by saying *ni modo* ("no way," or "tough luck"), meaning that the setback was destined.

One example of how these different approaches to difficulty play out concerns a response to disease and treatment. Elizabeth Treviño tells the story of Don Eleazar, a Mexican lawyer in his sixties diagnosed with terminal cancer.[11] He gave strict orders that he not be given any opiates. Eleazar did not want his senses or his consciousness dulled. A devout Catholic, he believed that God had been lavish with his gifts and that he was being permitted to share in some small way in Christ's pain. Don Eleazar's fatalistic perspective meant that he did not try to change the order of things but instead strove to accept them as presented. Contrast this with someone who, faced with the same diagnosis, tries every therapy and medical intervention available. Neither is wrong. Eleazar saw his situation as his fate, and his task as accepting it with dignity. Another might see the same situation as a challenge and focus on overcoming or beating the odds.

This variable of fatalism and free will is important in understanding cultural conflict. If someone whose identity is invested in free will crosses paths with someone more fatalistic in orientation, miscommunication is possible. The first person may expect action and accountability. Failing to see it, she may conclude that the second person is lazy, obstructionist, or dishonest. The second person may expect respect for the natural order of things. Failing to see this respect, he may conclude that the first person is irreverent, manipulative, or inflated in her ideas of what can be accomplished or changed.

Respect

Another cultural variable related to identity and meaning is the concept of respect. When I teach diverse groups of people, I find that they often speak of respect as though it were a shared idea. It seems intuitively true that respect is respect is respect. Yet this understanding flows from the Golden Rule—"Do unto others as you would have them do unto you"—and not the Platinum Rule—"Do unto others as they would have you do unto them." The Platinum Rule challenges us to look from the starting points of the other, rather than assuming our own starting points are shared. For example, *respect* in the United States and *respeto* in Mexico have quite different meanings.[12]

In the United States respect is bound up with so-called objective, universal values of equality, fair play, and democratic spirit. One respects others as one might respect the law, and the idea does not necessarily have emotional overtones. In Mexico *respeto* is quite a different phenomenon. Its meaning arises from powerful human relationships such as those of father and son, *patrón* and *peón*, relationships in which the parties recognize that they are unequal in power and influence. It requires strict deference toward the senior person. *Respeto* flows from protected to powerful parties, especially when there are possible threats. In Mexico *respeto* is likely to be more personal and conditioned by circumstance, while respect in the United States is more a matter of choice to which individuals voluntarily commit themselves.

Different ways of seeing and conveying respect exist whenever we cross cultural boundaries. In some national cultures, formal modes of address communicate respect. Responding to the U.S. or Canadian gesture of friendship, "Call me by my first name," may be uncomfortable and awkward for some because of their association of respect with formality. Although students in my graduate classes typically call me Michelle, there are still some from Africa and Asia who look as though they have something distasteful in their mouths when they try to follow suit. They remain much more comfortable calling me Professor LeBaron rather than having to continually override their discomfort when they use my first name.

Respect, like any relational dynamic, goes both ways. Respect for different starting points and ways of making meaning is important for educators in multicultural settings. For example, a graduate student from Taiwan studying in the United States turned in writing that seemed exaggerated, general, and poorly supported. When asked to revise his work, supporting his views with others' perspectives, he was resistant. He saw no reason to change his diffuse approach, pointing out that many American writings are equally biased, including editorials in the leading newspapers. Why should he strive for a different standard? Why should he take the flourish out of his writing, aiming for something more dry and less lively? Why should he acknowledge other individual scholars when he was part of a community of inquiry in which everyone was contributing to knowledge?

His professor reviewed his work again. It was logically tight and well constructed. As she worked with him to teach him U.S. academic writing conventions, she also realized that his approach was bound up with his identity and starting points. From his diffuse cultural perspective, broad generalizations made sense. From a communitarian viewpoint, everything is interconnected and can be discussed in a holistic, generalized way. The U.S. American approach to writing, emphasizing logical, part-by-part analysis, asks something else of students. Gradually, the student and the faculty member came to an understanding of these different starting points, and he developed a way of writing that included some elements of the style required at U.S. universities. He later observed that he now knew how to write two ways—as his Taiwanese self and as his American self. This facility helped him navigate in each cultural context, built his credibility, and saved his face.

Face Saving

Face is important in all human relationships across cultures, though it plays out differently. Closely aligned with the desire to save another's face is a preference for tact and indirectness. To preserve face is to choose not to confront. It is to preserve honor and reputation, a sense of self-regard and competence. It is to protect from embarrassment and to recognize worth. David Augsburger tells us that in the Eastern and the Southern hemispheres, the idea of face extends beyond self-regard to esteem for the other as well.[13] How does face show up in day-to-day interactions?

In some instances the desire to save face may lead to miscommunication and unnecessary escalation. Imagine a supervisor so concerned with face saving that he does not confront a supervisee about her suboptimal performance. Instead, he tries indirect means to communicate displeasure. The signals do not get through. Since her performance appraisals have been adequate, the employee is surprised to receive a notice of termination. Shocked, she asks why no one ever told her that her performance was not meeting the grade. It is not a comfort to her to know that her supervisor valued harmony over conflict, choosing to save face rather than confronting her.

In another organizational setting the director of an office was so concerned to maintain her face that she set up conditions where she did not hear employee concerns or criticisms. She cancelled the tradition of brown-bag lunches at which her predecessor had met regularly with employees "just to talk." She proudly asserted that she maintained an open-door policy but seemed not to notice that no one walked through the open door. Employees feared retribution and difficulty if they disturbed her harmonious view of the office, though there was considerable serious conflict among them.

Not all attempts at face saving are negative of course. Face saving can preserve room for maneuvering, as in the case of a Chinese organization arranging for a low-level official to convey a negative decision to American colleagues who had proposed a joint research initiative. The Americans were able to go back to the senior officials and negotiate an arrangement, cognizant of the limitations conveyed by the junior official that were important to, but not binding on, his superiors.

Related to the idea of face saving are the concepts of truth and lying. Although Americans and Canadians in dominant culture groups may content themselves with the belief that truth exists and does not vary across cultural boundaries, there is evidence that understandings of truth and lying do indeed vary considerably. For some, truth is absolute and objective, waiting to be discovered and revealed. For others, truth shifts with the context and has subjective components. I remember my mother explaining to her mother why she had not seen my father wear her birthday gift to him, a sweater. "It's so lovely, he wanted to save it to wear to the office," Mother told Grandmother. I listened with attention, knowing that my father had never worn the sweater in the months since his birthday.

Later, I asked my mother about this. She told me it was "just a little fib" to save Grandmother's face and avoid telling her that my father did not like the sweater. By not using the word *lie,* she communicated to me that there was a kind of sliding scale involved in truth telling and lying and that some untruths were less problematic than others.

Augsburger tells the story of a traffic accident in a non-Western country in which a U.S. expatriate consultant was hit (but not seriously hurt) by a car driven by a local official.[14] A conversation ensued in which the consultant's request for truth telling and an acknowledgment of responsibility from the official was met with proverbs and offers of friendship, since "fate has brought us together." The American's desire for an acknowledgment of the truth seemed strange to the driver, who suspected the American of trying to lay the foundation for a monetary claim. The driver's desire to save face by not replaying the events but instead moving on to more positive topics was experienced by the American as an obstruction. Each walked away quite frustrated with the other, and their communication was more parallel play than deep encounter.

Cultural fluency means being attuned to our own and others' needs to save face. It means considering indirect means even when our reflex is to charge straight ahead. Applying the Platinum Rule is to imagine what loss of face might occur for others rather than imposing our own understanding. Face and face saving are almost always part of conflicts and are frequently misunderstood or minimized across cultural boundaries. When face is lost, the accompanying shame and embarrassment mean this loss is unlikely to be named.

Time and Timing

Early in this chapter we explored differences relating to time as one of the most common sources of cultural miscommunication and conflict. In the Western world, time is quantitative, measured in units that reflect the march of progress. It tends to be monochronic—logical, sequential, present-focused, moving with incremental certainty toward a future the ego cannot touch and a past that is not part of the present. Novinger calls the United States a *chronocracy,* in which there is such reverence for efficiency and the success of economic endeavors that the expression "time is money" is frequently heard.[15] In the Eastern and Southern hemispheres, time feels more like an unlimited, continuous spiral, an unraveling rather than a strict boundary. Those using polychronic time tend to see birth and death as part of the spiral, because the universe continues and humans, though changing form, continue as part of it.

A passage that Novinger translates from a Mexican novel illustrates a polychronic perspective: "When she was asked how she could carry on two conversations at once, Emily replied that such a practice was genetic to all the women in her family. And that some, like her aunt Milagros, were capable of following up to four. It probably was because of the country in which they lived, because in Mexico so many things happened at the same time that if you did not follow several things at once, you always ended up lagging behind what was really going on."[16]

A good place to look to understand the polychronic idea of time is India. From a traditional Indian perspective, time is seen as moving endlessly through various cycles, becoming and vanishing. Time stretches far beyond the human ego or lifetime. There is a timeless quality to time, an aesthetic almost too intricate and vast for the human mind to comprehend. Consider this description of an *aeon,* the unit of time that elapses between the origin and destruction of a world system: "Suppose there is a mountain, of very hard rock, much bigger than the Himalayas; and suppose that a man, with a piece of the very finest cloth of Benares, once every century should touch that mountain ever so slightly—then the time it would take him to wear away the entire mountain would be about the time of an Aeon."[17]

I have seen differences in time play out in painful and dramatic ways in processes involving Canadian government representatives and First Nations people. In a negotiation process related to a land claim, First Nations people told stories of their people and their relationships to the land over the past seven generations. They spoke of the spirit of the land, the kinds of things their people have traditionally done on the land, and their sacred connection to it. They did not begin at a point seven generations before and trace a chronology; they spoke in diffuse, circular ways, weaving themes, feelings, ideas, and group experiences together as they also remembered past injustices perpetrated by government policies.

When it was the government representatives' chance to speak, they projected flowcharts that showed internal processes for decision making, speaking in present-focused, specific ways about their intentions for entering the negotiation process. The flowcharts were linear and spare in their lack of narrative, arising from the bureaucratic culture from which the government representatives came. Two different conceptions of time: in one, time stretches, loops forward and back; past is present in this time and the future. In another, time begins with the present moment and extends into the horizon in which the matters at hand will be decided.

It is hardly surprising that neither side felt satisfied with the process of negotiations. No one named the differences in how time was seen and held, and no one turned his or her mind to how a negotiation process might accommodate these two quite different notions. And yet the notions of time were there, just as plain as the noses on their faces, impeding them from proceeding in concert or feeling their steps were synchronized. These notions of time affected not only the way each group thought of solutions but the way each group saw its involvement in the process, what was relevant and meaningful, where stories fit, and what criteria solutions would have to meet. These ideas affected their identities and how those identities played out in the process. And because these differences about time were unnamed and unacknowledged, they remained unaddressed.

Chronology, the scope of time, is seen differently across contexts, interconnected with the ways meaning is made and spirituality is understood. In many spiritual traditions the domain of spirit is seen as operating outside human space and time. Decisions may be made from this view that look irrational to those who do not share it. If time is an unraveling ball of twine, a helix, an unfolding of stories already written, or a play in which much of the set and other actors are invisible, then meaning also spirals, connected with eternity. From this time perspective, people in conflict may ask themselves about right order, about how they can yield to fate or destiny while serving others, or about how dreams birthed generations before can be realized. Embedded in this relationship to time is a sense of relations to others, to generations past and future, and in some traditions, to Spirit or the will of God.

Some have drawn parallels between landscape and cultural conceptions of time. Paul Belbutowski relates Arab ideas of time to the desert.[18] For the Arab with experience of the desert landscape, he suggests, its vast and shifting nature symbolizes oneness with God and a rhythm opposite to that of the Western world and its conception of time. A "constant everydayness" flows from this idea of time, in which it becomes less important to keep appointments precisely than to be in harmony with God. From the ability to feel oneself "outside of time" comes a more elastic way of approaching it.

Another way of thinking of time is to consider behavioral norms associated with time boundaries. There is probably a grain of truth in these descriptions of Mexicans, Americans, and Canadians leaving a party. It is said that the Mexican says good-bye, and this signals the beginning of a leave-taking ritual that will stretch into the next hour. The American may leave quickly without saying good-bye at all, not wanting to interrupt the party. And the Canadian will say good-bye but apologize for leaving.[19]

Whether these generalizations hold true over time and generations, the way we relate to time is surely cultural. Swiss trains usually run exactly as scheduled; Mexicans often defer meetings or tasks to *mañana*. The differences relate not to personal traits of industry or inefficiency but to completely different relationships to time. Taken to extremes, the Western European or American view of time can be efficient yet oppressive; the Southern or Eastern view of time can give us immediacy yet have a negative impact on productivity.

Continuing Cultural Fluency

By now, we have taken a quick trip through some cultural patterns and ideas that will help us navigate new terrain. We have considered how cultural differences are expressed and maintained through communication. We have looked at key ways cultural starting points differ, affecting how we see the world and relate to others in it. The challenge we face is formidable: to keep these guideposts with us and at the same time remember that our guesses may be wrong. To be culturally fluent is not to perform sterile analysis in our minds but to engage with others in unfolding insights into our cultural ways of being. As we do this we bring curiosity and openness to outcomes, knowing that intercultural interactions will take us places we had not dreamed of being. Some of them will be sublime, some uncomfortable. All will be rich with learning.

Along the way, we continue to add to our fluency, remembering to suspend judgment and embrace a spirit of inquiry. We look for connection and integration as well as difference and separation. The Indian god Siva, with his third eye, is a talisman for us in this process. Siva's third eye is said to contribute unifying vision. If you travel in South Asia, you will see many women wearing a third eye just above the bridge of the nose. Some will be jeweled, others colored, some ornate, and some quite plain.

Intrigued, you stop to ask a local about the meaning of the third eye. The answers you get will vary, reminding you that cultural fluency is about taking a 360-degree view as much as possible. Some will tell you it is a fashion accessory, a decoration. For others it represents cultural identity and belonging. A Bangladeshi friend explained her view of it this way: from the third eye we hear and see beyond what is expected or usual. Suppose we hear hoofbeats on the road. Our minds might envision a horse. The third eye reminds us it may be a zebra. Remembering to think outside our expectations, we continue by examining the role of mindful awareness in cultural fluency.

CHAPTER FOUR

Mindful Awareness as a Path to Cultural Fluency

To practice *mindful awareness* is to pay exquisite attention. How is attention paid, and to what? What does culture have to do with paying exquisite attention? Consider these meditations on self and awareness:

> Self is defined by others. A vast expanse of muddy rice fields in spring. Men, women, and children planting seedlings. Songs of joy, rhythm of awe, appreciation for neighbors lending helping hands. Red dragonflies in the sunset sky. Gatherings and endless laughter over bottles of rice wine after a day's work. Self is born and raised in the circle of others. Self dies, embraced—or sometimes ostracized—by others. Others define self.[1]

> Self-awareness is standing back and evaluating myself in context. I have two cultures inside—a small culture that comes from my close family and a larger culture in which the small one is embedded. My small culture evoked feelings, emotions, and passions—a vision of what I wanted to be. My larger culture drew the ground rules and laid the foundation for what I should be. The two were often at loggerheads. In the small culture was warmth, a cocoon where I had no need to rebel. I railed against the confined picture of women the larger culture showed me.[2]

> What is it to be aware? It is to wiggle toes in the early morning cold of a mountain lake when the only other motion is the lifting fog. It is to run on the beach until my feet give out

underneath me. It is to soar in the air, pulled by a parachute or
a dream, seeing everything below and taking it in to buoy me
on the journey. It is to know that I love and am loved, yet to
recognize that I am inside a circle that only I inhabit. No one
else has my feelings, my thoughts. I run with them like a kite in
the wind, or I surrender them to the evening's quiet, and they
show me everything.

These three meditations show quite different sensibilities of
awareness and self. The first shows a communitarian starting point,
where awareness comes from the self in relation to the group. The
second describes a family culture embedded in a larger group, in
which both groups define and shape awareness and possibilities.
The third reveals an individualist starting point, in which the individual self is the focus of awareness. All three reveal different cultural starting points and different ways of conceiving self and
awareness. All three contain images of nature in which self is held,
celebrated, freed, and experienced. All three depict boundaries
within which the self is unfolded in relation to others.

Awareness of our selves as situated within boundaries drawn by
our cultures, worldviews, and individual habits of attention contributes to our cultural fluency. This awareness is an essential complement to understandings of cultural dynamics. The fluency with
which we apply our understandings grows as our awareness of the
filters through which they pass increases. Becoming aware of these
filters, maintaining awareness in the moment, and choosing culturally fluent ways to engage others is the gift of *mindful awareness.*
As we develop this capacity, we notice with more intention and
presence how our inner terrain—responses, perceptions, meanings, identity—dances in our communication and conflicts, bringing us closer together or further apart, keeping us curious or
shutting relational doors.

Mindfulness is an idea much written about lately in the West,
arising from centuries of Buddhist practice in India and Southeast
Asia. Three complementary routes to developing mindful awareness are

- Using introspection and self-observation to discern how our
  habits of attention and unnamed assumptions shape who we

are, what we see, and how we relate. In this way we become conscious of ourselves apart from the usual bounds of time, image, and habit.

- Expanding our capacities for conscious awareness of ourselves and others, both our inner and outer worlds. As we grow in our capacity to be attentive in the moment, we develop insights into our own and others' meaning-making processes, choice points, and ways of being in the world.

- Focusing on a single object or process—the breath, a mantra, a tree. As we do this we exclude all other thoughts and ideas from our consciousness, developing an intense inner quiet and awareness. These disciplines are part of meditation, yoga, tai chi, and other practices. They enhance concentration and the capacity for mindful awareness.

In this chapter we consider how mindful awareness is related to our stories of self and other and how we can cultivate it, especially when we encounter conflict. As we trace the storylines of our lives, we begin to notice ways our early experiences and the assumptions that flow from them have shaped who and how we are. This foundation informs six practices that help us cultivate mindful awareness.

Developing Awareness in Context

Whatever our cultural starting points, we have blind spots in our awareness—places where images simply do not appear in our fields of vision. Cultural fluency means to engage others with a spirit of inquiry, learning about the ways our and their perceptions differ rather than seeing only the familiar picture that shows us the world as we would like it to be.

We each find ourselves struggling sometimes, straining against the boundaries that surround us. These boundaries are perceptual, born of our tendency to see ourselves and our ideas as normal. But they are more than this. These boundaries come also from the wider worlds that surround us, worlds that carry histories and stories of division, separation, and oppression.

These stories cannot be overcome by good intentions or high levels of cultural fluency. They are part of our identities, mirroring larger social realities in our relationships. After a difficult racial dialogue involving African-American and white participants, a white facilitator came face to face with this reality. One of the African-American participants, Jerry, was angry at her because he felt she had cut him off in the dialogue. She had asked him to pause in his comments because he had come in late and she did not think he understood the full context of the dialogue.

After the dialogue ended they talked about this incident for more than an hour. In the end Jerry got to the bottom of his discomfort: "I don't think I can ever trust you," he said. This was a statement that went beyond Jerry's experience with this facilitator. He was speaking about pervasive distrust between blacks and whites in America, no matter how well-intentioned and enlightened the people involved may be. This kind of distrust is hard to transcend in individual relationships because it seems to be in the very air. And this kind of distrust is not exclusive to blacks and whites: it exists between Native Americans and those with immigrant pasts; between wealthy and poor residents of neighborhoods; between rival religious groups of the same national origin, like Hindus and Sikhs.

Trust of course is not just present or absent. It accumulates incrementally, though it can be destroyed in an instant. Trust is not necessarily a prerequisite to resolving conflict—if it were, we would never even begin to address some of the most vexing problems among us. Trust can be built through experiences of reliability and connection with others. Often an opening for these experiences comes as we glimpse something precious or shared about another. Perhaps it is an aspect of their identity; perhaps it is something they care about or are devoted to. For example, when we learn that another served in the Peace Corps in Zambia as we did, we sense the bond that comes from overlapping circles. If we learn that a stranger shares our passion for bird-watching, or that he too loves the poetry of Czeslaw Milosz, we may also feel positively toward that person and a foundation for trust begins to be laid.

Whatever we do, whether we are mediating between feuding neighbors, deciding on a new policy with coworkers, or giving a presentation in a new city where we don't speak the language, we seek to build trust with others. Trust comes when we make ourselves vulnerable and see that the other does not exploit or hurt us. The process of building trust is often greatly helped by mindful awareness—paying attention to ourselves, others, and the dynamics of our interactions from moment to moment. We begin with introspection and self-observation, an exploration of our memory and subconscious.

Exploring Our Inner Terrain

Learning about our own inner terrain, our cultural autobiographies, is an ongoing journey. We cannot remember everything in every moment, and the strength of our responses sometimes surprises us when we encounter conflict with others. Following these surprises to their beginnings, we inquire about early experiences that shape who we are, what we see, and how we respond to others.

How do your earliest experiences shape what you see when you encounter others? To explore this, take a few minutes to create a timeline of turning points or remembered events that relate to your dawning awareness of culture and difference. Who were you taught you were, and who were your people? What were their stories, and how did those outside your group figure in these stories? Were they friends or adversaries, oppressors or allies? What lessons did your people extract from the history that connected them? How do these lessons play out in your present, in the ways you respond to strangers and your responses to conflict?

What did you learn was possible as a young child? Were you told that you could be anything you dreamed, or were you warned that you would have to work twice as hard as anyone else because you were a woman, a person of African descent, or someone from a poor family? How were you treated by those from other groups, and how did you respond to this treatment? Did you have the luxury of being unaware of difference, or did you collide with it early because your identity did not have the privileges attached to it that others' identities did?

Early stories and experiences influence the ongoing ways our identities are composed in the present. As we become aware of our personal starting points, we have new choices, dawning as we grow in ways of seeing outside ourselves. Eventually we move from our internal universes to recognizing that there are many cultural worlds operating in a parallel flux around and among us. Glimpsing these worlds, we see pattern and rhythm, shape and intricacy. Choosing any one of them, we see worlds within worlds, like a hall of mirrors reflecting each other in endless succession. Consider three different beginnings and the ways the places and people that are part of our growing up affect our dreams. First, mine:

It was 1964, nighttime. I was a young girl sitting on the stubbly grass in the backyard of my prairie home, looking up at the stars. There were so many of them and the distance to them seemed so vast that I felt very small in comparison. I wondered what ripples my life could make in the timescape of eternity. What would I do; what would I see? So many plans to make; so much was up to me. The idea of eternity made everything seem so much more immediate and remote at once. I crawled into my sleeping bag and dreamed the heroic dreams of youth, dreams of time traveling and achieving, and somehow, in all of that, making a difference in the world.

My experience seemed common to me; wouldn't children all over the world on the verge of adolescence have similar grand dreams and plans? The answer, I learned much later, is no. Listen to the experience of Venashri, a South African woman of Indian descent who grew up during the era of apartheid: "Strangely, even as I think about it now, I don't remember having any dreams as a young child, not about the future, or about the life I wanted to have. I think a large reason for that was that I had no examples around me about how much one could dream—non-whites did not have much hope of progressing to anything much and dreaming was not necessarily encouraged."[3] Venashri's horizons were much different from mine, shaped by the context where she was raised. Although her context shifted as apartheid ended, external factors alone were not determinative of her future. Venashri had a deep concern for others, a quick mind, and a supportive family, and so she transcended the limitations that discouraged her young self from dreaming.

Another young person, Eleftherios, grew up in geographical and political landscapes that shaped his dreams in important and searing ways. He was born to a Greek Cypriot family who became refugees following the Turkish invasion of Cyprus. Eleftherios's dream was always to be a farmer or a fisherman but never a politician. His early physical environment was very strange, unsettled, and unwelcoming. Survival was the most important thing. Surrounded by the deprivation of the refugee experience, his dreams of becoming a self-sufficient farmer or a fisherman made perfect sense.

Three youths, worlds apart. One on the island of Cyprus, militarized and tense. Another on the edge of the vast city of Durban, South Africa, a place of concentric circles where the whites were at the center and everyone else radiated outwards in color-gradated ripples toward black. Me in a dusty city on the perimeter of the vast North American plains ringed by Aboriginal communities I knew about only dimly. We all went to school, though facilities varied a great deal between the refugee camps of Cyprus, the Indian community in Durban, and the oil-rich Canadian prairies.

I learned to be self-reliant, independent, hard-working, sensitive to punctuality and efficiency. In my classroom the teacher posted everyone's name and, beside each name, tiny cardboard models of books for every title the person read in a month. The student with the most titles won a free pizza. Thus I learned early that achievement is an individual enterprise, and more is better. It never occurred to me to help others to increase their book counts; on the contrary I liked to be out in front. It brought me acknowledgment, satisfaction, and encouragement to continue achieving.

For both Venashri and Eleftherios, self and community were not as separate as I had been taught. Here is how Venashri writes of her identity in relation to others:

> I am a bright, shiny thread in a rainbow blanket. As I weave in and out with other equally bright threads I stand out for I am a unique color and composition. At the same time I am also subsumed into this vivid, loud display of color in this magnificent creation that blankets all. My complementary relationship with the other unique threads allows me to be noticed and to be cloaked all at once. We come together in a beautiful, knitted rhythm of patterns and yet this very joining is what makes our unique lines and individual patterned routes more visible. I am because we are.[4]

Eleftherios experienced early confusion about his identity. His family taught him that Greek and Turkish Cypriots had coexisted in Cyprus for many years. But all around him were fellow Greek Cypriots who saw Turkish Cypriots as their enemies, without acknowledging the way the communities had once coexisted. Within his Greek Cypriot circle, Eleftherios learned that he was a part of a cohesive group. He remembers the sense of community and connection in the refugee settlement where he lived, though even people from the nearest village were treated as foreigners. Resources were scarce and survival was paramount. Individual survival depended on working together in close family circles.

Culturally different, Eleftherios, Venashri, and I were raised with different ideas about who we were, how we were to be, and how the world works. We understood time and place differently; we saw our places in the world differently. Our ideas of family, propriety, necessities, friendship, and learning were different. Only later would we come to know of each other's ways of life. As children we learned the songs that would accompany us all of our lives, no matter in which place we would sing or in which key. These familiar songs do not determine everything about us nor do they explain us completely, but they resonate strongly through the ways we compose our personalities and make our choices.

Of course, even early in our lives, we were not without diverse influences. Venashri traveled to the center of Durban, where she saw places where "special people who were much better than you lived." She never visited the African townships where black Africans lived; in the hierarchy that was apartheid, black Africans were the "garden boys" and maids who came into her Indian community every day for work.

Eleftherios met Turkish Cypriots as an older youth when he was part of facilitated dialogues set up by international organizations. Only through these experiences did he finally experience some of the similarities that those from the other side of the green line shared with him.

And I eventually came to meet First Nations people from the reserves on the periphery of my city, though in our encounters on city streets we were shrouded in entrenched social layers that prevented us from coming to know each other until we met in the less confined space of universities.

Each of us learned early our connections to family, neighborhood, regional and national cultures. We learned about our generations, our genders, and our religions, each giving us messages about what was "proper" and "appropriate." Each of us was taught about right and wrong, though we were taught differently about what they mean and the consequences for wrong choices. Each of us paid attention selectively, noticing different things about our worlds according to our unique perceptions and preferences. Early on we all came to see that people within our own groups were different from each other, and we observed contradictions and surprises. We watched shows on television that brought other worlds into our homes, though many of the shows taught us more about myths than living cultures.

As we grew, our personal choices proceeded, interwoven with the cultural contexts in which we lived. Like people around the world, we developed as individuals in counterpoint with cultural messages from our groups. Sometimes we rejected the messages our cultures gave us. But even then we could not escape them, finding them triggered, like the song that won't leave our heads, when we least expect or welcome them. We vary by personality as well as context: we are extraverts or introverts; we pay attention to danger or expect safety depending not only on our upbringing but the decisions we made in relation to it.

Then one day strangers find themselves in contact with one another. They are curious, intrigued by the exotic other. They may have been warned of this "other" by parents and elders who distrust the mystery that surrounds them and the values they hold. Motivated by curiosity, they set foot in each other's worlds. And as they do this, the possibility of conflict arises. Conflicts do not necessarily follow, but as they try to do things together, their differences and the horizons they reveal may interfere with their effectiveness. They may share a goal yet want to get to their destinations in quite different ways. If they are to go together, how will they travel? And what tools are needed for the journey?

These questions arise for all of us as we work and play with others. Because the questions are never comprehensively answered, the journey metaphor is an apt one. Whenever we seek to help others or address our own conflicts, keeping inner terrains—our own and others'—in our awareness is an ongoing challenge. Here is what one participant in a workshop wrote about it: "Of course, I know that I have many identities. But so often in America, we think of ourselves as situated at one end of a singular spectrum of two opposites. Remembering that we are multifaceted, as are those with whom we are working, is an ongoing revelation in managing conflict." This ongoing remembering is central to mindful awareness.

Thinking About Who Others Are

In any conflict interaction we encounter layered challenges. One challenge is to maintain a spirit of inquiry about the other—who they might be, what they want, and what it means to them. This is not always easy. Feeling defensive and angry we may find it difficult to maintain curiosity and deepen our understanding of the other. But though we may not understand the other, we often remain focused on her—the other as unreasonable, as calculating, cold, or cunning—the other as exacerbating the problem. We wonder why she can't see the reasonable thing to do. We wonder why she is so closed, so convinced of her views, so difficult.

Carried by the emotions of conflict, we are focused on what we see standing in the way of a good outcome, and what we see is the other. Yet the other is only part of the dance. We may find it difficult to perceive our role in the conflict and what it means to us. Consider this simple exercise that reveals how we respond in unfamiliar settings. It involves a trip to Alphaville, an imaginary place with a distinct culture and rules of communication.

In Alphaville, people respond to outsiders only with the words *yes* or *no*. It is inappropriate to respond with more or different words to anyone not raised in Alphaville. With this understanding, groups of eight choose two *cultural consultants* to volunteer to gather information about the culture of Alphaville. These consultants become outsiders, subject to the yes or no communication norms. As they stand outside the seminar room, preparing their strategy for gathering information about the culture of Alphaville, the residents of Alphaville are briefed privately. The instructions to the residents are simple: answer yes to any question posed by a smiling questioner and no to any question posed by a questioner who is not smiling.

In come the consultants, trying earnestly to get information from the residents of Alphaville. They introduce themselves, explain their purpose, and begin to ask questions. Because the consultants smile at some times and not at others, they receive contradictory responses. The more serious they get about obtaining accurate information, the more no answers they receive. Still, they persist, trying to make sense of the responses and the strange cultural signals that they do not understand.

Sometimes the exercise may be paused and the consultants advised to pay particular attention to nonverbal cues to assist them in understanding what is going on. Typically the consultants get even more earnest, carefully attending to the body language of the Alphaville residents. Almost never do the consultants crack the code and realize that it is their own behavior of smiling or not that determines the responses, rather than the literal meanings of words.

We tend to look for causes and factors outside ourselves rather than in ourselves or in the relationships among us and others. It is difficult for us to move outside our associations with meanings and to imagine that others have completely different ways of understanding and making sense. For the consultants, yes and no mean affirmative and negative, respectively; seldom do they recognize that the same words may be used with quite different meanings in different cultural contexts. It is also very difficult for the consultants to realize that the arbitrary answers they receive relate to the dynamics between them and the residents of Alphaville rather than to rules internal to the culture applied by individuals.

Anthropologists, historians, and others crossing boundaries of time or context have long faced the challenges encountered by the Alphaville consultants. With all the goodwill in the world, it remains difficult to get outside our own frame of reference and understand another culture or way of being from the inside out. For example, indigenous peoples in North America and elsewhere were labeled savage, wild, and uncivilized by succeeding waves of explorers, missionaries, and settlers. At times they were idealized and romanticized, perpetuating the myth that they were simple-minded and childlike. Neither of these ways of seeing indigenous peoples took their worldviews or cultural ways of being into account as they made sense in context.

In engaging conflict across cultures it important that we take these lessons to heart, cultivating mindful awareness of our assumptions, projections, and metaphors for understanding the world and others in it. From this place, we recognize that others are best understood through dialogue and attempts to see them as they see themselves. Awareness of our inner terrains as they inform what we see and shape our conflict behaviors and expectations is central to effectiveness in conflict.

Exploring Intrapersonal Choices in Conflict

Consider the many identities that compose you. They are not fixed but fluid. They are not equal in influence but come into prominence depending on a variety of contextual, personal, and cultural factors. Together, cultural and personal influences make up your identity, your ways of being in the world and communicating with others. I find it useful to think of them as a set of lenses through which I see others and perceive myself. Because of our different combinations of lenses, we see the world, other people, and our choices quite differently.

Figure 4.1 depicts a way of mapping some of these identities. It is meant to be a personal snapshot, one that changes depending on the time and context in which it is approached. At the center is *Essence,* also called *Source* or *Core.* Our Essence is that which is essential in us. It includes cherished meanings, purpose, and values—the things we deeply care about—and identity—who we believe ourselves to be in the context of others and the world. The center relates to the big picture and our relationship to it, whether informed by religion, spirituality, or secular values. It is the purpose, meaning, and values of our Essence that ultimately direct our course. They are central to the lenses we look through, searching as we do for pieces that fit our puzzles and stories that speak to the mysteries that weave their ways through our lives.

The second circle radiating out from the center relates to ways we pay attention. These ways of paying attention vary with personality preferences and learning styles. From the work of Carl Jung come the ideas of *extraversion* (getting energy primarily from external sources) and *introversion* (getting energy from within).[5] Jung also posited that we take in information differently, some of us preferring sensory channels of seeing, hearing, touching, tasting, and smelling (*sensing*) and others responding to the whole picture, the abstract, imagined universe of possibilities (*intuiting*). At the per-

Figure 4.1. Cultural and Personal Lenses.

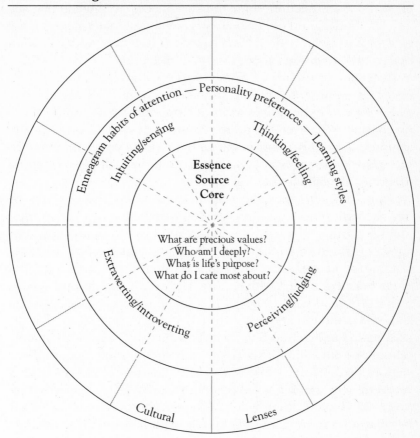

sonal level we also make decisions differently, some of us gravitating toward objective, external standards (*thinking*) and others to subjective, personal factors (*feeling*). Finally, we are oriented to our environment and others in different ways, some of us preferring a perceiving style that Isabel Briggs Myers and Peter B. Myers call *judging,* in which closure, planning, and certainty are paramount, while others prefer a *perceiving* style that is open to ambiguity, spontaneity, and change.[6]

The ways we pay attention at the personal level make up one set of lenses through which we look, influenced by personality preferences and learning styles. Some of us attend to danger, others scan for connection, some of us see first what is needed by others. The Enneagram of Personality is a rich tool for exploring these ways of paying attention.[7] It is based on the idea that each of us makes early decisions about how to compensate for the less-than-perfect state of the world. Some of us respond by achieving, others by retreating into an observer mode, and others by sampling a wide range of experiences without stopping to feel pain or dwell on conflict. Whatever our preferred mode of paying attention and avoiding discomfort, our personal habits are further refracted by the cultural messages we have received, and which of our cultural identities are salient at any given time.

Now look at the periphery of the circle, where there are a number of blank spaces. In these spaces, write some of your cultural identity groups. These groups may relate to a wide variety of cleavages. Informed by your childhood and formative experiences of how the world works and who you and others are in the world, they are nuanced and thick with texture. Each of them is its own system, with a group-informed logic of relating to others, making sense of situations, and engaging in conflict. These identities are diverse, relating to family, church or sacred community, sexual orientation, school or educational experience, age, generation, geographical region, profession or discipline, activity group, national origin, race, ethnicity, gender, able-bodiedness or disability, socioeconomic status—and many other factors. You probably have so many identities that you cannot name all of them, especially since the identities visible or salient to you at any one time depend on many contextual factors.

These cultural identity groups form the outer boundary of the circle, creating another a set of lenses through which images are received and transmitted. Their influence extends right into the center of the circle, informing Essence and shaping the ongoing ways meanings, values, purpose, and identity are composed.

As you look at your choices, ask yourself what messages cultural groups have given you about conflict—naming it, framing it, and taming it. What was and was not considered a conflict that could be talked about in each of these groups (naming)? How was the conflict addressed? Who could be involved and who was outside the circle? What kind of approach was acceptable and unacceptable (framing)? Was your attention directed to making peace within yourself, to confronting others, or to learning something from conflict so it could be prevented in the future (taming)? The various lenses in your cultural array will surely have given you different messages.

One of my most striking examples comes from contrasting the messages I received as an attorney in training and as the only daughter in a middle-class family in the 1950s and 1960s. From the former I learned to confront conflict in ways that stressed competition and closure: seek it out, name it clearly, and find ways to get and keep the advantage. From the latter I learned that girls do not engage conflict. They are receptive, agreeable, and lovely. They are peacemakers and so should set an example for others of equanimity and patience. With these two very different sets of messages, how do I navigate conflict when it emerges in my life?

It is quickly obvious that the right answer is, "It depends." Am I in a courtroom or my family's living room? Am I participating in a spirited debate or a gentle dialogue? Context makes a great deal of difference. At the same time, there are times when the setting is unclear, rendering my decision-making process more difficult. What if I am with a group of female lawyers from middle-class families? What if I am at a family gathering where someone asks me for help with a legal problem? At these times I am faced with mediating within myself before engaging with others around me.

Imagine you are with people from a number of different cultural groups to which you belong—family members, professional colleagues, sports group or book club members, those with whom you share a disability, people with the same ethnic or racial origin, people from your generation or your religious group, and so on. And imagine that a conflict arises among them. From which set of cultural messages would you draw in composing a response? You may well have a preferred style of responding to conflict—whether avoidance, accommodation, compromise, competition, or collaboration—but even these styles look different depending on which perspective you look from. To my attorney colleagues, compromise looks like giving in. To my family group, attempting collaboration to address conflict with elders may look disrespectful.

When conflict is with my sibling, a whole different set of strategies is appropriate. From a feminist perspective, avoidance may be tantamount to loss; from a Japanese cultural perspective, it may be an appropriately cooperative strategy.

As you consider different messages about conflict and conflict handling that you have received from different groups, ask yourself how you choose, harmonize, and reconcile different cultural messages. When you are in a mixed cultural group, which set of messages fits most easily for you? If you feel disempowered, which set of strategies will you reach for? If someone or something threatens one of your basic beliefs, will that change your preferred way of operating? This internal mediation process is something going on inside most people most of the time. It is largely unconscious, responsive to changes in context and mood, and varies depending on communication dynamics with others.

For those intervening in conflicts, observing this internal mediation process is important. Realizing that everyone is continually making choices from a variety of options implicitly invites other ways of seeing and approaching situations into the room. Recognizing that recent events sometimes cloud our abilities to maintain perspective, we can look for ways to step back, see the big picture, and reopen our awareness of choice.

An example of this awareness comes from a woman who attended a workshop on conflict and culture. As we were mapping our cultural lenses, she described the pervasive influence of two components of her identity:

> When I arrived at the course, it marked the end to probably one of the most difficult weeks of my life: my roommate Mary, an alcoholic, had gone on a four-day drinking binge early in the week, and we, her roommates and friends, were at the point where we did not know how to help her or how to tell her that we could not live with her anymore.
>
> It came as no surprise that the two identities I was most aware of were: me as Mary's friend and me as a non-alcoholic. . . . My context prevailed for the whole weekend, and every discussion was met with personal inward reflection on how my own situation related to that idea. . . . This realization led me to

a deepened understanding of myself. Now I see that my own identity is not fixed, but every situation highlights different aspects of myself that are important. It is therefore essential for me to step back from my immediate context, acknowledge those parts of my cultural identity that are informing my starting points, and approach situations with self-awareness and openness.

A dynamic, multilayered interplay of choices goes on constantly within us. Seeing how we mediate among those choices is an instructive exercise when done out of the fire of conflict, where our responses tend to be automatic rather than thoughtfully chosen. A related question is this: How do our favorite ways of dealing with conflict—those that fit best with our personalities, the settings we tend to be in, and our various cultural influences—compare with the expectations predominant in the cultural groups we encounter most often? For example, if I typically act in an assertive way, do the groups I tend to be a part of welcome assertiveness in a woman of my generation, class, ethnicity, race, and so forth? To the extent that our preferred choices are welcomed by a number of our identity groups, we have to do less *code-switching*, changing cultural strategies as we change settings.

It is also instructive to consider the number of times we find ourselves in the minority, or outside the norm, in the settings we frequent. When we feel that one of our identities is threatened or in danger of being eclipsed, that identity may become especially salient to us. If you are the only African-American in a group of Latinos, the only straight woman in a group of lesbians, or the only Christian in a group of Druids, your minority status may make you, and others, acutely aware of the identity that separates you. Possibilities of distorted perspectives and attributions grow, since it is almost impossible to tease out when and how conflicts relate to that minority identity and when other factors are involved.

Although our strategies for resolving conflict change over time as we learn new skills and enter new relationships, excavating and naming these cultural messages is a useful exercise. In a kaleidoscopic, dynamic way, they contribute to the lenses through which we see conflict.

A Cultural Rorschach: What Do You See?

Consider this situation to see how this kaleidoscopic process works. You are walking down an alleyway at dusk. It is dimly lit, and as you walk you become aware of some voices. It is hard to tell if the voices are angry, agitated, or excited. You realize they are speaking another language, though you are not sure which one it is. Walking farther, you see three people standing together. Because of the fading light, you can see only silhouettes of the figures. They are moving, now toward each other and then away. You can't really see what they are doing. Are they teasing, pushing, threatening, or playing? Should you be alarmed or not? You step closer to see, but they are in the shadows of a doorway and you cannot quite make out what is happening. After a few minutes you emerge from the alley and you can hear them no longer.

Notice what happens when you can see, but not fully, and hear, but not completely enough to understand. The natural human tendency is to try to make sense of what we experience. We search for the story, the logic, that ties the people, the talk, and the actions together. When we cannot find it, we fill in the blanks. We impute motives that may or may not exist, we imagine reasons for events, we find a frame to suit the picture emerging in our minds, a picture that may or may not have a close relation to what actually happened.

This kind of filling in the blanks is what a mediator did when his Chinese clients suddenly switched into a Chinese dialect in the midst of a session to resolve a conflict. Though the mediator spoke no Chinese, he let them continue because their tone sounded constructive and he wanted to show cultural sensitivity. After a time one of the men got up and went outside. As the mediator was asking the man who remained to fill him in on the agreement the two had apparently reached, the first man came back with a knife, intent on attacking the other man. The story of unfolding peace the mediator had imposed on this scene could not have been further from the truth!

Our tendency to fill in the blanks and make meaning of events is in operation every day. Even in a walk along the beach, you might find yourself watching the seagulls, noticing that they are all standing facing the same direction. Your mind turns to why they might do this, and you generate theories and possibilities. There are many perceptual tests that show us our tendency to make meaning. When we read a sentence in which a word is missing, we often automatically fill it in, unaware that it is not there. If we see a series of events that seem disconnected from each other or people acting in ambiguous ways, we ask why, how, what. We then come up with answers in the form of our favorite guesses, excavating these answers from our own cultural databanks. The more those we observe are culturally different from us, the more likely we are to be wrong.

I have seen this tendency illustrated powerfully when I show groups of people a videotape with shadow figures, much like the alley scene I described.[8] White U.S. Americans and Canadians make assumptions about motive, identity, and meaning that reflect their cultural lenses. They tell a variety of stories that make sense of the shadow behaviors, and they are surprised when their assumptions do not hold true. They often assume that the actors' racial identities are similar to theirs. When a Korean commentator reflects his assumption that the figures are Koreans, the whites in the audience sometimes gasp with surprise. In a scene of apparent physical aggression, most people believe the figures are a man (aggressor) and a woman (victim), even though the silhouettes are discernibly two women. Cultural assumptions about who is likely to be physically aggressive override perception, leading to an erroneous interpretation.

We are never blank slates. What we see and understand is always a product of our unique blend of lenses, operating in a context that gives us cues about what meaning to make, what conclusions to draw. Our cultural lenses influence how we perceive ourselves and others in conflict, what options we see for addressing that conflict, and how we pursue those options. As we grow in awareness of these lenses, we add the other components of mindful awareness: attending to our choices in the moment as they are shaped by our lenses and improving our concentration to make this possible.

Paying Exquisite Attention: Mindful Awareness in Practice

Paying exquisite attention reduces the number of times we realize only later what we could have known or done in the moment. We ready ourselves to pay exquisite attention as we bring our inner landscapes into awareness, noticing where they lead us naturally and how they open or block our way forward with others. There is much written about paying attention in this way. Six practices to develop this quality of attention across cultural contexts relate to multiple ways of knowing:

- Somatic ways of knowing—physical attunement
- Emotional ways of knowing—emotional fluency
- Spiritual ways of knowing—centering in purpose and connection
- Imaginative ways of knowing—releasing our hold on our *givens* (what we accept without question)
- Integrative ways of knowing (combining all of the previous ways of knowing)—focusing and meditation, caring and love

Somatic Ways of Knowing

Somatic ways of knowing are essential to mindful awareness. We know ourselves—our feelings, meanings, identities—through our bodies. We feel in or out of alignment, stuck or fluid, tense or relaxed. Our bodies literally express these states, and they provide ways to shift into new states. Essential to developing keen somatic awareness is *physical attunement and physical fitness.*

Physical fitness is important because tiredness, ill health, psychosomatic disturbances, poor diet, and environmental stresses can interfere with our capacity to pay attention in the moment. We are not automatons who function solely from the neck up. We are whole selves, needing nurturing, nutrition, rest, refreshment, and connection. Recognizing this, we attend to our own physical needs and those of others with whom we live and work. We seek to strengthen ourselves so that we can become instruments of inspiration, our bodies clear channels for receiving information about our feelings, our stuck places, and the interpersonal, intercultural dynamics in which we participate.

Taking a walk with an adversary may serve the ends of physical fitness and relational change simultaneously. Recently, I was angry with a friend over a miscommunication we had experienced. We decided to take a walk. As we walked, our measured steps punctuated the silence that turned into conversation, tentative first words merging into more risk taking and sharing. She spoke about her vulnerability as a new arrival in the United States, never knowing for sure "what the rules were." I spoke about my assumptions that we shared the same general understandings, assumptions that were not always correct. Because we were not looking at each other, we felt the space to express ourselves. Because we were moving, it gave momentum to our words, and we both felt much better by the time we had circled the lake. Physical movement was the instrument through which we tapped the emotional fluency we needed to restore our relationship.

Emotional Ways of Knowing

Emotional ways of knowing are understood and enacted through our bodies. We feel things in the pits of our stomachs, in our heads, the back of our necks, or our shoulders. These feelings bring us closer to or further from others; they help us maintain contact and alignment with ourselves. Emotional fluency—befriending our emotions—helps us access emotional ways of knowing.

Emotional fluency means to make friends of emotions, recognizing that they are not everything yet they are important guides. Emotions are guides to action—they suggest ways to act and respond. We are not slaves to them, yet we attend to them as markers of what matters to us and others. Our emotions pack a huge punch when we are not aware of them. If we seek to push them away, they can turn into the ball held deep underwater: when it is released, it shoots out with a lot of force. If we deny them, they can surprise us, infusing a situation with volatility beyond our expectations.

Having access to the full range of our emotions is important, even if we choose not to directly express ones such as rage, shame, or frustration. Most of us have come across others who are generally angry, whose anger spills out into differences with waitresses, gas station attendants, the person in the tollbooth. They may keep playing in that minor key unless they find a way to get more acquainted with their emotional innards and to fluently engage them in some intrapersonal dialogue.

Emotional fluency also means recognizing that cultural patterns shape how emotions are understood and expressed. National, regional, linguistic, socioeconomic, gender, and other identities give us messages about what to feel and how to express feelings. Try to unearth some of your messages by asking: What is it that someone from my region [or area or country] would just not say or do in a conflict? What were the limits on my emotional expression as a child? How do the groups I am a member of respond to emotions, the uncomfortable and the comfortable ones? Encountering others, it is helpful to ask the same questions, to catch a glimpse inside their worlds.

Emotions, as feeling impulses, guide us back to what matters most. Befriending them is another key to mindful awareness.

Spiritual Ways of Knowing

Spiritual ways of knowing refer to the experience of connection to that which is greater than ourselves. Some call it Spirit, Essence, or Source. Some know it through nature, others through silence, exquisite music, the laughter of a child. Our spiritual ways of knowing whisper that we belong to life in unseen ways and that these ways inform our purposes and our passions.

Centering in purpose and connection means learning the terrain of our inner core, however we experience it and whatever we image it to be. With mindful awareness of the big picture and our relationship to it, we resist acting quickly on the more transient emotions and reactions that conflict may generate within us. Rather, we refer back to Source or Essence, the values we cherish, the things we deeply care about, and who we believe ourselves to be in the context of others and the world. Our Source gives us a sense of perspective, grounding us in the big picture of what has meaning for us and how our purpose guides us. When conflict throws us off balance and divergent ways of being and perceiving obscure the reasons, centering in what we feel most passionate about individually and collectively informs our choices with mindful awareness.

Sometimes it is hard to access what we treasure, so focused are we on the barriers in front of us. We get distracted, thinly spread, and tired. Our identities are more bound up with conflict and survival than with connection and mindful awareness. Then it is time to apply this practice to ourselves, following Yeats's advice on climbing back to powerful understanding when he wrote

> I must lie down where all the ladders start,
> In the foul rag-and-bone shop of the heart.[9]

As we bring to mind what matters most to us, we welcome those parts of ourselves that are vital but dusty from neglect and distraction. We find a place where what we know becomes clear again along with why we are investing in certain relationships and pursuits. From here, we have choices about which of our givens we keep.

Imaginative Ways of Knowing

Imaginative ways of knowing take us out of the limitations of our perceptions, giving free reign to the dreaming parts of ourselves. Imagination is very powerful. It shows us new visions, and our feet follow suit, manifesting results in our lives. To invoke imaginative ways of knowing, we have to let go of our assumptions about how things are and what cannot be, at least temporarily. One of the first steps in accessing imagination is to uncover our assumptions about what is normal and natural. These assumptions tend to be carved into our ideas and perceptions in deep-seated ways that are mostly invisible to us. The practice of releasing our hold on givens asks us to make them explicit.

Releasing our hold on givens reminds us that our worlds are constructed. Our ethnocentricity tells us that we (or our group) are the reference point around which others are constellated as alternatives or variations. This is a small and limited way of seeing the world. We tend to live by our thoughts as they shape what we see and how we behave. Releasing our hold on the givens of our thoughts, we uncover new choices about which thoughts we give power to and which we set aside. This opens the possibility of inquiring about the thoughts of others from inside their frames, or worldviews, which is a key part of cultural fluency.

It is staggering to realize the power of our embedded givens to shape our choices, relationships, and our very lives. It was not until I was in my fourth decade that I realized the power of the frame of abandonment I carried with me. Raised by a devoted but work-addicted father and an invalid mother, I felt that I had been on my own from my early years. Only after my father's death did I recognize the strength of his love for me and how it had sustained me. This realization led me to see my grandparents' roles in clearer relief: they too had loved me fully and readily, telling me stories, folding origami with me, taking me on walks through their remembered childhoods of adventure and struggle.

As I came to realize that I was not abandoned, I was better able to welcome love and connection in many areas of my life. A key story had been reframed, and my life changed in ripples because of it. Only as I released my original story was I able to imagine other ways of being in the world. It had literally stood between me and change.

This is an example of an individual given shaping expectations and experiences throughout life. So, too, our cultural givens shape what we see, the roles we adopt, and how we engage others. Visiting a Hutterite colony in Alberta, Canada,[10] I saw men and women eating on opposite sides of the communal dining room. This segregation of the sexes is a part of the group's cultural gender roles, reinforced by social activities, dress, and organization. Women wearing layers of skirts and scarves over their hair are encouraged to make flower arrangements, knit, do needlepoint, and make rugs. Men dressed in black pants and high-collared jackets tend the fields and play hockey, football, and lacrosse in their leisure time. How strange our cities must seem to them, where young women and men dress in similar jeans and T-shirts, where plenty of girls take auto shop and boys freely study home economics.

Our givens are different, and they shape our identities and meanings in profound ways. To release our hold on our givens is not to abandon them, it is to recognize their existence, their effects, and our reactions to alternatives. It is to carefully separate out the recognition of difference from the negative judgment that can accompany this recognition without our even being aware. This is not to suggest that mindful awareness means suspending our ability to assess or choose. Rather we become more mindful of the path our choices take and the way this opens and forecloses options to us in our relationships, both conflictual and smooth. Another way to enhance our awareness is through focusing and meditation.

Integrative Ways of Knowing

Dividing ways of knowing into somatic, emotional, spiritual, and imaginative draws attention to the unique gifts each brings. But these ways of knowing are interconnected. Imagination uses the body—our mind's eye—to soar and invent images. It relies on feelings to guide the flow and connects to the big picture, however we conceive of it in our lives. Each of the ways of knowing is interconnected with all of the others. The last two sets of practices of mindful awareness bring them together: focusing and meditation, and caring and love.

Focusing and *meditation* are sets of practices that help us concentrate and expand our mindful awareness. Most of us live in the realm of "monkey mind," in which a variety of thoughts are constantly running around and through our brains. To quiet the mind, inviting concentration and focusing, is to make space for inspiration, intuition, and reference back to our Source. We literally clear our minds, uniting our focus on one point or process. We clarify our feelings as the noise of the day recedes.

Meditation may be accompanied by chanting, or it may be done in silence. It is a time apart from our everyday selves, a time in which we devote mindful awareness to our inner selves and the realm of the transpersonal. As anyone who has meditated in a group will know, the presence of others engaged in parallel intention is very powerful. As we meditate, our sense of vitality and energy is restored, and we are better able to receive others and attend to our own emotions and inclinations.

Canadian and U.S. dominant cultures tend to be preoccupied with *doing* at the expense of *being*. Meditative practices put some weight on the other side of the balance, helping us right ourselves, freeing us to see more clearly. Imagine how surprised a group of senior government managers were when a consultant told them she had inserted an item at the beginning of their packed agenda. It was a fifteen-minute period of quiet meditation. Leading them with guided imagery, she showed them into a quiet place within themselves, suggesting that they find there the symbols or talismans that would be helpful to them over the course of the day. Interrupted in their habits of moving quickly, they registered surprise and appreciation for the meditative interlude, asking her to lead one again the next time they met.

The managers' attention on doing was interrupted by this practice. They saw how it helped them work together with more clarity and concentration. Whatever path is taken to learning meditation and focusing, it will make a difference in our capacity to pay attention.

Caring and *love* are at the very center of mindful awareness. Of what are we to be aware? Surely our relationships with self, others, and the big picture, however we define or name it, are in the middle of what matters. Culturally, this may be seen differently (for example, is the individual the point from which relationships radiate, or is the group in the center?), yet love and caring are part of every cultural context. Martin Buber observed that all true living is relating and that love is a cosmic force, the only force capable of "giving intuitions of eternity."[11] Recognizing that our conflicts arise in relationships, we hold onto our capacity to care as a resource for bridging the differences that divide us.

To keep caring alive as a resource in our lives, we need the discipline to notice and consciously remove barriers of fear, greed, and prejudice. Love brings us to awareness of connection, a mutual resonance. It need not be romantic or even personal, for love in its largest sense transcends the personal. Listen to this story about the great violinist Yehudi Menuhin and the composer Béla Bartók. Menuhin played a Bartók composition in the composer's presence and later reflected: "Immediately with the first notes there burst forth between us an electric contact, an intimate bond which was to remain fast and firm. In fact, I believe that there can exist between a composer and his interpreter a stronger, more intimate bond, even without the exchange of words, than between the composer and a friend he may have known for years. For the composer reserves the core of his personality, the essence of his self, for his works."[12]

If we bring the essence of ourselves to our conflicts, sharing what we care about as well as inviting others' passions into our circle, we may be surprised at how our sense of the other is stretched. Across cultures, vehicles like music, art, and experiences in nature communicate volumes even when people have no language in common. Our creativity is summoned when we consider using a range of ways to bridge differences. We will explore other practices that tap creativity in Chapters Seven through Nine.

Mindful awareness helps us choose vehicles that help us cross the waters of difference. The waters contain both crocodiles—the threats within difference—and mermaids—the beauty within difference. To cross successfully we need to marry our cultural fluency (which we built in Chapters Two and Three) and mindful awareness (which we acquired in this chapter) with conflict fluency. Cultural fluency gives us the language to communicate about the stories that cultures have traced deep within us. Mindful awareness shows us how those stories shape our identities and meanings and how practices from multiple ways of knowing can help us engage each other with flexibility, fluidity, and attention. Conflict fluency complements and intersects with cultural fluency and mindful awareness, since we need both to create synergy from experiences of difference. What we do when faced with difference is influenced by our cultural frames and our fluency with a range of choices in conflict. These choices and lenses are explored in Chapter Five.

CHAPTER FIVE

Conflict Fluency

Do you speak more than one language? At first blush this question seems to ask about fluency with more than one linguistic system, for example English, French, Arabic, or Japanese. In this chapter the question has a different meaning. Here, we consider conflict as a language, and our fluency with it. Does engaging conflict come easily, are there a number of choices when facing it, are transitions through it smooth? Are we aware of different cultural starting points related to conflict, and how the language of conflict plays out in various ways across a range of cultural contexts? Do we know how conflict flows and plays out in our cultural contexts and within our individual psyches? Have we seen how conflict intertwines with who we are and what we care about? All of these matters are components of conflict fluency.

Consider these examples:

June and Geneviève, both women in their thirties, live next door to each other in an apartment complex. Late at night, June raps on Geneviève's door, demanding that Geneviève cease practicing an operatic aria. June says it sounds like gargling or an animal in distress and that the sound is far too clear through the paper-thin walls. Geneviève retorts that she has an important audition in the morning and no other time to practice. Each calls the other selfish, and June returns to her apartment shaking her head in frustration.

∾

Tomiko and Keiko are also next-door neighbors. One morning they meet as each is leaving her apartment. Tomiko compliments Keiko on her daughter's discipline in practicing the violin. "You must be very proud of her dedication in practicing before school every day, and looking forward to her career as a performer," says Tomiko. Keiko demurs, "Actually, she has only just begun playing. We don't know what her future will be. We had no idea you could hear her playing in the early morning. In the future she'll practice during the afternoon so she does not disturb you."

Both pairs of women are concerned with noise. The noise has the potential to erupt into a conflict, a difference that matters. June and Geneviève are overt and confrontative, proceeding from individualist starting points. Tomiko and Keiko are indirect and deferential, proceeding from communitarian starting points. Tomiko and Keiko arrive at a mutually agreeable conclusion, though whether it will work for Keiko's daughter remains to be seen. June and Geneviève might achieve a more constructive outcome if they used their direct communication strategies to inform an exchange about ways to manage the lack of soundproofing that work for both of them.

Both pairs of women could increase their conflict fluency. This does not mean that they should change their approach to communication or their ideas about living in community. It does mean that each of them could increase her awareness and choices for responding to conflict. Within any cultural context, there are choices, and choices increase when we recognize starting points and cultivate cultural fluency.

It might help all four women to realize that conflict, or differences, play out on three dimensions at once: material, communicative, and symbolic. The material dimension is the *what* of the conflict, the communicative refers to *how* communication takes place, and the symbolic dimension is *where* meanings and identities play out through conflict. Although the issue was noise in each case, and communication took place that fit the cultural context, symbolic dynamics ran through the heart of each conflict. June and Geneviève saw themselves as autonomous individuals, expecting and valuing privacy. Their individualist lenses supported their assertive, contesting engagement with each other. Tomiko and Keiko placed face saving over confrontation and saw community harmony as more important than individual entitlement.

The symbolic dimension shows us the importance of identity and meaning-making as they relate to face, face saving, perceptions, cultural starting points, and worldviews in conflict.

Because June and Geneviève had cultural starting points different from Tomiko's and Keiko's, they engaged differently in the four faces of conflict: naming, framing, blaming, and taming. *Naming* describes how we come to be aware of differences that matter and how we label this awareness to ourselves and others. *Framing* refers to the way we define our conflicts, deciding what and who is involved, drawing boundaries around what the conflict is and is not about. *Blaming* encompasses our ways of dealing with the conflict, from competitive to cooperative to avoidant. And *taming* has to do with closure—how we bring a conflict full circle, or not.

Each of these faces of conflict looks different in different cultural contexts. For Keiko and Tomiko naming was implicit and indirect. For June and Geneviève it was explicit and confrontational. Keiko and Tomiko framed the issue as involving the two of them in community. They did not see Keiko's daughter as having a voice in the chosen outcome, though Keiko's daughter's cooperation would be needed to effect the solution. Keiko, acting in a conflict-fluent manner, could assure Tomiko of her consideration of Tomiko's comfort and talk with her daughter to find a less disruptive time for her to practice.

June and Geneviève framed their conflict as incompatible individual lifestyles. They competed with each other for the right to pursue their chosen activities, silence for one and opera singing for the other. This approach to blaming ended in a narrowing of their relationship, leaving less scope for bridging this particular difference and other differences that might arise in the future. A more conflict-fluent response might have been to resist closure at that inopportune time, coming to agreement on a time for Geneviève to finish rehearsing that evening, with a plan to meet when each was less stressed and tired to talk about lifestyle, privacy, noise, and other neighborly issues.

Of course, it is easy to be fluent with conflict after the fact. It is much harder to bring mindful awareness to a conflict interaction. To be fluent with conflict means to be at ease with it, to have a range of choices for addressing it, and to recognize its visceral impact even as choices are exercised. It is neither to always avoid conflict nor to consistently engage it directly; neither to try always to prevail nor to consistently accommodate. Fluency means choosing appropriate strategies in specific situations, strategies that take everyone's cultural identities and meanings into account just as linguistic fluency helps speakers choose the right word or phrase in context.

Is Conflict Fluency a Good Thing?

It is useful to distinguish between developing conflict fluency and being a conflict junkie. Conflict fluency does not mean that we create conflict just because we are confident of our ability to negotiate it, as we might if we were conflict junkies. It does not mean that we rush to escalate conflict at the first blush of difference. Conflict fluency means

- Cultivating a repertoire of ways to engage conflict constructively and productively, with respect for a range of cultural starting points
- Recognizing that conflict itself is neither positive nor negative; it is our choices about conflict that damage or improve relationships
- Developing an experience bank of creative ways to dance with conflict that are culturally responsive, aligned with personal values, and draw on multiple ways of knowing
- Befriending conflict as an opportunity for learning, mutual and individual
- Applying emotional fluency to conflicts
- Learning the contours of conflict in different cultural contexts so that cultural fluency and conflict fluency complement each other

Conflict fluency, as defined here, is surely a good thing. It is a good thing because conflict unchecked, unacknowledged, and unengaged can escalate into damaged relationships and negative outcomes. Conflict fluency is useful because it calls us to remember that our differences are not necessarily divisive and conflicts are not necessarily pathways toward violence or ruptured relationships. Our differences can also connect us to each other and teach us a great deal as we summon the courage to face our shadow selves even as we step into our shining selves.

In this chapter we explore three dimensions of conflict as building blocks of conflict fluency. Then we trace four faces of conflict—naming, framing, blaming, and taming—as they unfold in different cultural contexts. Finally, we reflect on each of the dimensions of conflict fluency in turn. This foundation informs dynamic engagement, the ways of effectively bridging cultural conflicts presented in Chapter Six.

Three Dimensions of Conflict

Figure 5.1 delineates three dimensions of conflict. This tool helps us remember that there are three categories of things going on in most conflicts: *material, communicative,* and *symbolic.*[1] Too often, conflict is seen and responded to only in its material and communicative dimensions, leaving out much of the context—the wholeness of the people, their histories and their identities. Resolutions grounded only in these two dimensions tend to be limited and fragile, rather than seeded in the foundation of relationship and the rare gifts that come from glimpsing reality from another's eyes.

The symbolic dimension is that part of conflict outside our analytical reach—it evokes our identities and ways of making sense of the world when they collide with the identities and meanings of others. This dimension reminds us that all conflict is relational and all cultural conflict involves us at the unconscious parts of our beings, those parts where meaning is made and identity constantly formed and reformed. Since all conflict is relational, finding constructive ways to relate to each other is our central task, no matter what the issues or precipitating events of the conflict.

Relating constructively in the midst of conflict is not as easy as simply wanting to relate, and it often requires surmounting perceptions of the other as misguided, less capable, less able to access "common sense," or even evil. Relating constructively is more than using an integrative approach to address material aspects of problems; it is more than practicing a range of communication skills designed to bridge miscommunications. It means that we have to draw on mindful awareness of self and other, our capacities to con-

Figure 5.1. Relationships: Smooth and Conflicted.

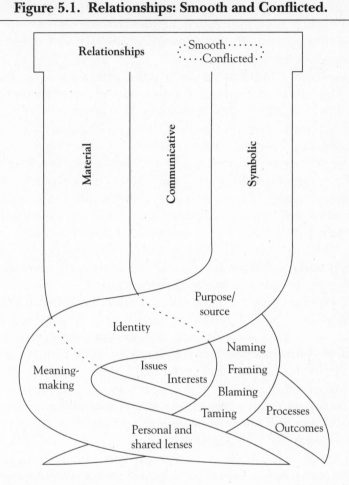

nect, our imagination, and our intuition in reaching across the chasm of conflict.

Consider the three dimensions of conflict: the material, the communicative, and the symbolic. The material dimension, as you might think, is the "stuff" of the disagreement: the chocolate both children want; the watershed that could be logged, preserved, or used in a variety of ways; the corner office that two staff people feel entitled to in the new premises. The material dimension is amenable to analysis, identification of interests, and problem solving. But these tools are often not enough to address the aspects of the conflict that relate to communication gaps and other, more profound differences.

Sometimes conflicts revolve around communication, the second dimension in Figure 5.1. Often they escalate through miscommunication or misunderstanding. So it is worth inquiring into the communicative dimensions of a conflict, watching to see whether misperceptions, misinterpretations, or wrong assumptions can be addressed to promote progress. Much of the training of mediators and facilitators takes place in this sphere: the skills of listening, summarizing, questioning, paraphrasing, restating, and reframing are all part of it. Clarity in communication is an important goal both for any third party and for the parties who are trying to navigate a conflict. Clarity will be achieved only if cultural fluency and mindful awareness are part of communication: there is no universal way to communicate in conflict.

Even when the parties are culturally fluent, many conflicts cannot be solved through material analysis and improved communication alone. They arise, develop, and are sustained in the murkier realm of culture and worldview differences, made more opaque by a variety of personality preferences and distinct systems of meaning. Put simply, we all have different common sense when it comes to conflict; different ways of understanding ourselves, others, and the world; and different approaches that issue from these distinct understandings. We have different starting points and look to different currencies. Though we all share the human condition, we understand it in fundamentally different ways, ways that sometimes clash, bringing pain and, too often, violence.

And we do not understand every aspect of our conflicts. There is much we do not comprehend, whether we are looking at the much-analyzed Palestinian-Israeli conflict or an issue in our own family or workplace. Even if we had perfect analytical understanding or could perform flawless communication, we would still get barbed on each other's identities, still contest ways of making meaning, still find ourselves at odds with those we call "the other" and even those we thought were part of our group.

In the third, symbolic dimension of conflict, what has meaning to us and how that meaning plays out in our lives becomes clear as the seedbed of resolution. Who we are, who and what we celebrate, who and what we forget, who we see ourselves to be individually and collectively, and who we aspire to be are all a part of the ways we get into conflict and the ways open to us to get out. Meaning-making and identity are part of our conflicts, giving body and texture to our stories. They are the sparks that give us uniqueness and also the holes in our roofs through which water pours in on our vulnerability. For our meanings and our identities are not only about who and what we are but also about how we have hurt, what we have lost, and what we never had but have always yearned for.

Conflict fluency asks us to take the symbolic dimension into account, recognizing identities and inviting divergent ways of making meaning into our awareness. As we do this, communication improves and material issues can be dealt with. When we have conflict fluency we cultivate simultaneous awareness on all three dimensions: material, communicative, and symbolic. Whichever dimension is in clearest focus as we engage conflict, the other two are probably just below the surface.

Before conflict is engaged it comes into being. It is named by someone or some group; it is the subject of framing, blaming, and possibly taming. Conflict fluency calls on us to explore how these faces of conflict arise in a variety of cultural contexts.

Four Faces of Conflict

As we saw in Chapter One, naming conflict is a cultural act—conflict takes on different labels and forms of existence in different cultural contexts. Once a conflict has been named, or acknowledged, framing becomes an ongoing process. Framing relates to the shapes and boundaries conflict takes on as well as the ideas about who is and is not a party to the conflict. Blaming refers to the whole constellation of possible approaches and processes for addressing the conflict. Cultural contexts shape which of these alternatives are acceptable and appropriate and how they are applied in practice. Taming refers to the outcome, resolution, or coming full circle that brings closure to the conflict. Not all conflicts have all of these faces. Some go on for years, digging deeper into the territory of blaming or framing, without moving into any phase that could be called taming.

Naming Conflict: Where Is It and Where Isn't It?

People in different societies engage in conflict very differently. Peter Adler writes that "[t]he Leopard Chief tradition of Central Africa, the disentangling ceremonies of Melanesia, the peace pipe rituals of Native America, and the song duels of certain Eskimo peoples are all part of a rich tapestry of ideas, models, and tools for managing controversy."[2] In each of these contexts, and hundreds more, there are variations in what people call conflict. When does the needle register a conflict on our inner seismograph? The answer is, of course, it depends.

Have you ever found yourself in a dispute with someone about whether or not the two of you are in conflict? "Why are you angry at me?" you ask. "I'm not," he replies, with an edge in his voice. Is there a conflict here? Is there a difference that matters? There are ripples in the relational waters, and where one person perceives a conflict, something is usually going on at some level. That something may be bound up with culture as well as mood, individual communication styles, context, and many other factors.

Just as it is important not to ignore culture, it is important to remember that it does not explain everything. I ask a man in a shop a question. He does not reply. Is it gender, race, or generation that is coming between us, or is he simply distracted and not aware of my presence? Just as culture does not explain everything, every miscommunication is not a conflict.

At the same time, our kaleidoscopes of cultural lenses lead us to see conflict in different ways and to label it differently. In response to a question about conflict put to a woman in Costa Rica, she said, "Ah, no, here we don't have conflicts. Conflicts are what they have in Nicaragua. Here we have *plietos* ['disputes'], *lios* ['messes'], *enredos* ['entanglements'] and *problemas* ['problems']."[3]

For some Hawaiians, interpersonal conflict is imaged as a blocked pathway. Conflict blocks the flow of positive feelings among people. A colloquial expression for it is "all jam up."[4] In this view conflicts may exist between people even when individuals are unaware of them. Their lack of awareness does not prevent possible damage from a conflict.

The Chinese interviewee referred to in Chapter One reported that he had encountered no conflicts over decades of living in

Canada. He had experienced a peaceful, ordered life, and no events had been so tumultuous as to activate the conflict needle on his internal seismograph. Indeed, as discussed, he probably does not use the same seismographic interpretation manual as people from other cultural backgrounds, generational and national, do. Also, the gender and age of his interviewer may have influenced his reticence. This is not to suggest any deficit but to propose that he paid attention to harmony, rather than dividing his world into conflict incidents, a decisively Western approach.

The very idea of studying conflict as an academic discipline is a Western one, and programs have flourished in U.S., Canadian, and Western European universities in line with a cultural tendency to break things up into discrete units of study. Although conflict is a global phenomenon known to most societies and cultures, it is named, framed, and tamed quite differently around the world. One Vietnamese participant in a workshop described her cultural perspective this way: "Imagine that our relationship is like water in a bowl. We do everything we can to protect the bowl, to keep it fresh and tranquil. If something happens and the bowl breaks, the water will fall all over the floor. We can get sponges and cloths to try to get the water back, but the water will be dirty, dispersed. We will never be able to get the water back into the bowl as it was, nor will the mended bowl ever be as strong and beautiful a container."

From her perspective, naming a conflict and then applying a series of techniques to resolve it was a poor second choice. A far superior focus of attention was on keeping the bowl intact and the water pristine. If this meant failing to name a difference or failing to confront others when they did something contrary to her preference, it was a small price to pay for the integrity of the bowl. We can see some of the same approach in the exchange between Tomiko and Keiko, described earlier.

The tendency to name conflict directly or to confront another is more frequent in cultures with an individualist pattern (described in Chapter Three). When the individual is the unit around which meaning is composed, then damage to a relational bowl may be less catastrophic than a possible injury to the self or one's personal agenda. Conversely, when the bowl, or the community, is at the center of importance, then the relational system may fracture beyond repair when it is damaged, and it is therefore much more necessary to guard and protect it. Paying primary attention to networks of relationships is typical of a communitarian cultural pattern.

Of course neither starting point is superior and neither is absolute. We may be communitarian with our immediate families and individualistic with coworkers; we may be encouraged to act as individuals by our families and later join a religious group to which we feel collective allegiance. As with any cultural patterns, context and timing may trump conditioning. The degree to which a person is independent or interdependent will vary, as will the way the qualities of independence and interdependence are seen from individualist and communitarian perspectives. Both perspectives value relationship, but they value it from different starting points that nod in different directions when conflict surfaces. Cultures also shape what happens once a conflict has been named or experienced.

Framing Conflict

Framing refers to the ways we understand, interpret, and hold conflict. To frame something is to give it boundaries, to define where it begins and ends, what it is and what it is not. Framing conflicts is a cultural act, relating to what we do and to what we see as appropriate, possible, relevant, and outside the bounds. How we frame a conflict also relates to what motives we attribute to others, whether we see others' actions as part of a pattern or as isolated incidents, and how we see our own role and the conflict dynamics unfolding. Framing is also influenced by structures, power, hierarchies, and roles, and how we see ourselves within these elements.

Framing, the way we think about a conflict once we have named it, affects our interactions and communication, which in turn subdue, escalate, or contain conflict. Suppose a European woman gets off a plane in Tokyo and is greeted by a Japanese colleague she has never met. Their communications during their first few minutes together are not smooth—they seem to have different ideas about how much help she needs and in which order to do things. But she does not think of this as conflict until he asks her age. Now she is really taken aback, affronted. Depending on her awareness, she may frame the question as a local norm, a mystery, or rudeness. If she attributes the question to rudeness, a conflict could certainly escalate. If she understands that Japanese forms of address vary according to age, then she may swallow her surprise and cooperate in giving her colleague the information he needs to address her respectfully.

There are many instances of conflict escalating because communication nuances like this are not understood across cultures. Conflict may also be exacerbated by differences in communication norms. Some of these differences are quite subtle. Raymonde Carroll writes that conversation among French and Americans is often a series of miscommunications, with each person opaque to the other.[5] While French and Americans in conversation may believe they are attributing the same meanings to verbal exchanges (framing similarly), they may actually understand these exchanges and their roles in them quite differently. Carroll reports that the French complain that Americans in conversations are "boring, that they respond to the slightest question with a lecture, that they go all the way back to Adam and Eve" in their responses. Americans encountering the French may find them changeable, insincere, and abrupt as they toss the conversational ball among themselves, interrupting at pauses to keep things lively.

Carroll, a French anthropologist married to an American, suggests that these differences stem from the two cultures' quite different metaphors for conversation. The French, she says, view conversation as a spider's web: "delicate, fragile, elegant, brilliant, of harmonious proportions, a work of art."[6] The words of the conversation are the spider, generating the threads that bind participants. Participants in the conversation are obligated to nurture it, to keep it from dying, and to watch over its development as though it were something alive. They rely on nonverbal behavior to signal each other about changing the topic or shifting focus, cues that are often missed by more subject-focused Americans.

Americans, she suggests, see conversation more as a jazz session. People can come in and out, play solos while others accompany them, and disappear into the night while the music is still playing. They enjoy the spotlight, playing without interruption in a style that is their own. Other participants follow the solos, adding their encouragements in ways that do not disrupt the performance.

Carroll tells the story of a French professor visiting the United States who met an American historian at a party. The French professor inquired about the American's opinion of a new historical book. His goal was to toss out a conversational ball that he expected to be lightly and promptly returned. It was a way of exploring the possibility of connection through conversation. The American responded by explaining his views of the book at length. He was surprised to be interrupted by another Frenchman, who joined the conversation and interrupted with a joke. Only later did the American realize that his conversational partner had glanced around the room, attracting the attention of the second Frenchman who came over in response to the first professor's signal and interrupted the American's monologue.

These different ways of framing, or understanding, conversation may lead to miscommunication and conflict. For the French, conversation commits the initiator to another person, indicating a desire to maintain or create ties, while for Americans, conversation may be more casual, a way to pass time. These generalizations are not always accurate; they hold true or not depending on the context and players. It is not enough to know that the conversationalists are French and American respectively. We have to ask which American and which French person is involved. For both we must ask, is their heritage African, Latin, Scandinavian, or something else? Are they new to the culture or long ago acculturated? What is their generation, their education, their gender, their purpose in meeting? Depending on who is involved and the context in which they are interacting, the patterns will shapeshift and play out differently. But Carroll's observations about the shapes and rhythms of conversations in each context remind us that knowing broad patterns can help us decode cross-cultural communication.

Implicit Framing Rules. Just as communication and expectations are framed differently, conflicts are framed differently according to cultural contexts. When Canadians watched a videotape with no soundtrack that showed silhouetted figures in a series of interactions,[7] they interpreted what they saw as an argument escalating into violence, culminating in a stabbing. When I showed the identical videotape to a group of government managers from Taiwan, not one of them mentioned a weapon or physical injury. Instead they suggested the tape showed a conversation where there were gestures and communication between friends or colleagues, culminating in an embrace or a dance. Was the difference in their interpretation unrelated to culture or were the implicit rules about naming and framing conflicts quite different for the Taiwanese officials? Although these are by no means systematic research findings, they show sufficient difference between the groups to raise the possibility that framing is quite different when done through Taiwanese cultural lenses and Canadian ones.

We need not go as far as Taiwan to find examples of implicit rules about framing conflicts. Within organizations, rules are framed and understood implicitly. The question of who must follow these rules and how these rules apply may lead to conflict. Consider the story told of Charles Revson when he was head of Revlon Corporation. Revson insisted that everyone sign the time of his or her arrival in the office in a book kept at the reception desk. A new receptionist was in her first week on the job when a man she had not seen before walked into the reception area and took the book. She went after him, calling, "Excuse me, Sir! But that book is not to be removed. I have strict instructions." Revson turned and stared at her. "When you pick up your last paycheck this evening, ask them to tell you who I am."[8]

Contrast that event with this story about Tom Watson when he was chairman of IBM. Watson approached a secure area with a group of visitors but was not wearing his badge. The female security guard stopped him and requested that he show his badge, in spite of her associate's urgent whisper that this was the chairman himself. In response, Watson stopped, along with his whole party of senior officials from the company and the Pentagon, and sent for his badge. "She's quite right," he said. "We make the rules. We keep 'em."[9]

In the Revlon case a receptionist's attempt to enforce the rules with the head of the company led to a conflict that ended her employment. In the case of IBM a subordinate's similar behavior led to a positive acknowledgment of her judgment. Revson framed the issue as insubordination while Watson framed it as diligence. In the IBM instance no conflict emerged because Watson did not enforce a culture of hierarchical power. In the Revlon case conflict had a serious effect for the employee, who had failed to appreciate the implicit rules of the hierarchical culture in which she was operating.

Private and Public Framing of Conflict. Home. It is one of the primary settings in which cultural messages about framing conflict are conveyed. Conflict is done in many different ways in homes. In the home where my mother grew up neither her father nor her mother ever disagreed or argued in front of the children. Years later my grandmother confided to my mother that they did have differences, but they resolved them by talking them through in the privacy of their bedroom before going to sleep. Despite this familial modeling my mother and father engaged in frequent arguments in front of me and my brother, at home and in many public places.

As I described this years later to a Japanese friend, she automatically assumed that my parents had even more intense disagreements in the privacy of our home. But it was not necessarily true. Her expectations of public propriety led her to think that an attempt would be made to cover public disagreements. But my parents did little to cover their disagreements, shouting at theme parks, in restaurants, and at family gatherings when conflict erupted between them. Strangers and extended family members responded to these outbursts mostly with embarrassed avoidance. Individualist notions of privacy meant that others did not intervene. In communitarian cultural contexts, there are different mechanisms for surfacing and addressing conflicts publicly.

In the Solomon Islands, for example, conflict is seen as an entanglement to be disentangled. Because an entanglement or a knot impedes the usual flow of things, it needs to be addressed. When an entanglement arises, a village meeting may be convened to address it or prevent further entanglement. People come together to "make a way," sharing feelings and stories in a public setting.[10] The whole village is involved in addressing a conflict that began between two people.

Framing and Parties: Who Is Involved and Who Is Not? As the example from the Solomon Islands makes clear, cultural ideas about who is a party to a conflict vary a great deal. It may be the whole village; it may be a small group. Often the parties in a conflict change over time. Conflict may begin in one unit in an organization but spread to include many others if it is not effectively addressed. Across cultural contexts, different metaphors govern the identification of parties. In communitarian settings, relationships are like webs or constellations. Every part of the web, every star in the constellation, is related to the conflict and may be a part of attempts to bridge it. In individualist settings, relationships are more like connect-the-dots puzzles. Only the discrete dots that form the outline of the picture are part of a conflict, not others that fall within or outside the lines.

In this story from Taiwan the definition of parties was broader than the humans present. There was a conflict over the widening of a road. A local government agency had determined the road widening was necessary, but local residents protested because there was a temple at the roadside where a number of them prayed. There were meetings about the project and considerable anxiety lest the resident God of the temple be angered by the interference and bad consequences follow. At last a solution was reached—a plan to widen the road as planned and temporarily relocate the temple away from the construction. Once the construction was finished, a new, larger temple to the same God would be built at the roadside.

Before this solution could be adopted, everyone involved had to be consulted. Everyone, in this case, included not only local residents, but the God of the temple. The proposal was put to the God via divination, and the God's approval obtained. What would have happened if the divination had yielded less than an affirmation of this solution? The Taiwanese explained, "There are ways to influence the outcome of these things." In this public conflict, a cultural ritual involving all the parties, human and divine, had served to bring about a satisfactory resolution.

Framing and Intervention: Who Can Help and How? The degree to which conflict is public or private varies, as does the extent to which intervention from outsiders is appropriate or possible. Indeed the definition of an outsider or an insider is a cultural question. Are insiders people in the immediate family, the extended family, the neighborhood, the community, or the church, temple, or mosque? Is gender or class or generation the dividing line between insider and outsider? The answer, once again, is it depends. It depends on the kind of issue, the changing norms of the group, and the wider cultural contexts to which parties belong.

Depending on where the line is drawn between insider and outsider, different forms of support, involvement, and intervention are possible. Consider the story of a South Asian household consisting of a husband and wife, their three children, and the husband's parents. Conflicts arise about how much domestic work the wife should do, how much her mother-in-law should do, and how the children should be raised. Much is below the surface, but even the surface of their relational waters is increasingly tumultuous, as tempers are short and the husband and children feel pulled in several directions.

No one is calling the situation a conflict, but several small conversations are going on between different family members, both those living in the house and those in other households. Family members are aware that there are problems and that they seem to be worsening rather than dissolving. Getting wind of the difficulty, two elders from the temple—a man and a woman—come for tea. They talk generally about community interests and observe a series of social rituals. Toward the end of the visit they discreetly raise questions about how things are going in the home. They offer suggestions embedded in stories and cautions. And then they leave.

During a mediation training in Canada a tableau like this was presented. The participants were from several ethnocultural groups, but they were acculturated to dominant culture norms and were learning a prescriptive, linear approach to mediation. South Asian volunteers played out roles similar to those just described. To the mediation trainees, accustomed to a direct approach to communication, the talk meandered into seemingly irrelevant stories, negotiated via incomprehensible social rituals. Because so much of the conversation was subtle, evocative, and indirect, they wondered whether anything useful had happened. They saw cajoling without attributing blame and inquiry without confrontation. They were not sure where the closure was or whether the family members actually received any useful assistance. The family members reported that they experienced the visit as a helpful, supportive interaction in which the boundaries between public and private were observed, while the curtain on family privacy was pulled back just enough for some help to be received.

A more direct approach would not have worked in this instance. Nor would a more formal naming or framing of issues. What worked arose organically from the setting of the family, the culture, and the intersection of both. Mohammed Abu-Nimer, writing about Middle Eastern Arab approaches to conflict, observes that skills like active listening or repeating what has been just said to be sure that you understand, do not translate well into those cultural contexts. He maintains that methods like this that are too programmed or formal will not work. In Arab culture it is more effective to listen to and reflect on what the speaker says without using a structured technique like reflective listening.[11]

Similarly, intervenors known to the parties are preferable to outsiders in Middle Eastern Arab settings. Abu-Nimer reports that in conflict resolution training workshops in Gaza and Jordan, "most participants reported that professionalism is not a sufficient or legitimate base for intervention in public or community conflicts and certainly not in interpersonal disputes. Legitimacy is gained through the third party's relationship and influence on one or more of the parties. Such legitimacy is derived from age, clan, tribe, political position or other sources of social status, and not from neutrality or impartiality."[12]

Responding to this preference, Abu-Nimer held conflict resolution workshops for *mokhtars,* powerful local mediators who were selected by their clans to mediate family, community, and interpersonal disputes. These mediator-arbitrators rely on hundreds of years of traditional conciliation, arbitration, and mediation. They intervene using what they call *sulha* (conciliation) and *wasata* (mediation). Working with these "natural" third parties, blending traditional and Western approaches, yielded a wider range of possibilities for complex cultural conflicts. The groups were able to address not only how conflicts are framed differently but also how they are processed.

Blaming: Addressing Conflict

Just as there are an infinite variety of ways to frame conflict culturally, so there are many ways to address it, ways that involve responsibility and accountability in diffuse and specific ways. To resolve a conflict is to move beyond blaming or seeing the solution solely in terms of the other's behavior. How blaming plays out is a cultural question.

David Augsburger's story of a hit-and-run incident,[13] introduced in Chapter Three, illustrates several cultural differences in the ways each party approached blaming, including contrasting emotional styles; opposite views about fate and personal responsibility; differing expressions of face, honor, and dignity; and quite different ideas about friendship and relationship. Augsburger reveals only that the event took place in a non-Western country and involved a Western expatriate and a local high-status official.

The expatriate, called Mr. Smith in the story, is not seriously hurt but is affronted that the official, Mr. Isphahany, did not stop at the scene after hitting Mr. Smith with his car. Mr. Smith seeks Mr. Isphahany out at a local exclusive club and confronts him, asking why he did not stop. The two men have a long conversation in which Mr. Smith seeks a linear discussion of the issues, recognition of fault and responsibility by Mr. Isphahany, and a "reasonable resolution," leading, among other things, to documentation of his injuries for insurance purposes.

But what is reasonable to Mr. Smith is not what is reasonable to Mr. Isphahany. Mr. Isphahany offers to give Mr. Smith a reduced membership to his club, to have him tended to by his personal physician, and to become friends. Mr. Smith gets more and more frustrated since he is looking for quite different things. To Mr. Isphahany, fate has brought them together, and friendship can result. To Mr. Smith, the objective is to clarify personal responsibility and conclude the incident.

Some Americans reading this story wonder if Mr. Isphahany was sincere. Was he using his cultural ways of being to circumvent Mr. Smith's desire for accountability and documentation? From a dominant-culture American view, these possibilities present themselves. Applying cultural fluency we look at the situation as much as possible through each party's eyes. In Mr. Isphahany's context there is greater acceptance of the dealings of fate and less emphasis on personal responsibility than in Mr. Smith's home setting. What seemed to be obfuscation to Mr. Smith may have been sincere puzzlement on Mr. Isphahany's part. In our quest to understand, we hold open the possibility that miscommunication exacerbated this conflict.

This example illustrates that blaming, or ways responsibility is assumed, has a great deal to do with different ideas of power, hierarchy, status, and individual responsibility versus collective fate in different cultural contexts. It also has to do with where the fault lines lie in local cultures, something not always obvious to outsiders. For example, a misdeed by a teen in a U.S. context may be dealt with through individual consequences and blame, while the same misdeed in a more communitarian society may be seen as bringing shame to the family and the neighborhood. Members of the family and the community in the latter context are thus necessarily involved in making reparations and helping the teen to avoid misbehavior in the future. Restorative justice and family group conferencing are attempts to introduce a communitarian approach to engage family and community members in rehabilitation of individual offenders.

The nuances of conflicts and fault lines are not always visible to those outside the cultural context. Cynthia Cockburn tells the story of going from the United States to work with women in Northern Ireland to help build a women's support network to advance the cause of women politically and socially. Before she arrived she thought that the most divisive issue would be religion. As she worked there she began to see it differently: "In the case of the Women's Support Network, I saw *the* bridge as being one that would bring Catholic/republican and Protestant/unionist women together. Now I was beginning to understand that these particular women found *this* span relatively unchallenging. . . . [M]any lived in mixed relationships, their post-school education had lifted them out of sectarian environments and involvement in the women's centres had furnished experience of cross-communal contacts."[14]

Cockburn found that there were many less obvious dimensions of difference to be bridged. Conflict did not emerge so much over religious chasms as over radical nationalism versus moderate nationalism versus unionism and over secular leftism versus cultural orthodoxy. Blaming happened over differences in views about abortion, violence, and feminism more than over differences in religious affiliation. Understanding the way blaming worked in this context involved understanding the cultural contours of the society, contours visible only after sustained work in the setting and the development of relationships.

Taming

Taming conflict refers to bringing conflict to some kind of closure, calming troubled waters or managing the differences that have surfaced. Where specific issues have surfaced, it may mean resolving them. If improved relationships are sought, transformation may be the desired end of taming. Sometimes, taming may mean finding a way to coexist, even in the midst of divisive differences.

What does closure look like in different cultural contexts? It may look like silence. It may look like informal, unspoken understandings. It may look like a written, signed agreement. It just depends. Do those involved want acknowledgment; apology; restitution; punishment of a wrongdoer; deterrence of future wrongdoing by a wrongdoer or others in the community; community reconciliation; a formal agreement; an informal understanding; better working relationships; a way to manage past, present, or future difficulties; or restored harmony in the family or community? Do they want resolution, transformation, or simply to be left alone? Do they want to air as many of their feelings as possible and have them mirrored back by the one they see as being on the other side, or do they want an indirect process that will save their energy and face for other encounters?

John Paul Lederach, writing about different approaches to taming, suggests that a number of paradoxical values present themselves to be balanced in any attempt to transform conflict.[15] These paradoxes involve

- Justice and mercy: How do we balance the values of compassion and forgiveness with the desire to create right relationships based on equity and fairness?
- Empowerment and interdependence: How do we empower individuals while nurturing mutuality and community?
- Process and outcome: Can we pay attention to the how of what we are doing even as we strive to work together for outcomes that transform conflict?
- Personal change and systemic change: Do we begin with individuals or work first to change the system? How do we address the ways that the personal and the systemic interconnect?

The way each of these values is observed and the weight it is given in the quest to tame conflict will vary with cultural context, type of issue, and many other factors, including history, timing, players, setting, and complexity. Behaviors will be conditioned by what seems normal and appropriate to those involved, and these values are shaped by cultural messages. In U.S. criminal law for example, punishment of the wrongdoer and deterrence from future wrongdoing is an accepted norm and goal. Justice is emphasized over mercy. From a Tibetan Buddhist perspective, this approach fails to take account of poverty as the root cause of immoral behavior and the responsibility of the state to ensure that civil disorder is minimized by providing the necessaries of life.[16] Tibetan Buddhists practice mercy toward lawbreakers and invoke a more communal idea of justice and responsibility.

The values of empowerment and interdependence also play out differently across cultural contexts. Consider a noise-related conflict between two tenants in the same building in the United States, one is twenty-something and one is elderly. Coming together with a mediator, each talks about her lifestyle and daily schedule. Together they search for solutions that will answer as many of their individual and shared interests as possible. Each is seen as a relatively autonomous individual, empowered to negotiate on her own behalf. Each assumes a right to her lifestyle as long as it does not infringe on others' rights. The mediation process is empowering for the tenants, helping them maintain control over their lives and retain decision-making power as long as they can come to consensus.

The response to a similar conflict would look completely different in another cultural context. Suppose a noise-related conflict arose between a youth and an elder in a traditional Masai community in East Africa. In accordance with clear, prescribed rules and roles in the community, no confrontative conversation would take place. The Masai believe that it is impossible to know truth until they become old and that deference is to be shown to elders. The onus would be on the youth to accommodate to the elder's preferences, in recognition of the two parties' interdependence and relative status.[17]

The tension between process and outcome plays out in a variety of ways across contexts within national settings. For some deep-rooted conflicts, bringing people together to talk with each other is a huge step forward. Prolife and prochoice activists divided over abortion have engaged in dialogue in several U.S. and Canadian cities over the past several years. Although they were surprised and pleased to come to know each other, tension surfaced in ongoing groups over whether to plan joint actions or continue talking and exploring. Members of some groups planned joint actions to combat female and child poverty or to develop the viability of adoption as an option for unwanted pregnancy; members of other groups continued talking, examining the many aspects of their differences and commonalities. Whether group members are comfortable with a focus on process or on outcome depends not only on the issue and the cultural context in which it plays out but on other factors like a preference for closure or open-endedness.

Lederach's final paradoxical continuum, between a personal focus and a systemic focus, draws our attention to the inherent challenge in conflict transformation work. Even as we work to change systems in the direction of equity and harmony, ongoing personal work also needs to be done. In protracted, destructive conflicts, this work involves healing deep feelings including anger, grief, and loss. A focus on individual change does not erase the need to look at the wider system and its potential to birth new conflicts; a focus on changing the system yields tasks that must be done at the personal and interpersonal levels to support the desired change.

This tension between an emphasis on a personal and a systemic focus plays out in multiple settings, from classrooms to town halls. It is intertwined with identity and meaning-making: do we prefer to make meaning through sharing personal experiences or working for systemic change, and how do our cultural identities shape those choices?

In a Canadian classroom, issues of identity and meaning-making played out in some painful ways. The group was made up mostly of lawyers, men and women, from several Canadian regions. One of the group members was a First Nations woman, Sandra. Sandra often focused her comments on ways the political and social system needed to change to address equity and fairness for all residents of Canada, especially those who are the historical victims of racism and oppression. Though Sandra was initially quite involved in the class, her engagement waned as she heard things that alienated her. When a fellow student spoke of multiculturalism in Canada in glowing, if slightly patronizing terms, Sandra stopped focusing on the system. She spoke passionately of her personal experience of being a member of a First Nation, a member who had to fight for her membership because of intermarriage, a member who carried an identity card with a number proving her status.[18] She spoke of the stigma of this identity, and her resentment at the daily indignities that accompany it.

Sandra was experiencing the tension between the personal and the systemic levels as they played out in her life and her experience of the class. The pain of listening to others talk about the system in positive terms turned her attention to the personal, the personal that is very much interconnected with political and social systems. As members of the class responded, some focused on her personal experience and others on ways the system does or does not need to change. The facilitator tried to balance these contributions, while acknowledging the deep feelings Sandra was expressing.

What did resolution, or taming, look like in this context? It did not look like a "win-win" outcome or anything close to that. It did not look like transformation or even neat closure. It involved recognizing that it is essential that we weave our personal experiences into abstract or intellectual discussions and also use those experiences to inform our ideas about reform and change. Taming meant temporarily shifting the agenda to receive and sit with the feelings in the room. While class members needed and wanted to move through the class material, failing to address what had occurred and its relational ripples would only have chilled the group climate, limiting participants' ability to move forward.

In the context of the class, taming was accomplished. Did it mean closure for Sandra? Surely a few moments in a class could not provide closure for her lifetime of hurts. Did it mean that everyone sat comfortably after that, ready to move on? No. In fact several members of the class referred in their papers to the way they had continued to process this experience internally and in dialogue with each other days and weeks after the class ended. Some of them felt enriched by the experience; others struggled to understand Sandra's perspectives and experiences and the impassioned responses, both supportive and challenging, of their classmates.

Taming means to bring things full circle, but it is not just one point in time. Taming happens at different rates for different people; it looks different depending on cultural context. Sometimes, pieces fall into place long after an issue has been addressed, and some pieces are never woven into the fabric of our ongoing journeys. Conflict fluency reminds us to attend to the ways these unwoven threads may play out in subsequent conflicts.

Weaving Conflict Fluency into Our Relations

When we began this exploration, I defined conflict fluency as including six elements. Now that we have an awareness of the cultural dimensions of naming, framing, blaming, and taming conflict, we can examine each of these elements more closely.

Conflict fluency means cultivating a repertoire of ways to engage conflict constructively and productively, with respect for a range of cultural starting points. We learned our responses to conflict as children. Those of us who hid may find ourselves still hiding. Those of us who stood up to the bullies may find ourselves still defending. As adults, we can choose to broaden our repertoires, stretching our comfort zones and trying on less comfortable ways of being. We do this recognizing a range of cultural starting points that turn our heads in particular directions when conflict arises. No set of prescriptive directions will do. We learn to engage various starting points (our own and others') through experience, the willingness to take risks, and a spirit of inquiry. As we make choices we realize that conflict itself is not positive or negative—it is exercising our choices with mindful awareness that matters.

Conflict fluency means recognizing that conflict itself is neither positive nor negative; it is what we choose to do with and in conflict that damages or improves relationships. In most ongoing relationships and interactions, conflict arises. When I bring my relational history to mind, I realize that I have sometimes bridged those conflicts adroitly and sometimes fanned their flames. Fear, insecurity, and lack of mindful awareness have led me and others to escalate our differences, hurting others around us in the process. When I have been able to summon mindful awareness, I have had more choices and been able to craft better outcomes. When everyone involved drew on conflict fluency and cultural fluency, we were able to progress more constructively and fluidly.

Focusing on choice in conflict brings up difficulties for some people. Where there is long-standing oppression or subjugation, how can there also be choice? We do not always choose the conflicts in which we find ourselves, but we still have choices. We choose how to receive others. We choose how to name and frame the situation. We choose whether taming is appropriate or whether the conflict should be escalated to catalyze social change. And these choices have profound effects on how conflict develops.

Conflict fluency means developing an experience bank of creative ways to dance with conflict that are culturally responsive, aligned with personal values, and draw on multiple ways of knowing. Conflict is often not soluble through analysis or problem solving alone. When it is woven into our identities and the meanings we hold dear, we cannot analyze our way out of the corner. We can only draw on our creativity and imagination—our capacities to re-vision and re-create—as resources to help us across differences. If we could think our way through the difficult conflicts that have divided so many—Palestinians and Israelis, Greek and Turkish Cypriots, French and English Canadians, Native and dominant culture Americans and Canadians—we would have done so. We need to put all that is within us at the service of composing identities that live in peace and finding meanings that do not delegitimize others. This task is so multifaceted and interwoven with history that we will work on it incrementally well into the foreseeable future, or until we fail.

Conflict fluency means befriending conflict as an opportunity for learning, mutual and individual. In working around the world I have met few people who embrace conflict as an opportunity for personal and cultural change. Far more of us are resistant, reticent, and afraid of the punch conflict carries. Yet when I change the question, asking people to identify moments richest in learning, they often name conflicts or differences that led them into learning. As we recognize the gifts that conflict offers us—clarity, expanded awareness, deepened relationships, new ways to understand ourselves and others—we may find it a little less threatening. At least we may see reasons to engage it with energy and invite others to do the same.

Conflict fluency means applying emotional fluency to conflicts. We have seen that mindful awareness is an important foundation for conflict fluency. Stereotypes notwithstanding, mindful awareness does not mean screening out emotions from our conflicts or ways of bridging conflicts. Just as we need to be fluent with the pathways and shapes conflict takes in our cultures and individual psyches, so we need to learn to listen to, but not automatically react from, our emotions. Just as conflicts change and transform, emotions pass through our consciousness—informing, guiding, nudging, and releasing as we enter into dialogue with them.

Conflict fluency means learning the contours of conflict in different cultural contexts so that cultural fluency and conflict fluency complement each other. It is not always easy to discern the cultural features of conflicts or understand how they operate. Even as we learn about a particular cultural context, much more remains below the surface. As we apply our understandings of cultural starting points, we realize that these points are layered. We may understand that one person puts individuals at the center of the circle and another puts the family, clan, or community at its heart. The challenge is to continue in mindful awareness of these starting points as we engage conflict.

It is tempting to revert back to our own reference points during the process. For example, from an individualist starting point, the solution to a conflict involving indirect communication might be to use direct communication. An individualist starting point may also lead to the identification of solutions to conflict reliant on individual initiative. A communitarian cultural perspective may be that many problems would be solved if people were more conscientious, obedient citizens. Advice from people at one starting point to people at the other end of the continuum may be irrelevant, impractical, or even insulting.

Rather than resorting to our own cultural common sense when conflict arises, it is important to hold a range of starting points in mindful awareness. Then we can seek to weave together a process that makes sense and feels comfortable for everyone involved. This is the process of dynamic engagement, the subject of Chapter Six.

CHAPTER SIX

Engaging Difference

I was about to give a lecture to a hall full of people recently when I looked out and saw my kindergarten teacher, Muriel, in the audience. She was smiling broadly, exuding the same magic she had when I was a child. Though I had not seen her for many years, I knew her instantly. Gray hairs had replaced jet-black ones and her skin had a translucence I had not remembered, but at seventy she looked as engaged and poised for adventure as when we had first met forty years before.

In that moment memories of the times we shared years before flooded in—the songs she taught me, the horizons she showed me, the care she lavished on me. I realized then with powerful poignancy that the approaches I talk about for bridging conflict have their seeds in my very early life. In my times with her I learned openness to new worlds, adopting her contagious spirit of adventure. I learned to listen to my inner wisdom and to trust it, even as I maintained curiosity about what made sense to others. I learned to try new things, trusting that she would be there to mark even the mistakes with acceptance and wonder.

As I reflected on the gifts of seeing and talking with Muriel after so many years, I realized that an essential part of bridging cultural conflict relates to choice: the choices we make as we tell stories about our worlds and the people in them. Not only is the choice *to* engage difference important—for without this choice we are doomed to lives as parallel solitudes or, worse, reciprocal destroyers as we aim to wipe out difference in the mistaken belief that this is possible—but the choice of *how* we engage is essential to our success. This is the central question addressed by this chapter: how can we engage with differences in ways that bring about generative, creative resolutions while supporting or even deepening relationship?

Many books about bridging cultures or resolving conflicts present skills and stages as ways across difference. Few address the who and the how: who are we in this work, and with what spirit are we most likely to succeed? In Chapter One we began exploring these questions, traversing the nuances and fault lines of culture, tracing it as an underground river influencing conflict, constant yet dynamic, vital yet vulnerable. Cultural fluency was explored in Chapters Two and Three, as we considered how starting points and currencies shape our identities and meaning-making. Mindful awareness, the subject of Chapter Four, showed us the role of awareness in applying cultural fluency. Together, mindful awareness and cultural fluency informed our exploration of conflict fluency in Chapter Five. All of these elements—cultural fluency, mindful awareness, and conflict fluency—form the foundation for bridges across cultural conflict. Mindful of relationship as the center of our efforts, in this chapter we explore dynamic engagement and a dialogic spirit as ways through conflict.

Dynamic Engagement and Dialogic Spirit

Dynamic engagement with a dialogic spirit is a series of ways through conflict. It draws attention to action and attitude, doing and being. It is a series of interconnected, fluid, and adaptable components that run through many successful efforts to bridge conflict. These efforts look different—and are different—across cultural contexts. This is to be expected. Dynamic engagement reminds us that change is a constant across cultures, so we must change too if we are to mine the riches cultural conflicts offer us.

Dynamic engagement brings the central importance of relationship into focus. Analysis and logic alone cannot guide us through difficult conflicts, so tied are they to our cultural common sense. Instead we must engage relationally with those involved to invent and live into new ways of relating. Our abilities to communicate, bond, and empathize with others are needed when we are in conflict just as much as when we seek to make a new friend or connect with an old one. Indeed, engagement is needed even more in conflict because the foundation for trust and connection may have been shaken.

Engagement itself is not enough. *Dynamic engagement* means relating to others with mindful awareness of the constant change in us, them, and the world around us. Conflict often limits our horizons, keeping us stuck, cornered, or narrowed in our perceptions; dynamic engagement aims to free us to invent new ways of being, smoother ways that are generative, more fluid, and more attuned to possibility. How do we prepare for and sustain dynamic engagement with those on the other side of conflict, those whose views may violate our values or challenge our sense of how things work? We do this through embodying a dialogic spirit.

A *dialogic spirit* is a state of being. It is to be open, inquiring, and receptive, to find meanings that are neither mine nor yours but something co-created. In this chapter, as we traverse eight components of dynamic engagement, we also explore how a dialogic spirit helps shift conflict. When we are finished, we will have a map through difference, ways of thinking about cultural conflict that pose questions and open possibilities to us as we go along. This map relies on our willingness to tap our growing cultural fluency and conflict fluency as resources for understanding and to invoke our mindful awareness as we attend to the changing dynamics through which we move.

Components of Dynamic Engagement

Conflict happens when a difference surfaces that makes it difficult to proceed harmoniously. It may happen over material things; it somehow interrupts the flow of relationship. It causes us to narrow our perspectives and batten down the hatches to minimize potential losses. Looking below the surface we see that conflict often involves collisions of identities and ways of meaning-making. Because many of us are uncomfortable with conflict, we often avoid acknowledging it until it has wreaked considerable damage to physical things or our relationships, or we seek to short-circuit it. When we can no longer deny or avoid conflict, we often seek to "fix" it as expeditiously and efficiently as possible. Depending on our cultural starting points, we may suggest solutions, apply ourselves to problem solving, or find a trusted elder to help.

Sometimes conflict is solved quickly. But when cultural or worldview differences separate us and others, it is more difficult to effect a quick fix. And when these cultural or worldview differences have played out over time, shaping the other into negative images in our minds and lodging as hurts and scars within us, then quick fixes are out of the question.

No one process will work in all conflicts across all cultural settings. Every process has built-in cultural assumptions about naming, framing, blaming, and taming conflict. The components presented here are offered not as prescriptive parts of a process to bridge conflict but as touchstones—places to refresh, envision, and center attention. They will come alive as they are used in a variety of contexts, adapted to local conditions, and completely changed when appropriate. They are seeds more than fruit; sparks of ideas more than a set of plans. They speak not just to what but to how. They invite ongoing adaptation rather than rigid application.

It is important to acknowledge the cultural dimensions of dynamic engagement. Dynamic engagement involves attending to conflict, dialoguing, and designing processes that reflect the cultural common sense of the parties. Approaches to conflict are very different across cultural starting points including individualist and communitarian, high- and low-context, and specific and diffuse. As discussed in Chapter Five, norms of indirectness and attention to face-saving may mean that conflict issues are addressed without any face-to-face conversation or collaboratively designed process. Some conflicts are never named or processed at all—at least not in ways outsiders would recognize.

This is why dynamic engagement is not a prescription but a series of touchstones. Naming a conflict may be a private or public matter. A process may be designed collectively, or it may be devised by people not directly involved, to help parties to the conflict save face. Each of the components of dynamic engagement discussed here is meant to stimulate imagination and ideas about the ways particular conflicts in specific cultural contexts may be addressed. Other components may be added; some may be skipped.

The eight components of dynamic engagement, depicted in Figure 6.1, are a flow, not a straight line. They may help us unlock stuck dynamics. They are designed to be used in a variety of sequences, to be mixed and matched when appropriate. They are depicted in chart form for ease of reference, but actual conflicts follow courses that eddy around these markers, sometimes slowly and sometimes quickly, sometimes doubling back. The components of dynamic engagement are animated by a *spirit of dialogue,* helping us to substitute inquiry for defensiveness and engagement for competition. The components of dynamic engagement are

- Attend, assess
- Suspend judgments, expand perspectives
- Receive the other side
- Create a shared circle of experience, opening to shifts and postponing problem solving
- Design a way through that reflects cultural common sense
- Reflect
- Integrate
- Quest

We will meet each of these dimensions in turn, focusing on the *doing* and the *being* parts of each component. The components are discussed as they apply to an actual cultural conflict that is part of a larger negotiation. Because the conflict is about relationship and identity, the way it is resolved will have an important effect on the course of the negotiations.

In New Zealand, two Maori tribal groups are in the process of negotiating land claims settlements with the government, referred to as the *Crown.*[1] These two Maori groups, who call themselves *iwi,* are meeting for the first time with representatives of the Crown. The *iwi* are represented by fifteen people, all males over the age of fifty who have been involved with the treaty claim process for many years. The Crown is represented by six officials from different ministries and offices. They are a Crown elder (an older male *iwi* who works with the Crown to advance treaty settlements), one other male, and four females in their twenties and thirties. The Crown team is led by a woman in her late thirties who is new to her position. They meet on a *marae* (meeting place) belonging to one of the *iwi.* The story that unfolds is told as seen through the women's eyes.

At this initial meeting the *iwi* and the Crown representatives discuss technical aspects of the treaty negotiation process and exchange information. Questions are answered primarily by two female members of the Crown team, because they have had the

Figure 6.1. Dynamic Engagement and a Dialogic Spirit.

Attend, assess	Spirit of inquiry	Awareness increases, perspective broadens, starting points are explored
Suspend judgment	Spirit of release	Judgment does not block perception; enemy-image does not crowd out humanity
Receive "the other side"	Spirit of witness	Identity becomes more complex, meaning-making windows are opened; empathy and trust grow
Create a shared circle	Spirit of engagement	Multiple ways of knowing are welcomed and dialogue and indirect actions open possibilities; past hurts are acknowledged
Design *a way through* that reflects cultural common sense	Spirit of creative action	A variety of modes are used to engage conflict—direct and indirect, verbal and nonverbal. Processes make room for commonalities and differences and a variety of cultural starting points. Problem-solving is one of a range of methods. Being is balanced with doing
Reflect	Spirit of perspective	Dialogue about *the way through* with achievements, requests, appreciations, and regrets all welcomed. Reflection may be private or public, individual or collective, diffuse or specific
Integrate	Spirit of acknowledgment	Shifts and accomplishments are marked with rituals and acknowledgments as the basis for future engagement. Ongoing progress is monitored
Quest	Spirit of inquiry	Relationships continue with collective attention to creating positive spirals

SHIFT—
HAPPENS THROUGHOUT
PROCESS

most experience with these people and this claim. Toward the end of the meeting, one of the *iwi* representatives stands up, visibly furious. Barely controlling his anger, he confronts the Crown representatives, asking: "What is the Crown doing, sending up young white women to talk to us about the treaty settlement process? We do not even let our own women work on our claims!" Another *iwi* follows, saying, "We have our own bright young things who are more than capable of working on the claims, but we consider the claims to be sacred, and it is something of an insult for us to be spoken to by young people representing the government."

Attend and Assess

A conflict has surfaced. It is felt in ripples throughout the relationships of those present. How to approach it? In the first instance the Crown representatives do nothing. They simply attend and observe, assessing the situation and not wanting any of their actions to worsen it. Recognizing the high-context starting point of the *iwi*, among whom age is venerated and the status and identity of negotiators is critical, they know they cannot simply respond with a defense or justification.

Attending and assessing is not passive, though it may appear so from the outside. It is a useful thing to do when conflict first surfaces, unless safety or lives are at stake. Resisting the urge to act, the mindful person takes stock of events, ideas, and the cultural lenses and assumptions of everyone involved. With a *spirit of inquiry,* genuine questions are posed to self and, where appropriate, others to enlarge the scope and understanding of the conflict and how it has arisen. Attending and assessing will look different across cultural contexts. It may be an internal process or the subject of dialogue within a group. As part of assessing and attending, it is essential to bring context, history, identities, and the ways meanings are made into focus. Is this a conflict centered in the material, communicative, or symbolic dimensions of relationships? Is it part of a pattern? What is the physical experience of this conflict; where does it live in the bodies of those involved? What are the emotional dimensions of this issue? How does intuition speak to this issue and to what underlies it? How do past events affect the course of this conflict? Is this a matter for urgent attention, or is there space for reflection? (Remember that many times, matters that seem to require urgent attention benefit from careful thought and reflection. Urgent action in the absence of imminent danger can escalate conflict.)

Attending and assessing is an information-gathering phase, but the information gathered is not just the usual who, what, where, when, why, and how. In addition, cultural fluency, conflict fluency, and mindful awareness are employed to increase the parties' understanding of the cultural and symbolic aspects of a situation. The mindful person also looks within, inquiring how personal lenses color what is seen and also hide things from view. Fluency with conflict helps temper reactions in the direction of observation and attention, preserving options and choices.

Suspend Judgment

Having stopped, breathed, and attended to all the levels of conflict, the mindful person, with a *spirit of release,* actively suspends judgment and expands perspectives. This is a difficult thing to do, and one that attracts a lot of resistance. When we are in conflict with another, the last thing we want to do is suspend our judgments, which are often negative and numerous. We tend to think our perspective quite expansive enough; often it seems clear to us that the problem of narrow vision is theirs, not ours.

It can also feel as though suspending judgment is giving in or losing our moral compass. This inhibition arises from two things: the fear of losing some part of our identity or meaning that is dear to us and the related fear of losing the negotiation or the outcome we desire. It is important to remember that suspending judgment is not agreeing with the other; it is simply releasing our judgments, setting them to the side to see what else we can let in.

In the case of the Crown and the *iwi,* the Crown negotiators are offended, indignant, and dumbfounded by the statements of the *iwi.* They remember that several ministers in the government they represent are women. They wonder why these men are refusing to live in the real world, why they are trying to impose their cultural values on others. The Crown negotiators have attended to what was said with a *spirit of inquiry,* and they have realized that the *iwi* begin from a different starting point than they do. But inner protestations and judgments follow this realization; the Crown negotiators summon discipline to interrupt their self-protective mechanisms and suspend their habit of judging.

As they put their judgments to the side, they realize again that to reply at all may seem to add insult to injury. They also notice that there is some disagreement within the *iwi* groups; some of the *iwi* are embarrassed that the Crown representatives have been subjected to such ill-feeling. Releasing their judgments, the Crown negotiators resist labeling the *iwi* with pejorative adjectives or responding defensively. As they hold their silence, the Crown elder on their team speaks for them, saying, "These young people are not as young as you think and they are people of capacity."

As I mentioned, all of these exchanges are taking place on a *marae*. Traditions dictate how communication takes place here, including *karakia* and *mihi* (prayer and greetings or introductions, in Maori language) at the beginning of the meeting. Important aspects of identities, meanings, and symbols are conveyed via these openings. The high value the Maori place on maturity means, for example, that a man does not speak on the *marae* if his father or older brother is alive. Only those who are mature can work on claims in the view of some tribal groups, since claims are *tapu* ("sacred").

This exchange is part of a series of meetings in which the parties are preparing for negotiations, coming to know each other and sharing a range of experiences. The foundation is being laid for constructive relationships, which are central to effective negotiation. Suspending judgment and resisting action, the Crown negotiators open the door to a *spirit of witness*, in which they can receive the other side.

Receive the Other Side

Rather than reacting, the Crown representatives listened to what was said, even as it was said in anger, with a *spirit of witness*. What is a *spirit of witness*? It is a quality of attention that involves stepping outside our usual habits. Judgment is suspended and a space is made for the experience of others. A *spirit of witness* requires a quiet, receptive mind and an internal dialogue with that part of ourselves that would leap into action protecting us, telling it, "Please just sit still and let the words wash over like a wave. It is important to hear them, and to hear the spirit within them. Let them be on the shores and seep into the sand. Hearing them does not mean adopting them; it means receiving them in all of their nuances and passion. It means not deflecting or denying them. It means recognizing that my brother or sister is speaking." Acknowledging our connection to another, we receive what is said in a new way. We do not agree or disagree; having a *spirit of witness* is about making space for another in our hearts and using our minds to receive what is said. There will be plenty of time later for weighing, assessing, or responding.

From a witness state, the Crown representatives listened further to the *iwi* representatives. A variety of views were shared. Some *iwi* apologized outside the formal meeting for the behavior of their brothers. They explained that the frustration of the *iwi* arose from the high turnover of Crown negotiators and that it took the form of this attack on age and gender. The Crown representatives later learned that vigorous debates continued among the *iwi* after the meeting ended, with stern remonstrations from those who felt the outbursts were inappropriate and unrepentant justifications from the two men who had voiced their objections. Hearing all of this, the Crown negotiators experienced the context as more clear and the speakers as more understandable. This issue had not arisen from nowhere. Past hurts, resentments, and distrust arising from a history of racism and oppression fueled the passion expressed by the two men. Making the context bigger through listening with a *spirit of witness* helped the Crown negotiators feel empathy for the *iwi*.

Create a Shared Circle

The next part of the process, creating a shared circle, arises from listening with a *spirit of witness*. In some cases it may look like sitting down together around a round table and sharing views. In others it may be a walk side by side, observing nature. In still other situations no direct conversation is ever initiated. Indirect communication or conciliation by others is more appropriate. Creating a shared circle need not involve direct communication or confrontation. It is to draw a notional circle in our minds with a *spirit of engagement* that includes those we are in conflict with and ourselves. Having drawn this circle (however much we may not want to be with the others in a shared space), we ask ourselves, what next?

In this case, the what-next involved listening, waiting, and considering the perspectives of each side. The Crown representatives were mindful that while their departments have turnover and employment benefits, the Maori have no ability or choice to resign from the negotiating work. They expect to work with the Crown throughout negotiations, placing a high value on strong relationships with the minister and members of the Crown team as a means to develop a successful agreement.

The what-next actually took place over several months, as negotiations were set up and begun. Unlike the previous components of attending, suspending judgment, and receiving the other, creating a shared circle may be a more visible, active step. One way into this circle is to pay attention to metaphors used in communication and to use these metaphors to inform choices about how or whether to engage the other directly.

In this conflict, metaphors were very important, in part because of the rich oral tradition of Maori language. Used with a *spirit of engagement,* metaphors helped advance the conversation without escalation. One elder spoke saying, "I don't mind being told what to do by a cat, but I won't be told what to do by a kitten." The Crown elder responded with this saying, "The glass elver grow up to have a big sting in their tails" (a reference to baby eels that develop into big adults). The Crown elder was meeting the image proposed by the kitten metaphor, suggesting that the young women representing the Crown were not as innocent or powerless as the *iwi* might think. Another *iwi* member argued that the age and gender of the Crown representatives was not relevant, that it was more important for the *iwi* to concentrate on getting the ancestral lands returned to the *iwi.* He used a proverb that, translated, means, "The land is permanent, man disappears."

As negotiations continued, a shift took place. It did not happen all at once. It happened as the two men who had spoken out against the women were elected as negotiators for the official process. Both women continued into the negotiations as representatives of the Crown. Neither side had choices about who was on the other side: the minister delegated her representatives and the *iwi* elected theirs. As they negotiated the terms of the process, a constructive working relationship evolved. Part of the reason for this improvement was the performance of the women over time: the *iwi* representatives saw that they were competent, committed, and consistent.

With one circle drawn around them (the circle of the official negotiations), they came to work together with a positive *spirit of engagement*. The shift to a positive, constructive climate meant that they began to expect positive things from each other, not negative things. They began to hold each other in high regard. They developed trust. Through the Crown representatives' willingness to acknowledge the history and suffering that marked the *iwi's* past, progress was facilitated.

Shifts and Turning Points

The spiral spanning Figure 6.1 illustrates the shifts that occur as people engage constructively with each other, changes that may be small or very significant. Whether they seem like a blip on the radar of a negotiation, or a major shaking of the earth, shifts are marked by people paying attention differently to each other and the issues. On one side of a shift, people are guarded, defensive, and tense. On the other, there is at least a little more openness and willingness to let in information that contradicts assumptions or stereotypes. Trust and empathy can be built. Relationships may grow.

Shifts happen throughout dynamic engagement, marked by emotional "ah-hah's" and cognitive realizations. They are not associated with any one part of the process, though they may happen more frequently as foundations of trust are built. The dialogic spirit that accompanies each part of dynamic engagement is an essential component of shift. Shifts may be precipitated by an intervention from an outsider; sometimes they arise as a result of a shared physical experience like having a meal or going on a field-trip. Sometimes, shifts feel dramatic, much as attaining a summit gifts the climber with a fabulous panorama. Other times, as in this instance, there is no one event to point to. It is enough that there is listening and respect along the way as material issues are addressed, and a space made concurrently for deep ties to identity, values, and meanings to be made visible. In the case of the *iwi* and the Crown, sharing metaphors, abstaining from confrontation, and acknowledging history helped smooth the tension of the conflict, contributing to a positive spiral in their relationships.

Design a Way Through That Reflects Cultural Common Sense

Moving forward, the Crown and *iwi* were able to make substantial progress in the negotiations. With a *spirit of creative action,* each side invited the other to contribute rituals and steps that its members found meaningful. Prayers and traditional greetings were important symbolic rituals for the *iwi*. Agendas and clear, written terms of agreement were important signposts for the Crown. Both Maori and English were spoken at the negotiation table. References to history were frequent, and these were seen by the Crown negotiators not as digressions (the stereotypical Crown perspective) but as integral to the process (the traditional *iwi* perspective, in which time is circular, not linear). Similarly, the *iwi* shifted in their behavior toward the Crown.

At the ceremony marking the signing of the Terms of Agreement between the *iwi* and the minister representing the Crown, one of the two men who had been the most vociferous opponents of the two women told the minister: "Your officials are wonderful ambassadors for the Crown. Their professionalism is only matched by their beauty." In meetings that followed he continued to sing the praises of the women and to rebuke anyone who was impolite to them. The female Crown representatives saw this behavior as a kind of indirect apology, not explicit but still appreciated.

Not every conflict will be addressed with face-to-face meetings. A variety of ways for facilitating communication, involvement, and input to decisions exist across cultural contexts. Face-to-face involvement, once a relational foundation has been laid, may allow for deepening of relationships and generative collaborative work.

Reflect

When we reflect on this conflict in a *spirit of perspective,* one of the things that stands out is that the process took time. No one stepped in as a formal mediator, though the Crown elder did several things to bridge the conflict, both overtly and behind the scenes. The Crown elder had insight into the cultural traditions of the *iwi* and acted with awareness of these ways of thinking, knowing, and being. Although neither negotiating group was successful in changing the composition of the other (a solution both might have preferred at various points), the groups found a way to work together. This way was not ideal for the Crown negotiators. They appreciated the positive regard of the *iwi* who had first rejected them. But his comments about their attractiveness were not in the realm of political correctness they had come to expect in their own European– New Zealand cultural context.

Still, the process showed them that trust and respect are iterative, earned. Similarly, it demonstrated that shifts do not necessarily accompany specific events but build over time, like waves, even if they seem to emerge suddenly. They do not come about in one meeting; they are the product of investment in relationship. These lessons informed decisions about future treaty negotiations processes within the ministry. The final part of the bridging process, integration, is an essential link to capturing the rich learning arising from cultural conflict.

Integrate

As the Terms of Agreement between the *iwi* and the Crown were signed, this phase of negotiations drew to an end. With a *spirit of acknowledgment,* the knowledge and experience of the Crown negotiators about the *iwi*'s different cultural starting points was passed on to others in the ministry. Both women and men continue to represent the Crown in negotiations, but awareness of Maori values and perspectives helps them prepare and respond to concerns. Relationships are maintained, and continuity of responsibility preserved where possible, so that agreements can be implemented with less difficulty. A *spirit of acknowledgment* animates this part of the way through, as lessons learned in relationship are integrated into the foundation from which new questions and possibilities emerge.

Often integration is accompanied by rituals that mark time shared and accomplishments. Rituals range from spontaneous to traditional and include everything from a shared meal to the passing of a talking stick once more around the circle so that everyone can reflect on what has happened. Rituals give a sense of closure, leaving everyone more aware of achievements and the relationships that made them possible.

Quest

As milestones are marked, new questions and avenues for joint work emerge, again animated by a *spirit of inquiry*. With the confidence born of incremental achievements, participants continue to work together. In ongoing relationships, the quest is always recurring. The quest runs through good times and bad times, spiraling into positive shifts when people work together effectively and into negative places when they are stuck. It is a quest not only for results and accomplishments but for experiences that speak to our deeper parts, where meaning is made and identities are constantly invented. It is a quest carried out with a *spirit of inquiry*, setting preconceived notions about others aside as much as possible. In our quests, individual and collective, we need a *spirit of inquiry* to discern our path, our direction, and ways we can work together.

Applications Closer to Home

Though the eight elements of the dynamic framework have been presented in sequential order, they may not play out this way in every conflict. Dynamic engagement is a continuous set of components through which we can ascend incrementally or slide quickly down, depending on the relational dynamics in the negotiation or communication. Several of the components shown in Figure 6.1 can exist simultaneously, and it is possible to move out of sequential order because all the parts are connected. The dialogic spirit that animates the components breathes resilience and vitality into dynamic engagement, counteracting resistance and defensive-ness; it is this that makes movement and true relational empathy possible.

This example of cultural conflict from New Zealand has assisted us in exploring dynamic engagement. What does dynamic engagement have to do with a development dispute, where the cultures involved are rural and urban, conservation and development oriented? How is dynamic engagement relevant to a racial or ethnic divide in a neighborhood or a classroom? What does it have to say to families in conflict, for whom religion, class, or generation may be fault lines? Let's explore questions like these, drawing from a range of examples, this time highlighting the second column in Figure 6.1, the ways a dialogic spirit helps us move through conflict.

Some years ago a class on gender and conflict was taught to twenty graduate students from the United States, Canada, and Africa. One-third were black and the rest were white. When one of the weekly readings made a reference to *white trash,* a student from outside the United States asked for an explanation of this expression. A white American student, Sylvia, attempted an explanation, describing the term as pejorative and class related. Then, searching around for more scaffolding for her fellow student, she used an analogy. "It's used the way the term *n——r* is used to describe blacks," she offered.

The class froze. Several of the African-American women sat in silence, seething. How could someone be so insensitive? The legacy of hurt linked with that term in the history of African-Americans was not commensurate with the term *white trash* at all. They said nothing, but their rage was palpable, and the class was stopped in its tracks.

Was this a conflict? Surely it was a conflict with identity and meanings at its heart. In a moment a whole history of oppression and racism flooded into the room for the African-American students. An expression of defensiveness quickly took over Sylvia's features; her conscious motivation had been only to provide help. If the students had been pebbles, an outsider would have been able to observe them quickly rolling to one side or the other as some members of the class aligned with Sylvia and others with the black students. The tension was thick. They looked to their teacher to provide leadership. It made sense to begin with attending and assessing, asking where the class was and what was possible from there. He tried to do so, searching the room for clues.

But it was difficult to engage the class members on the path of dynamic engagement. Their senses were certainly heightened. But a *spirit of inquiry* was not present. With the possible exception of the woman who had asked for clarification in the first place, no one was in a state of inquiry. All of them were experiencing reactive states—anger, panic, frustration, shock.

The teacher named the chasm that yawned in their midst and invited comment. A few people vented some of their feelings. Shortly afterward he called a break. He wanted to speak with the women involved, to gauge what needed to happen next. He wanted everyone to have a chance to move out of the space that seemed, paradoxically, both frozen and overheated. Until they moved from this space, a *spirit of inquiry* could not be embraced.

Embracing a *Spirit of Inquiry*

To truly embrace the potential of attending and assessing, a *spirit of inquiry* is essential. Only in genuine inquiry does our adrenaline give way to perspective and our vision broaden. How do we get to inquiry when all we feel is aggression? Physiologically and psychologically this takes time. Resisting the adage that tells us to "strike while the iron is hot," we choose to let it cool down. We take a break, move around, sit in silence—all ways of making room for inquiry. We know we are in a state of inquiry when we have a sense of inner spaciousness rather than heads and hearts entirely full of justifications, blaming, and rounds of triggers continually firing as we replay the original scene and other scenes from the past that it has brought to mind.

In this instance it took until the following week, with many intervening conversations, before members of the class were able to embrace a *spirit of inquiry*. In private some of the African-American women related stories of what the incident meant to them. They were unwilling to share these with the class but sharing them with the teacher and a few students helped them move from the defensiveness and anger they were feeling. The woman who had made the original analogy had work to do too to get out of a perceptual corner. She felt insulted and wronged by the responses of her classmates. Her stories were also shared in private, stories about misinterpretation and being blamed for things she did not personally do. In private the students could say things without worrying about inflaming others.

The following week everyone agreed to come back to class with a *spirit of inquiry,* an openness to hearing a fuller picture than had come out during the previous class. The students were still guarded, bruised, and passionate about their views, and they were committed to moving through the rough spot so that they could continue in constructive relationship as a class. Because they had developed a vision statement for the class early on, they were able to refer back to it as an anchor, a way to open a space in the conflict for genuine inquiry into the living stories that were fueling it. Rather than dueling with competing narratives, they held to their intention of letting ideas unfold among them in a spacious way, where differences were welcome.

Did the atmosphere transform quickly from stormy to sunlit? No, the process was more gradual and less obvious than that. When stories of insult and frustration accumulated over years are surfaced, resolution seems a distant possibility. It is enough to focus on incremental gains, addressing issues and communication in a *spirit of continuing inquiry* as forward momentum emerges.

A *spirit of inquiry* leads directly into the next facet of dynamic engagement: suspending judgment with a *spirit of release.* Almost as soon as inquiry begins, information is offered that has the potential to arouse defensiveness. If this defensiveness is internalized or deflected, the entire cycle of anger and arousal starts again, and the *spirit of inquiry* disappears. To move into a *spirit of release* is literally to let go of the reactions that arise, noticing them but not investing in them. This is a difficult thing to do, but it yields positive results when it happens.

Yielding to a *Spirit of Release*

One story of a *spirit of release* is more about internal cultural conflict than differences between people. Benjamin Zander, a professor of music at the New England Conservatory, announced at the beginning of the fall semester that he was assigning all of his students A's for the term. Here is what he told them: "There is one requirement you must fulfill to earn this grade: Sometime in the next two weeks, you must write me a letter dated next May, which begins with the words, 'Dear Mr. Zander, I got my A because . . .'"[2]

One student, from Taiwan, had been raised in a culture where musical performance centered on measurement and competition. Here is how he spoke about the effect this choice had on him and how it led to a *spirit of release:* "I am number 68 out of 70 student. I come to Boston and Mr. Zander says I am an A. Very confusing. I walk about, three weeks, very confused. I am number 68, but Mr. Zander says I am an A student. . . . I am number 68, but Mr. Zander says I am an A. One day I discover much happier A than Number 68. So I decide I am an A."[3]

This student discovered that he could choose to step into the possibilities that being an A student offered. He did not need to take on the label assigned by his national culture, which placed him near the bottom of the list. He saw a choice, and stepping into a *spirit of release,* he let go of the limitations infused in the old label, limitations as real as any brick barrier that might block the way forward. As he did so he was able to let go of his old image of himself, seeing more creative possibilities.

When conflict happens between people, the same process is possible. Suspending judgment with a *spirit of release* means setting aside our enemy image of the other, imagining that he makes sense inside his own circle, and stepping into that circle, if only with one toe. Consider the conflict about abortion that rages in the United States and Canada, erupting from time to time in violence, tearing apart communities and families. This conflict and the violence that attends it led two Washington, D.C., women to develop a dialogue process to help people on both sides of the issue talk with each other.[4] After months of a prolife, prochoice dialogue, advocates on both sides of the issue became practiced at a *spirit of release.* When I asked one of them why they kept meeting when others on their side might have seen dialogue as a dilution of their efforts, he turned to me with tears in his eyes. "I do it," he said, "because I see God in the eyes of the others."

A *spirit of release* makes the God visible where once there were only images of evil or bad intentions so fully projected onto the other that they seemed to emanate from her. Suspending judgment is a discipline that flows from this *spirit of release;* it is literally to let the judgments pass through and wait by the side of the road, turning our attention instead to the humanity of the speaker. It is to ask: Who is he in context? How does his world make sense to him? What don't I know about this whole picture that I can learn if I stop judging for a minute or an hour?

Entering a *Spirit of Witness*

Companion to the *spirit of release* is the *spirit of witness.* The *spirit of witness* accompanies our opening to receive the other side in all of their humanness. It requires sustained attention and deep listening. The kind of listening that is part of the *spirit of witness* is not everyday listening. It is listening in a time and way apart, listening for the sense of the words as well as their meaning. To practice a *spirit of witness* means literally to lend ourselves to the graceful place where whatever is said is held softly, without judgment or rejoinder. It is held with heart and mind at once in a space where the speaker is received for all of who she might be. This *spirit of witness* makes it possible for the speaker to reveal contradictions within, self-doubts, guilt, or regrets, rather than painting a uniform picture of justification. When we listen to another with a *spirit of witness,* we see a more whole picture of him. Chances are some part of us will resonate with the picture, and empathy will arise.

I saw a *spirit of witness* when a friend was dying. He had suffered a stroke and could not speak. As a local politician for a record number of years, he had favored development and championed local industry. He had many supporters, but he had also acquired enemies along the way. In one episode of his career he had promoted the construction of a large dam that produced massive environmental impacts and flooding of Native American land. There were strong, vocal protests and visceral feelings on both sides. At his bedside one day I witnessed a visit from a member of the local environmental coalition that had opposed the dam. She spoke to him of her respect for his passion and dedication. She listened to his silence, watching the expressiveness of his eyes as he struggled to talk. She held his hand. In that moment they received each other as they never had on the debating floor. Words were not the dominant mode of exchange, but exchange occurred anyway, and a window of connection was opened. Empathy was palpable in the room, and it seemed as though a third culture emerged, a bigger circle in which they were no longer adversaries, no longer clothed in their roles of development promoter and environmentalist, but something more. They were two people passionate about their community, two people who had invested a great deal and tried very hard, even if for different ends. This was a powerful experience of the *spirit of witness*.

Gathering a *Spirit of Engagement*

It is trite to say that two people can be divided by a problem or united in trying to fix it. Wanting to fix the problem is not enough when the divisions are about long histories of mutual hatred and pain. Gathering a *spirit of engagement* means helping everyone draw a metaphorical circle around the people and their problem, but not just that. The circle needs to be large enough also to encompass the people in context—their identities, meanings, perceptions, and stories past and present. Tempting as it may be to try to fix the problem once people are gathered in a common circle, other things may need to happen there before or instead of problem solving.

What needs to happen will look different in different situations. Perhaps it is creation of a shared history, composed in language expansive enough that both parties recognize their roots there. Perhaps it is a shared ritual or experience in which coming together is symbolized. Sharing a meal is one of the most universal ways of creating a shared circle: as we eat together, we literally engage as humans with shared appetites and desires. It helps if the shared meal is subject to a ground rule: that the issues that divide are not to be spoken of. Given this ground rule, people talk of other things and come to know new facets of each other, facets unrelated to conflict identities. Their pictures become more nuanced and alive, and the other more real. Sharing a meal, French and English Canadians find they are also merchants, parents, readers, singers, or amateur astronomers. Greek and Turkish Cypriots find they are also twins, gardeners, thespians, hikers, or birdwatchers.

Of course, sharing a meal is itself a cultural event. It is important to be sure that the food does not violate the beliefs or rules of the other. Are these people vegetarian, do they eat meat but not pork, do they use chopsticks or hands or cutlery? Finding a way to share a circle around food opens a window into many other aspects of culture. And it is not always a simple way. A facilitator was helping a group of Israelis and Palestinians with a community-based dialogue. They were talking with each other over a period of weeks, but relations were strained and difficult. Seeking to expand the *spirit of engagement* the facilitator suggested to the Israelis that they act from their tradition of hospitality. Perhaps they would prepare food for the Palestinians in advance of the next meeting. This hospitality is ubiquitous in the desert, and it seemed to be a culturally appropriate suggestion that was received favorably by both sides.

On the appointed day the Israelis were busy in the kitchen of the meeting place. Many dishes were being prepared, and attention had been paid to making sure that the foods did not violate Muslim beliefs. But as the facilitator walked into the dining room she noticed that there were not enough seats for everyone at the table. The Israelis then told her that they had promised to prepare food for the Palestinians. "But," they added, "we never said that we would eat with them." These Israelis knew the symbolic value of breaking bread together, and they were not yet ready to step that firmly into the circle.

A *spirit of engagement* calls on us to bring the full range of our intelligences and gifts to drawing and maintaining a shared circle. We bring our emotional selves, feeling with others; our intuitive selves, sensing what is left unsaid; our imaginative selves, extending a vision of what is possible into the future; and our somatic selves, acting out a new relationship even as we feel our ways into it. We bring our connected ways of knowing, attending to the big picture as it encompasses us and them, even as we know that we may call the big picture different names.

When we engage in creating a shared circle with others, we are necessarily changed. We do not necessarily change who we are or what we want, but we change our view of, and relationship with, the other. And this opens up more possibilities than existed before. We have shifted our relationship, nudged aside the enemy image at least enough to make it more complex, to recognize that inside the ogre is gold as well as dross. Extending a *spirit of engagement* further along the possible continuum, we may even come to see that inside the ogre is a thread that connects him or her to us.

Sparking a *Spirit of Creative Action*

A sense that we and others are in a metaphorical circle together in a way that has the potential to be constructive may make it possible to address conflict issues. A foundation of relationship and shared experience is helpful, providing resilience amid setbacks. How can differences be addressed across cultures? Far from being a prompt to revert to orthodox methods or linear progressions, this component of dynamic engagement is a jumping-off point for creativity. In fact the spirit most needed here is the *spirit of creative action*.

Have you seen it animate groups, this spirit? It is a collaborative spirit, welcoming ideas and differences even as progress is made. It is not so narrow that it offers only one way forward and not so broad that no focus is achieved. A *spirit of creative action* is not about expression for expression's sake; it is about creativity in the service of results. Proceeding from an awareness of cultural starting points and currencies, people work together with playfulness, humor, and a sense of adventure. They may run into conflicts along the way, but they have a base from which to untangle them.

Bring to mind an occasion that fits with what I have just described. What made it possible? Perhaps it was part of a church, mosque, or temple service project in which the shared commitment to help fueled the *spirit of creative action*. Or perhaps it was a class in which, after a difficult exchange, participants stepped into the space created by the dialogue, sharing deeper truths. It may have occurred in a family, an organization, a community. Wherever it happened, consider for a moment which words you would use to describe the feeling and the outcomes.

People typically use words like these to describe a *spirit of creative action: energized, generative, on fire, fired up, synergistic, fluid, open, effervescent, engaging.* They describe the process of coming together and achieving something as satisfying and enlivening. Problem solving is more possible when a relational base has been built and people know something about each other's identities and ways of making meaning. Other ways of moving through conflict are also easier, supported by the relational foundation that has been cultivated.

Even when this relational base is present, maintaining a *spirit of creative action* can test a group. One dialogue group of prochoice and prolife activists ran into challenges as the participants moved toward creative action even though they had talked together very constructively over several months. They had discovered considerable common ground even though initially their different views on abortion had led them to feel as though they were from different universes. Now they wanted to do something together, to share the results of their dialogue more broadly.

With some trepidation, they decided to compose and issue a joint press release. As they worked on it, they ran into new barriers. Though they had been able to listen to each other with *spirits of witness, inquiry,* and *release* during their dialogues, it was harder to polish the diamonds they wanted to share with the wider world. Questions of image and perception arose as participants from each side considered how they could present the common ground they had found without seeming to have betrayed their deep values and fellow advocates.

This kind of test arises frequently when we seek to take something we have developed out into a bigger sphere. The trust and safety built up among participants does not extend to the wider world, and translation of what has been experienced is difficult because it is based in relationships that do not extend beyond the boundaries of the group. Coming up against this challenge, group members decided to suspend their problem solving for a few minutes.

They went out on a walk, agreeing not to talk about the struggles they were experiencing nor about the issue of abortion generally. They talked about the sea, their families and communities, social reform, and faith. They talked about their work selves, their home selves, their public selves and their private selves. With the space and freedom they gave themselves, they became reenergized and again aware of their reasons for working together.

The energy in the room following their walk was palpably different. Stiff, tense, boggy exchanges were replaced by lightness and laughter. The *spirit of creative action* was again vibrant in the room, and it breathed life into the problem-solving process that continued until they agreed on the text of their release. Hearkening back to the source of meaning and "juice" in their lives had created a shift, freeing the *spirit of creative action* to spur them on again. The experience of completing the press release was later described by the participants as one of the richest parts of what they learned, yet one of the toughest.

Holding a *Spirit of Perspective*

Learning can be lost if it is not named, preserved, and marked. Have you ever found yourself learning the same lesson twice because you failed to internalize a realization? I trust I am not alone in having had this experience on more than one occasion. Learning is more than being in the vicinity of insights. It is an active state, drawing on a *spirit of perspective*. Learning asks that we move the lens closer and then farther away, looking at our progress and missteps from the peak of shared purpose and the microscope of our internal monitors. Mindful of our cultural lenses, we ask these questions: Who am I in this issue? Who are we in the issue? What have I learned, and how have we changed through these experiences? How have we changed in relationship to each other? To the issues? How have our cultural ways of being played out through this experience? In a similar situation, what would be useful to remember from this experience?

A *spirit of perspective* reminds us that experiences of euphoria and despair are exceptions in most lives. From them come nuggets that can be named and examined later in the light of time passed. Immediacy brings learning into focus; time helps us assess which nuggets are gold and which are to be discarded. Dialogue creates more opportunities for learning as we hear a variety of views about each other and the work we have done together.

We are often tempted to skip over this facet of dynamic engagement, especially when we feel relief at having accomplished something or unfrozen what was stuck. We probably feel fatigue and want a break. We are relieved to be out of that indeterminate place where the boundaries seem to shift and the markers are unfamiliar. Even the most conflict fluent and culturally fluent among us feel this. At the same time, it is important to choose a time for learning—checking in with self and others—that is not so remote from the experiences that they will no longer be fresh.

A particularly powerful experience of reflecting with a *spirit of perspective* came in a class taught on teaching and learning. We were a diverse group, with widely different cultural and educational backgrounds. When it was time to pass around the class evaluations, class members protested. The class had been run with a *spirit of dialogue,* and the evaluations were a departure. In compliance with the university requirements, class members finally filled them out individually. But in addition, we set aside a time for reflecting together on our learning, for which we prepared in some structured ways. We considered what stood out for us, what content had been most meaningful for us. We looked at the process of our class, what worked and what worked less well. Most significantly, we each brought and shared a metaphor for the class, opening up new levels of discussion that had never been plumbed in the class over the entire semester.

Why were the metaphors such a potent tool for reflection? They were an invitation into each other's sensing, dynamic worlds, worlds where meaning is constantly being composed. For example, participants saw the class as an orchestra rehearsal, a white-water rafting trip, a walk in the woods. Through such metaphors we talked about who we were in relation to the material we had read; we shared with each other some new aspects of ourselves. For the person whose metaphor for the class was a walk in the woods, an insight surfaced about her habit of standing apart from what is happening. She was in the woods, but she was a visitor. Others gave her feedback about the ways this stance affected them and the ways they responded to it even when they were unaware of her metaphor. With the person whose metaphor was a white-water rafting trip, a dialogue ensued about risk and safety as part of learning.

Welcoming a *Spirit of Acknowledgment*

The *spirit of perspective* that helps gather and mark learning culminates in a *spirit of acknowledgment.* This is the time for rituals, certificates, meals, planning, and other culminating activities. Rituals should not be artificial impositions; they are most powerful when they arise organically from the group. Over time, groups evolve unique rituals. They can be simple things, ranging from ringing a set of chimes to mark beginnings and endings to using an expression that has taken on meaning for the group. Sometimes they have playfulness or humor rolled up in them; at other times they are quite serious. With a *spirit of acknowledgment* we mark the ways that the learning we have achieved in dialogue has built our conflict and cultural fluencies. We look for internal and interpersonal connections among what we once believed and what we now believe. Letting inconsistencies fall from the bigger picture, we acknowledge shifts and celebrate growth.

Because we are culturally different and make sense of the world differently, we do integration differently too. A *spirit of acknowledgment* may or may not be named; it may be manifested quietly and privately or boisterously and collectively. Expectations about acknowledgment are infused with cultural understandings. In a diverse group, various levels of comfort with explicit naming and direct dialogue need to be balanced with preferences for indirect reflection. We make sense of our worlds, gathering our learning and forming new questions, in our own ways.

Different approaches to integrating and acknowledging learning were evident in a set of final papers from a graduate course on conflict and culture. The thing that amazed me the most was the diversity of the papers. The students had two choices: they could write a scholarly paper complete with references and citations, or they could write a reflective journal, integrating their learning and observations with case studies and experiences. In the stack of papers, diversity awaited me. From a group of people who shared similar educational backgrounds came everything from intensely personal accounts of recovering from childhood sexual abuse and the cultural messages that accompanied that journey to a superb critique of the philosophical underpinnings of the conflict resolution field as it relates to cultural relativism. Both were to be acknowledged as outgrowths of the class journey.

Embracing a *Spirit of Inquiry*

At the end of the class on conflict and culture we reflected on our experiences. We had come together with a *spirit of inquiry,* sharing significant experiences along the way. As students worked to integrate their learning, they made quite different meanings of it. My experience of reading these papers initiated a new quest: rethinking the design of the course. Were there ways it could go deeper, providing content and experiences that would be more pertinent given this broad range of interests, identities, and ways of meaning-making? With whom could I partner in taking a look at the cultural biases inherent in the design? What evaluation system would be flexible enough to adapt to such different assignments, yet provide a central core of learning objectives that could be fairly assessed? These questions launched me into a new quest, a quest to develop the course further to integrate a dialogic spirit with multiple ways of knowing. Completion, when done well, leads to new quests, and so the quests continue.

As we quest we do less arriving than continuing, trusting that dynamic engagement with a *spirit of dialogue* will serve us more than instincts that tell us to shut down, preserve what we have, and screen the other out. Practices at the personal, interpersonal, and intergroup levels are helpful in maintaining a dialogic spirit and accessing creative potential. In Chapters Seven, Eight, and Nine we will explore the ways conflict fluency, cultural fluency, mindful awareness, and dynamic engagement inform a series of practices for bridging cultural conflict.

PART TWO

Practices for Engaging Cultural Conflict

CHAPTER SEVEN

Deepening the Colors
Personal Practices to Help Bridge Differences

My friend and colleague Venashri Pillay has worked as a social worker in a traditional Zulu community in South Africa. When she began, she was frustrated by ongoing difficulties in establishing and maintaining relationships with the local people. Though she had grown up in Durban, in an Indian family, she found it difficult to bridge the gap between her formal training and the traditional beliefs of her clients. Finally she realized that she would make progress and develop positive working relationships with people only if she "embraced and acknowledged their traditional ways of solving problems." She modified her intake form to include non-Western, nonmedical interventions. She tells this story:

> A mother was referred to me with her child for his learning disability. I immediately recommended a visit to the local *sangoma* or *nyanga* (traditional healers). I even suggested one or two of the treatments he would want to initiate—rituals to appease the ancestors and cleansing ceremonies. I wrote all this down on the official hospital chart, demonstrating to the parent that I was not just paying lip service to her culture and traditions, but that I saw them as legitimate, important and helpful. Only once she followed this advice did I suggest a Western medical approach of various tests and analyses. In this way, I earned the mother's trust and respect, and this had a ripple effect in the community. Soon, other clients were coming

to me and following both their traditional routes to
healing and the complementary Western medical practices
I proposed.[1]

This story demonstrates ongoing inquiry and conflict prevention. Rather than trying to force compliance or rejecting the traditional beliefs of her clients, Venashri found a way to work with
them in partnership as whole people. Through her willingness to
learn about and legitimize her clients' traditional approaches to
problems, she engaged them in ways that addressed their psychological, spiritual, emotional, and physical needs. Venashri's holistic perspective, combined with flexibility and creativity, contributed
to her success. She deepened her relationship with her clients, and
from these relationships change and transformation followed.

Venashri's story reminded me of the dream recounted by
the potter M. C. Richards, in which a fire burned into her neighborhood, threatening her house.[2] Richards ran away as the
fire approached but noticed that a friend stayed behind as the fire
swept through her home. When the fire was over, Richards
returned to her house and found her friend still standing there.
The pots and precious things she had worried about remained
intact—only their colors were deepened. This dream reminded
Richards that conflict is not something to be run from; it can
deepen colors just as surely as adversity tests and also strengthens
friendships.

The common thread between Richards's dream and Venashri's
experience in South Africa is creativity. Each woman valued creativity. Venashri found creative ways to bridge cultural differences
in her work. Richards's dream reminded her that creativity is not
extinguished by adversity or struggle but may actually be enriched.
Each woman encountered conflicts or challenges and learned
from these challenges to welcome new ways of seeing, even when
those new ways seemed to upset the status quo.

As M. C. Richards observed following her dream, conflict—like
a fire—carries with it the potential for clarity and deepening. It
may spark feelings of renewed closeness and better alignment with
others and with what we care about. If we are to step into these creative possibilities, we need a series of practices that help us to be

ready, supple, and able to navigate the change and confusion that often accompany intercultural encounters. These practices work at three levels: personal (within us), interpersonal (between us), and intergroup (among us).

The practices presented in Chapters Seven, Eight, and Nine are intended to be a complement to the touchstones of dynamic engagement provided in Chapter Six. They condition us for preventing and engaging conflict, just as workouts prepare a runner before a marathon. They are designed to illuminate culture, the underground river that animates our conflicts. They are designed to help us develop clarity, flexibility, and intuitive wisdom—all important parts of an ongoing commitment to inquiry. They are designed to help us befriend conflict, even as it threatens to change our identities, our perceptions of others, and our ways of making meaning of the world around us.

Because we are attached to our identities, wanting to maintain a positive image of ourselves, and because we want to preserve our ways of seeing others and the world, we resist conflict. Brought face to face with conflict we have tried to resist or avoid, we analyze it. Analysis helps us feel that we are keeping the conflict at arm's length. But keeping conflict at a distance does not make it disappear from our lives. Conflict has a way of being durable, of resurfacing with new names, new subplots, and half-familiar lines until we finally do something to engage it differently than we have done before. These practices are designed to help us notice choice points and choose in the direction of conflict prevention when possible and dynamic engagement when conflicts are not prevented, drawing both on cultural fluency and conflict fluency.

To be most effective in bridging conflict we need our whole selves interacting with others' whole selves in genuine inquiry. Through an ongoing commitment to developing conflict fluency and cultural fluency, we continue enlarging our repertoires of skills and capacities. Creativity sparks us and moves us along when we might otherwise get stuck. A commitment to ongoing awareness and learning focuses our efforts. The practices described in this chapter help us to be ready to meet the challenges that present themselves daily in our diverse communities, workplaces, families, and inner lives.

Four Ways of Knowing

These practices draw on our human capacities for relationship, which are at the center of preventing and bridging conflict. Our relational capacities exist alongside our skills as analysts, communicators, and rational problem solvers. They draw on the right sides of our brains and our abilities to integrate what we know with all that we sense and feel. In my earlier book, *Bridging Troubled Waters*, I describe the following four ways of knowing that complement rational, reason-based approaches:

- Intuitive and imaginative
- Emotional
- Somatic, or body based
- Connected, or spiritual

Whether we are in the midst of conflict ourselves or trying to help others find ways through it, these ways of knowing are important resources. Our dreaming selves bring the gifts of imagination, intuition, and vision beyond the limits of time and space. From our feeling selves come the empathy and genuineness so essential to positive relationships with others. Our physical selves receive millions of important messages that communicate unseen dynamics and help us literally enact change. At the center our spirit selves breathe, making and remaking meaning, maintaining our clear view of the interconnections that link us to others.

These resources are always available. Yet we do not always draw on them in preventing and bridging cultural conflict. They are available to us personally and interpersonally. In this chapter, eight personal practices designed to build awareness, creativity, and preparedness for bridging conflict are described. While these practices are not useful only in solitude, each of them is centered in inner awareness and exploration. They are designed to build attunement (inner listening), alignment (inner and outer congruence), and stillness (inner peace).

These practices are by no means comprehensive, nor are they definitive. They are themselves a series of starting points. If a nugget within them stimulates an idea or a different approach, they have fulfilled their promise. They proceed from my cultural lenses and perceptions about what is often missing from the books and the training courses about resolving conflict. In presenting them I do not mean to ignore the many hundreds of practices in diverse cultures that nurture attunement, alignment, and stillness. Instead I hope to add to the momentum of creative approaches that support mindful conflict prevention and dynamic engagement. I challenge all of us to continually step outside our comfort zones, make intentional choices, and develop those relational resources so needed in this fractured world where competition and painful histories sometimes obscure our human connectedness.

Personal Practices

The following personal, or inner, practices are a range of ways to keep awareness attuned, help us question our givens when they exclude other people or ideas, broaden our experience beyond our familiar favorite channels, and generally keep us present to our choices and ways of seeing. They are things we can do by ourselves, though they may have an impact on others. They show us ways we see and stretch our seeing; help us cultivate awareness of choices, especially hidden choices; and assist us in finding places of renewal and connection within ourselves that ultimately feed our relationships with others. They are summarized in the following list, then described in detail:

Ways of Knowing	*Related Personal Practices*
Intuitive and imaginative	Writing into clarity
	Shapeshifting
Emotional	Sitting with resistance
	Writing a letter
Somatic	Listening with the body
	Catching and releasing
Connected	Shifting frames
	Continuing inquiry

Practices That Draw on Intuitive, Imaginative Intelligence

When we find ourselves faced with conflict, or simply notice differences among us, we often rely on intuition and imagination to show us ways through. Unfortunately, conflict may be accompanied by barriers that keep us from using our intuition and imagination. These barriers arise because conflicts, or differences that matter, touch us and challenge us in ways that stimulate defending, avoiding, justifying, and deflecting. When we are engaged in offensive or defensive action in response to an actual or anticipated conflict, it is difficult to also pay attention to our deepest intuitive selves and tap the vastness of our imaginations.

Intuition means knowing without being aware of the process by which the knowing arose. It is sometimes referred to as a sense or a feeling; it often comes unbidden and then may be welcomed or rejected before we are fully aware of its existence. Most people have had the experience of encountering dangerous or negative events that they might have avoided if they had followed their intuition. "I knew I should not have gone down that street," I say after I am delayed in traffic for an hour, or, "I sensed I should have stayed home," after I take the car out and get caught in a damaging hailstorm. Intuition, when invited into our personal practices, helps us recognize, normalize, and utilize wisdom in its most subtle forms.

Imagination is the partner of intuition—it is the capacity to see new possibilities. Intuition taps us on the shoulder with an inkling or a nudge; imagination helps us plumb the potential and usefulness of the insight or inkling.

Cultures may be more or less receptive to imagination and intuition as ways of knowing. From a gender perspective, U.S. and Canadian women are more likely than men to be perceived as intuitive and are more likely to receive positive social reinforcement for using intuition. This stereotype may disadvantage both men and women in the end. Men who learn as boys that intuition is soft and unreliable may have difficulty tuning into it later in life. Women may find that intuition is expected of them but that in certain contexts empirical ways of knowing are more trusted, because of intuition's lack of traceable origins.

Intuition and imagination need not operate in opposition to reason or empirical approaches. Both ways of knowing are needed, as intuition and imagination are not only complementary but helpful in the choice making that accompanies empirical methods. Men and women can increase their intuitive and imaginative ways of knowing. Two practices that help are writing into clarity and shapeshifting.

Writing into Clarity. *Writing into clarity* is the practice of writing on a chosen focus within the boundaries of a set length of time, a particular number of pages, or both. The focus may be diffuse—for example, writing about "what's up"—or it may be specific—for example, writing about a particular strained relationship or conflict. When we write long enough to exhaust what we know about any given subject, then interesting things emerge. As the conscious mind feels empty, we move out of our heads into the realm of intuition, feelings, and unconscious awareness. From this place our writing may generate insights or ideas that were out of reach only minutes before. We may make connections with past situations triggered by current events that we had not recognized; we may see whole new dimensions of a conflict that were not evident before. We may come to see what matters to us, and even to others, as we write while letting go of our conscious editor and monitor.

Why does the practice of writing into clarity work? It draws on the insight that we cannot solve the problems we face with the same thinking that got us into them. If we want to make a shift, to find new ways of seeing and deeper insights into ourselves and others, we have to move outside our mental habits. These mental habits are long-relied-on ways of paying attention and processing information, shaped by culture and personal filters, that lead us in predictable directions. The Enneagram of Personality[3] is one system that illustrates this phenomenon. According to the Enneagram, our habits of attention reveal some worlds and foreclose others, depending on where our attention is directed. Some of us pay attention to threats and danger, others are concerned with image and performance, and still others forget themselves and their agendas in the presence of others. Wherever our focus is trained, there are many realities—whole universes—that are not the focus. And so it is important to become more aware of, and move out of, our habits of attention.

Writing into clarity is to get beneath these habits of attention, entering a state in which we have exhausted what our habits can show us. As we step outside our ordinary consciousness, our intuitive wisdom is given voice, and surprising results may reveal themselves.

For some people, writing comes harder than it does for others. They may ask whether sitting in meditation for a period or walking or drawing could be substituted. Each of these approaches can be powerful, releasing intuitive wisdom as the chatter of our everyday mind is interrupted. I focus on writing because it is a discipline that requires physical engagement in the motor activities of writing, thus keeping the writer on task. Writing is also habitual enough for most of us that our conscious mind does not need to constantly monitor it. The conscious mind literally gets tired of coming up with answers to the question addressed in the writing and lets go, allowing other ideas, insights, and questions to emerge. This is the power of writing into clarity.

As you try this practice, look back over your writing after it is completed. Chances are, you will see a place where you shift voices, stepping out of the well-worn ideas you have tossed around and around in your mind and into a voice that comes from a deeper place. This deeper voice may sound more childlike, more adamant, or softer and gentler—it will have a tone and cadence different from that of your everyday voice. This is the voice that emerges when the defenses have melted, the image is set aside, the fears are subdued, and the deeper self is invited in. This is the voice of intuitive wisdom; it is the voice that teachers, parents, and mentors were trying to summon when they said, "You know deep inside what to do."

It is important that you write into clarity without worrying about others' responses. Anticipating an audience can inhibit this voice, as it may carry expectations and boundaries that limit what wants to be said. There is no need for polishing, proper spelling, or editing—this voice requires freedom and space to surface. There will be time enough later to fit what you have written into a plan of action or to consider the consequences of your insights. Writing into clarity is to put aside a concern with consequences and others' expectations for a set period of time, to allow intuitive wisdom to be given voice.

Writing into clarity is a good way to gain perspective about conflicts and our roles and choices within them because it puts us in contact with our inner selves. It invites our conscious minds to awareness of what is precious to us, what we long for, and what we deeply desire. It helps us sort out where we are in the stillness, apart from the maelstrom of events and interactions. It helps us tease out our cultural and personal lenses as we discern the essence of situations, conflicts, and options.

The benefits of writing into clarity may also be reaped among parties to conflict. In a group setting, a particular focus related to the conflict is chosen, and each person writes in silence for a set period of time. The writing is later shared, in whole or in part, by those who are comfortable reading aloud. A shared practice of writing into clarity sacrifices the safe cocoon of writing without an audience, but it may yield benefits as group members hear each other's genuine concerns and feelings.

For a group taking a course on women, culture, and spirituality, this writing practice helped broaden discussion, address differences, and prevent conflict from escalating. The course met for half a day once a week. The practice of writing into clarity was the first and last thing done in each meeting, with twenty minutes allocated for writing and thirty for writers to read from their work at the beginning and end of each class.

The group used these ground rules while writing: Write from your own heart and mind. Write the truth, and do not shield uncomfortable truths. Welcome feelings, questions, sparks, and *skraps*.[4] These ground rules applied to listening: Receive what is said as an acorn from a tree—in appreciation, respect, and open-heartedness. Suspend judgment and comment, and listen with compassion.

Upon coming together, group members wrote about their relationship to the reading material for the week and generally addressed the question, "What's up for me?" Before they left, group members spent silent time writing again, under the heading, "Closing reflections—appreciations, differences, and inquiries."

Each time a writing period ended, group members were invited in to read aloud some or all of what they had written. Passing or declining a turn was fine, so all members did not read each time. As one member read, everyone else listened fully and silently. No discussion followed the sharing, and no questions were permitted. The group followed its shared intention, listening to what was read as completely as possible. Clarity, not consensus, was the goal of the writing practice. Dialogue and discussion were used at other points in the class to facilitate communication among participants, while the writing stood alone, protected from challenge or criticism that might inhibit free expression.

In the early stages of the course, the writing tended to be light and not too probing. As the course progressed, fault lines among participants became more obvious, and this in turn was reflected in their writing. A reaction from a Roman Catholic participant, Cindy, was triggered when Marina, a Pagan woman, described a ritual involving nudity and body painting. Cindy said nothing in response to Marina's description of the ritual during the class discussion. But in the closing writing for that class, Cindy expressed her discomfort with Marina's description, and her rejection of the ritual as a part of sacred practice. She also described her fear at being in the class with Marina and others who might "undermine her faith."

Cindy's writing was received, as usual, in silence. No one responded directly at the time, and the class adjourned after others had read. The next meeting began with writing. The theme of the reading for the week was spiritual practices, individual and shared. Marina wrote about needing a refuge from the world in the wake of her cancer diagnosis eighteen months earlier. She described how she had turned her garden into a refuge and a place of spiritual renewal. She did not address Cindy's previous comments directly, except to say that when she reflected on some of the things she and her Pagan friends do, she imagined they might seem quite bizarre to outsiders.

Cindy wrote about the peace she felt in attending Mass the previous Friday. She wrote about the simple fulfillment she gets from cooking, baking, and doing things around her home. Cindy also referred to her experience during the interval between classes. She reflected that she had been increasingly uncomfortable after the class, feeling conflicted about how to maintain loyalty to her faith while learning about other traditions. She spent time talking with family and friends, many of them fellow Catholics. Finally she tried the practice of writing into clarity.

The confusion and resistance she felt melted as she wrote, leaving her in a more peaceful place. Her questions were not all resolved, and she still felt discomfort with the wide range of approaches to spirituality among her classmates, yet peace came as she realized that she could let go of her need to protect her faith. That faith was strong, shared in her family and community. She saw that it was protected by a force more potent than any she could wield alone, and so she no longer needed to defend it by screening out other voices.

The effects of writing into clarity for Marina, Cindy, and others in the class were very positive. The differences between them were not things that needed to be resolved. Each of them was free to pursue her spiritual practices as she saw fit. Writing proved a vehicle for the group members to express their feelings, reactions, and resistance without any management or attempts to control by others. Because the writing allowed feelings to be expressed without attempts to resolve or address them, thoughts and reactions did not get bottled up and relations in the class stayed positive.

Writing into clarity helps surface those parts of us that whisper, the wisdom we can access that is not always at our internal table. It is a way of integration, of moving toward wholeness in our relationship with ourselves. As we expand our awareness in this way, we become more clear about what we can offer others and more receptive to intuition as a vehicle for wisdom—our own and others'.

Because we are all multicultural beings, dynamically dancing with a myriad of influences, messages, and ways of knowing, being, and doing, a writing practice like this helps us acknowledge and honor our internal diversity. As we do this, we are more able to appreciate the diversity we see in others around us, recognizing in them the very contradictions, tensions, and confluences we have traced within ourselves. This awareness of our inner contours is one of the doorways to transformation. Shapeshifting, another practice drawing on intuitive and imaginative ways of knowing, helps us walk through the door.

Shapeshifting. *Shapeshifting* means recognizing the choices we make at many levels everyday and exercising intention, imagination, and even playfulness with a few of them. Shapeshifting is an idea that appears in the mythology of most major civilizations; it is a theme of folklore and a relation of magic. In the many stories of trickster figures that appear in diverse traditions, shapeshifting is a recurrent feature. Trickster figures are those that traverse boundaries, questioning givens and challenging the status quo. They are ingenious, inventive, wily, and spontaneous. Tricksters are also abundantly and fallibly human, not infrequently falling victim to their own clever plans and schemes, which endears them to us and causes us to welcome them back even though they are disruptive and mischievous.

To practice shapeshifting is to invite some of these elements into our lives, to suspend our usual common sense and transport ourselves temporarily into an altered time and place where different parameters apply. There are many ways to do this, and some cultural contexts may welcome experimentation more than others. Shapeshifting may be harder for those who begin with specific starting points than for those who start from diffuse ones, since shapeshifting involves playing with ambiguity and boundaries. It may find more opposition in fatalistic settings than in those favoring free will, because the former dictate acceptance of one's lot rather than challenging it.

But every cultural context provides outlets for shapeshifting, whether through dramatic expression, storytelling, or rituals. Lewis Hyde suggests that tricksters and their shapeshifting play an important, if paradoxical, role in maintaining cultures: "the origins, liveliness, and durability of cultures require that there be space for figures whose function is to uncover and disrupt the very things that cultures are based on."[5]

The paradoxes inherent in trickster figures' crossing boundaries and embodying both positive and negative qualities are evident in stories from many diverse cultures. For example, the Carib people of Brazil tell stories of Kalapalo, a figure seen as both the "father" of humanity and as a dangerous and angry "powerful being."[6] The Greek god Hermes is also called *mechaniôta*, which translates as trickster.[7] In the Greek pantheon of gods, Hermes is the last one born and the last to get his share of things. Yet Hermes, a classic shapeshifter, is essential to the functioning of the world. As Jenny Strauss Clay observes, his birth brought to "the fully articulated Olympian system of divisions and boundaries . . . the possibility of movement between its spheres and limits."[8] This movement makes change and adaptation possible and gives conflict its potential for transformation.

Shapeshifting helps us because it challenges the old notion that our personalities—and our cultures—are fixed, stable, consistent entities. As we entertain different ways to invent ourselves, dancing with paradox and imagination, we recognize our choices and our active participation in a constant process of inventing and reinventing our identities. Shapeshifting helps us remember that when it comes to human relationships, there is not one objective reality. Instead there are many possible perspectives, and that understanding is a key to intercultural fluency.

As a personal practice, shapeshifting is assisted by using metaphors. Metaphors are windows into the ways we order and see ourselves and others.

> Suppose André feels quite stuck or limited in the organization where he is working. Setting aside time for a shapeshifting exploration, he sits in silence and allows a metaphor come to him to describe how he sees himself in the context of the organization. He sees himself as a willow, with a complex root system that extends into others' root systems. The organization is a grove of trees, and he is the only willow. He is strong, yet bends when powerful winds blow. He appears delicate, but he is resilient.
>
> There is a lot of pressure on the organization to shift and change, yet the people there also are attached to some old ideas and ways of being. Trees do not get up and move about, at least not without a high degree of intervention. There is a sense that the old ways of doing things are not effective in the competitive world, yet other ways to move forward are not clear. As trees, André and his coworkers stand rooted, vulnerable to blights, storms, and the whims of developers who may see a lucrative opportunity if only the trees were cleared. Their beauty and history could be traded for future development without a second thought.

All of these thoughts come quickly on the heels of the metaphor that has suggested itself. Now, André engages in shapeshifting—letting his imagination have free rein, suspending further analysis. He asks himself, "What would I look like if I had the wings I have lacked as a tree?" He imagines himself as an eagle, a pelican, a heron—all large birds with discerning eyesight and inherent strength. As a pelican he would see the fish tumbling in the breaking waves; as a heron, the movement of the schools of fish through the shallows. As an eagle he would soar high above all of it, taking in the big picture. And these gifts—gifts of discerning movement or seeing the big view—all of these augment André's possibilities as a tree.

André closes his eyes, letting the sensation of flying span his body, stepping into the freedom and the buoyancy that attends it. Having embraced it, he steps out of the imagined experience and invites the tree and the birds to dialogue. He gets a cup of tea, and listens in. The birds love the willow, for its shade, for the rest it offers, for its stability. It is landmark, home, and shelter for them and their kind. And the tree is in awe of the birds for their flight, their ability to see different scenes, and their lightness.

Taking this experience back to his experience in the organization, André asks these questions: "What does the perspective of the birds add to my sense of myself as rooted and stable?" "How can I invite the gifts of mobility, lightness, and vision into my awareness of the situation of the organization?" "How can I introduce changing conditions and new ideas in ways that those who value history and roots will not feel challenged?" "How can I as a member of the organization develop wings even as I maintain the connections that have sustained and strengthened me?"

All these questions arise from using imagination in the practice of shapeshifting. Via a metaphor, André uncovered a sense of how he was seeing his situation—both its strengths and its limitations. He then allowed an alternative metaphor to enter, and followed it to experience its gifts and possibilities.

Finally André created a dialogue between the two metaphorical images to look for ways they might complement each other.

Shapeshifting is a powerful personal practice, with many possibilities for application to intercultural conflicts. Because it draws attention to metaphors and their boundaries, it can also help group members become aware of limitations and choice points.

Shapeshifting requires a set period of time, with boundaries of privacy and quiet, and a willingness to engage imagination. Sometimes a coach, counselor, or facilitator may help with this practice. No matter how implausible or strange the images that surface may seem, we follow them to see what they reveal. Whether shapeshifting is done as a personal practice or as a way to address conflict in groups, it can help us incubate creative ideas and open new possibilities. Stepping outside of what is known and given, shapeshifting liberates us to see what might be and to trace ways of living into it.

Practices That Draw on Emotional Intelligence

A great deal has been written in the past fifteen years about emotional intelligence. Emotional intelligence is the capacity to know and manage our own feelings and also to read and effectively deal with others' feelings.[9] To exercise emotional intelligence means to invite our feelings to the table of choice making and awareness, to welcome them as guides to action with a legitimate voice in our plans. This is not to let feelings take over, nor to conflate them with all of reality, but to recognize that emotions, too, carry messages that need to be heard if we are to tap our whole human capacities for self-knowledge and relationship.

As they do with intuition and imagination, cultural contexts may encourage or deny emotional ways of knowing, through norms for communication and behavior. When we cross cultural boundaries, we notice these differences more than we do when we stay within familiar groups. A Colombian colleague addressed this point recently in telling me about the marriage of her sister to an American. When he came into the family, she recalled, he was shocked at the ways her family apparently fought and struggled with each other over political ideas. "We feel something, we say it," was the way she described her family. Although families and groups in any setting vary, this Colombian family reflected a pattern of comfort with emotional expression different from the one the young American was accustomed to.

Wherever we are from, emotional intelligence is an important capacity. It helps us to relate well to others and to be attuned to our own feelings. If we are not attuned, we may act feelings out in ways we had not anticipated. Two personal practices that support emotional intelligence are sitting with resistance and writing a letter. Both of them welcome emotions into our circle of awareness but in quite different ways.

Sitting with Resistance. *Sitting with resistance* means to stay with those feelings we would rather avoid or push away. It will be immediately apparent that this practice is not the most pleasant one on the list. Yet it is worthwhile, because emotions to which we are resistant carry messages that we ignore at our peril. Resistant feelings often attend conflict because they seek to protect us from change and from taking in information contrary to our beliefs or our images of ourselves. But they are more than just barriers to be struggled against, dissolved, or climbed over. Resistance can be a rich labyrinth from which useful information may emerge and shifts may originate. An example illustrates:

In a conference session about early stories that have shaped our sense of self, a group of women from many countries are gathered together. The scene is Women's Worlds 2002, an international women's congress in Kampala, Uganda, the first gathering of its kind hosted in Africa. I am privileged to be there coleading a session on women's stories. After setting the stage and offering some of our own stories, my coleader and I turn the session over to the women in attendance. One woman shares the story of how she was told as a child not to climb trees. The area where she grew up was home to lush fruit trees, and the prohibition meant that her brothers got all the best fruit. She received only what they threw down to her or carried down from the trees. At the same time, as a girl she had the job of gathering firewood for the family cooking. Firewood was not plentiful and had to be collected by climbing trees and breaking off small branches. Here was a contradiction: she was told girls don't climb trees, yet she was required to climb trees to do her familial duty. No one explained why the fruit trees were off limits but the firewood trees were not. As a child she accepted the situation, gathering firewood until she moved away from her family home.

She reflected as she told the story that she had never thought of this contradiction before; she had simply accepted it and complied with her duty. Because she was taught to, and wanted to, hold her parents in high regard, she had not even considered the unfairness of the rule. As she sat among women listening to their stories, she could feel resistance within herself to thinking about or relating this story. She wanted to explore the way her life had been gendered, but she also had a strong desire reinforced by her cultural upbringing to respect the memory of her parents.

Hearing the stories of other women (some similar and some quite different from hers) and sitting with the resistance she felt until it subsided, she was able to tell the story. The resistance shifted, but it also cued her to tell the story not as an example of parental injustice but as an example of the gendered contradictions in her society generally, within which her parents did the best they could. This gave the story poignancy yet also mirrored the genuine respect and love she felt for her family.

This example illustrates something that is often true about resistance: if we sit with it, not pushing it away and also not completely identifying with it, a shift may happen. Resistance is like an old story told of Deer. It is said that Deer exemplifies the qualities of tenacity and quiet determination. One day, Deer was on her way to the top of the mountain. On the path, she encountered a monster, who tried to get her to change her route and to scare her into abandoning her mission. Deer did not respond with noise or fierceness, only with quiet resolve and clarity of purpose. As she continued on the path, neither pushing the monster away nor engaging it beyond stating her desire to continue on her path, the monster became smaller and smaller.

So, resistance is there to defend and protect us, screening out those things we may not have felt strong enough or ready to let in during earlier times in our lives. Because it is a relic of the past, tied to old fears and past hurts, it may melt when we hold it quietly, inquiring what it has to show us. Like the woman who collected firewood, we can trace the reasons resistance sought to divert us and take them into account as we expand what we are willing to see and share with others.

Another personal practice that lets in emotional intelligence is simple yet very powerful—writing a letter.

Writing a Letter. Have you ever tried to write a journal or a diary? Having facilitated journal-writing workshops, I observe that many people begin a journal but have trouble sustaining it. Some of us do write journals but find that when we later come back to them they are hard to understand or decipher; they are frequently missing important details that as we wrote we were sure we would remember. I was faced with the question of how best to write a journal when I sailed around the world with my four children as a faculty member on Semester at Sea in 1999. I knew we would see many things: should I write a travelogue? I knew I would experience precious things with my children: should I write a memoir? I knew it would be difficult to track all of what was going on at once: should I write a stream of consciousness diary that would serve as outlet if not reliable record? None of these ideas seemed quite right.

Then we had a visitor on the ship, Lady Borton, an American who lived for many years in Vietnam. She spoke to the heart of my concern: journal writing tends to be chronological and somewhat dry, with assumed connections and misplaced certainty that specific things will be remembered. She proposed that we write instead a series of letters to someone dear to us. Whether or not we ever sent the letters, writing them would let in emotional intelligence; in letters we share not only our impressions but also our feelings. We take others' feelings into account, imagining what they may feel in a particular situation, thus expanding our descriptions and making connections explicit. In letters we are aware of being in relationship, and so our writing is more likely to come alive, to be vibrant and full of the sparks and skraps that are an inevitable part of change and travel.

Using this strategy I wrote a number of letters over the course of the trip, letters that deepened a friendship and left me with a set of writings more complete and multidimensional than those in past journals. I realized as I reflected on this experience that letter writing like this is a strategy with usefulness beyond the boundaries of a trip.

The practice of letter writing can be used in multicultural settings in numerous ways. Students in diverse classes can be asked to write letters to the instructor or each other, introducing particular aspects of their identities or sharing an experience of handling a cultural conflict. When a letter is written, rather than a formal paper, emotions are more likely to be included as the writer's attention is on the relationship with the reader and not just the ideas. Sensory descriptions are more likely to be included as the writer tries to convey the nuances and particularities of experiences to a receptive reader. Because the process of letter writing includes envisioning a reader's response, the aperture widens more than it does for an academic paper.

Another way of using this practice is to ask members of classes to write a letter about a conflict experience to a mentor, hero, or heroine. This may be someone known personally to the writer or not; it may be a public figure or a family member. Letters written to mentors, heroes, or heroines bring to mind admired qualities, implicitly inviting the writer to relate their experiences to these qualities. When letters are written within real or imagined relationships, they nudge the writers to explain their perceptions, motivations, strategies, and disappointments. As these are explained, choices made during the course of a conflict become clearer. Letters can become the foundation for follow-up papers applying research findings and theories to conflict stories, stories brought to life through becoming the subjects of letters.

The practice of letter writing can also be helpful for diverse teams or members of organizations. Team members can write letters to each other at the beginning of a project, introducing themselves and expressing hopes for their joint work. These letters communicate something of each writer's identity and help form a foundation for positive relationship. They also convey what is meaningful to the writer, leaving the reader to discover nuggets of connection and questions or curiosities to pursue. When letter writing is approached in this way, it is useful to have face-to-face follow-ups to continue the conversations. When teams are functioning across distance, simultaneous electronic communication may be used for these follow-ups.

The practice of writing a letter is not new, yet it has fallen out of fashion in much of contemporary society. Letter writing is a personal and mindful approach to communication, conveying an intention to engage the reader personally. When letter writers use pen and paper, their choices of color, texture, paper size, and ink give clues about their emotional states, moods, and frames of mind. Encourage letter writers to experiment with choices of medium and to make intentional decisions about how they reflect their feeling states. All these aspects of letter writing emphasize the importance of emotional intelligence.

Letters have long been used in therapy and self-help groups to help people clear their minds of past traumas, express repressed feelings, and move beyond hurts. They are written to parents, to bosses, and to ancestors or descendents; they express regrets, resentments, anger, frustrations, hopes, or aspirations. Many of these letters are never sent. They are cathartic for writers, freeing them from the grip of victimhood or despair. They are a virtual dialogue, constructed not for the purpose of engagement with an actual other but for the purpose of setting things in a new place inside, creating a new alignment, or revealing the writer's own unexpressed feelings. They are very powerful vehicles as they invoke emotional intelligence and harness it in the discovery of new ways to move forward.

Practices That Draw on Somatic Intelligence

The third set of practices draws on body awareness to prevent and bridge conflict. The body is both receiver and transmitter, cueing us when something is amiss in our relations with those around us and conveying our feelings to others. Listen to people talking about conflicts they have experienced; they will often use words that reference the body. They may say things like, "I felt it in the pit of my stomach," or, "It was like an arrow had hit my heart," or, "The tension in the room was palpable." Moving through conflict, people also use somatic, or physical, references to describe shifts or breakthroughs: "I felt like a weight was lifted from my shoulders," or, "I was finally able to breathe more easily."

Somatic practices are those that draw on our bodies, our physical experiences of being in the world. We are not vaporous ghosts or unattached intellects. We have bodies. Through these bodies we feel, receive intuition and inspiration, and express ourselves. Our bodies may mean different things to us across cultures; we may groom them, feed them, dance with them, and conduct them differently. But we all have them, and so involving our bodies is an important source of connection across differences.

From the Cartesian mind-body split comes the dismissal of the body as superfluous to good decision making and working relationships. The body, carrier of passions and needs, is both mistrusted and indulged. Many cultural settings—bureaucratic, diplomatic, and academic—give us the message that we exist from the neck up. Good intercultural relations are treated as though they are matters of logic and reason alone. But then we realize that people have different logics and different ways of making meaning in the world. When we realize that these logics and ways of making meaning are connected to our bodies and our physical ways of being in the world, we open a different set of choices.

Our choices are richer when we heighten our awareness of our bodies as they send and receive signals. Two personal practices help: listening with the body and catching and releasing.

Listening with the Body. *Listening with the body* is just what it sounds like: it is to remember that the body is an instrument, finely tuned, that continually receives and transmits information about interpersonal dynamics, misalignments, and communication. Across cultures the capacity to listen with the body is critical: we may misinterpret language, incorrectly understand body language, and miss boundaries and cues set by others. But our bodies speak a language that is not as culture bound, letting us know when there is something we need to attend to, something that is "off" or out of sync, something amiss.

All of us listen to our bodies, though some of us do so only after they escalate in their messages to us and we are immobilized through illness or injury. But fewer of us learn to listen *with* our bodies, using them as the finely tuned instruments they are to bring in all kinds of valuable information.

If we are to cultivate this receptivity, becoming aware of our bodies is the first step. A body-based discipline is helpful here, such as yoga, martial arts, or dance. In each of these practices, body awareness is enhanced, and new neural circuits are created between body and mind that can be used in other settings. Meditation-related practices are also advantageous, since many of them include a focus on breathing, posture, and body awareness. There are many good books and programs to teach these practices, so I will not detail them here. Choosing a way to increase our somatic awareness is to befriend our bodies.

As we befriend our bodies, we come to learn their language. Bodies hold tension in different ways and in different places. They manifest messages differently. And we respond with different habits—some of us are accustomed to ignoring body messages, others of us take tension as a cue for exercise, massage, rest, or meditation. As we introduce receptivity to body messages into our habits, we tap the wisdom that our bodies have to offer. When we tap our bodies' wisdom, we are more effective in our own conflicts and as helpers to others in conflict.

> The usefulness of listening with my body came through in a group I was working with recently. A pattern of ongoing conflict had become established among the group members, revolving around different approaches to their work, approaches that they labeled progressive and traditional. The conflict was exacerbated by cultural miscommunication, although no one was quite sure exactly how the issues related to culture. It was not clear to me how much of the conflict emanated from group members' different ideological and political orientations and how much came from practical problems including different ways of using English (several of the group members spoke English as a second, third, or fourth language).

They were relieved, though wary, to be having some difficult discussions that had been deferred through longs-tanding
denial, avoidance, defensiveness, and misunderstanding. The
process was moving slowly but deliberately, and things were
being said that had been hidden over time. They began by talking in small groups about the climate in the organization and
what they had done to try to improve communication and
address conflicts. After these initial discussions I moved the
entire group into the next planned exercise, a paper-and-
pencil exploration of their cultural styles during conflict.

As we moved into this activity the energy level in the room
dropped. I felt exhausted, as though suddenly overwhelmed
with an intense need for sleep. I noticed that others were flagging as well. Listening with my body I began to inquire of
myself: "What is tired in this moment? What has drained the
lifeblood from this moment? What needs refreshment and revi-
talization?" Of course the obvious answers presented themselves as possibilities: perhaps people needed a break; perhaps
we had tried to do too much in too short a time. But the issue
seemed to be more than these garden-variety things.

I decided to ask the group the questions I had asked internally: "What's going on here? Have we missed an important
junction?" As they looked up from their papers, checking in
with themselves in the process, visible light bulbs went on in
some faces. As we paused and talked, we realized that the previous topic had been brought to closure too quickly and that
other things remained to be said.

The paper-and-pencil instrument that they were filling out
was taking them away from the immediacy of their compelling
conversation. They had been on the edge of a shift, then we
had stepped well back from that edge to the terra firma of a
different, lower-risk topic. But they had been ready to take the
risk of talking more frankly, and so a sense of tired disappointment had settled on both them and me as we collectively and
prematurely shrank away from the possibilities. As we shifted
gears back to where we had left off, momentum and energy
returned—both to me and to the group. Their discussion

deepened, and more was learned about the things that had divided them in the past.

I felt huge relief in my body. I was no longer tired but awake and alert to the possibilities unfolding in the conversation. My body had functioned as an instrument, cueing me to the needs of the group. Had I not been attuned to this message, or had I dismissed it as my own lack of enthusiasm or tiredness, I would have missed the opportunity to facilitate a deeper conversation. My ability to tune into my body arose from my somatic awareness, developed in ongoing physical practices. My commitment to aligning my inner and outer states led to the questions I posed to the group. Once we were back on track, I felt a stillness inside that confirmed the direction was a generative one.

Listening with the body is an ongoing process. Not everything we feel physically will have such a direct meaning for the whole group. But our bodies are instruments—barometers—that are hugely sensitive to that which is unseen yet present in the group. As we listen and name the messages our bodies receive, internally or to others, we have richer choices for moving forward. These choices are further enriched by employing another somatic strategy: catching and releasing.

Catching and Releasing. *Catching and releasing* is especially helpful in evoking creativity for bridging cultural conflict. It is a practice found in the accounts of many creative people, such as inventors, composers, writers, and mediators. Over and over again, these people tell stories about intense, concentrated work on a problem or a creation. The work seldom follows a straight line. There are spurts of progress and frustrating setbacks. Sometimes an impasse is reached and the way forward is murky or completely invisible. It is at these times that the catching and releasing strategy is useful.

Catching and releasing simply says that preparation and concentrated work are important to achievement but that the line from these activities to results is not necessarily straight or continuous. As important as it is to prepare and concentrate, focusing on a goal or a process, it seems also important to let go of the process, taking a break at times of tiredness, turning points, or impasses. Beyond the obvious benefits of recharging spent energy, releasing the focus also allows for other ideas to come into awareness.

The simplest instance of this for me occurs when I am trying to remember something, perhaps a person's name or the name of a book. I try very hard for a few minutes, and then I release the question, letting go of concentration and moving onto something else. Frequently, I remember the name I was searching for in the next few minutes or later in the day. This is catching and releasing—to work toward the result you are seeking as hard as possible, as though everything depended upon it, and then to let go of both the process and the striving, as though they mattered not at all. In the space created by the inner release, answers waft in, shifts happen, and strategies to unblock impasses reveal themselves.

Venashri Pillay, the South African social worker I referred to earlier, writes of a powerful experience of catching and releasing in her life. She was working in a U.S. city where her caseload included children with a variety of social, behavioral, and emotional problems that made it difficult to establish relationships with them. She was acutely aware of the cultural divides between these children and her and wanted very much to build bridges.

She says, "When I began working with 'troubled children' who had been labeled delinquent or incorrigible . . . , I knew I had to gain their trust and establish relationships with them. So I put all of myself into this goal of establishing relationships, trying to be the best social worker I could. But the more I tried, the more I felt that the distance between us was growing. Inside, I felt fatigued, drained, used-up. Eventually, I just became too tired from all the effort, and stopped, sadly resigning myself to the conclusion that I may not be cut out for this work.

"But when I was still and released my expectations, I noticed that things changed. The children began to move toward me. When I gave up trying so hard, the children finally had the opportunity to take some responsibility for establishing relationships with me. I realized that I was making all the effort and not really allowing them the opportunity and space to come toward me on their own terms. A new, mutual way of establishing relationship opened itself to me and the children, with whom I continued working successfully."

Venashri had discovered the wisdom of catching and releasing. She worked to *catch* the children's trust, demonstrating her concern and commitment. After she had done this, she *released* her expectations, waiting in stillness for whatever would come. This experience of stillness left her feeling less anxious and peaceful. And as she exuded these feelings, the children came toward her. She also learned to use her body as an instrument to let her know when to make an effort and when to let go as she found her place in her work.[10]

The practice of catching and releasing is related to somatic intelligence because the answers we seek arise from our bodies, and these answers are often related to movement. Tired of negotiating, we take a walk in a place that feeds our senses. Weary of concentrating, we find a beautiful image and drink it in with our eyes. Frustrated with our attempts to make progress on an issue or an outcome, we choose stillness and find energy. Needing to build a foundation for negotiation, we share a meal and find ourselves in a more constructive, open place than we were before. Our bodies thus become instruments not only to receive and process information but to move us from stuck places to smooth places, from impasse to progress. In partnership with other practices, the practice of catching and releasing helps us work and play across differences more productively.

Practices That Draw on Connected Ways of Knowing

Two other personal practices complement those already described. They come to us from the realm of connected ways of knowing, also called spiritual ways of knowing. From this realm comes the assurance that we are all connected. We may not always see the connections as obvious, and our connections do not erase or

diminish our cultural differences, yet they exist. From this understanding come possibilities that are eclipsed when we hold a picture of ourselves as entirely separate and disconnected. The
possibilities for connection are all around us, as ubiquitous in our
everyday relations as conflict. Abraham Maslow spoke to the connections among us manifest in our everyday lives when he wrote,
"The great lesson from the true mystics, from the Zen monks . . .
is that the sacred is *in* the ordinary, that it is to be found in one's
daily life, in one's neighbors, friends and family, in one's back
yard . . ."[11]

Two practices that help us use connected ways of knowing to
see our everyday lives more clearly are shifting frames and continuing inquiry.

Shifting Frames. The practice of *shifting frames* comes from the ther-
apeutic and narrative literatures. Simply, it is the idea that we operate with certain frames, or ways of seeing the world and the issues
we face. These frames give our worlds order and structure and lend
coherence by forming an outline around what we attend to. They
point our attention in particular directions and also away from
other directions. Our frames have many dimensions. They offer
orientations to time and space and approaches to communication.
We frame our worlds differently depending on our starting points.
Some of us frame our worlds in terms of the past; others focus on
the future. Some of us attend to what is near to us that we can
touch and manage; others focus on abstract, expansive ideas and
connections. Finally, some of us are linear in our approach to communication; others communicate in spirals that circle back and
connect in ways both complex and multidirectional.

These frames relate to cultures because our cultures influence
the frames we use, and give us messages about which approaches
are most valued. Of course there are differences within cultures—
not everyone in a given group follows the norms or adopts the preferred frames of the group. In the practice of shifting frames, it is
important to become aware of which inner frames govern our
understanding of a conflict or a situation.

As we become aware of our frames, those overarching structures that direct our attention, we also realize that these frames
can change. This is not to suggest that we change our opinions or

feelings but that we relax our boundaries for a time and watch what happens. Often, shifting frames can lead to increased insight or empathy with someone whose frames are different from our own. The inner practice of becoming aware of frames and their capacities to reveal and hide is an important part of developing cultural fluency.

The practice of shifting frames is simple: notice one part of how you see an issue, whether related to time, space, or communication. Then change that dimension. If you are focused on the past, try modulating into the future. If you are focused on the concrete here-and-now, try zooming out to the big picture. If you are seeing a situation in a linear, analytical way, try reorganizing the way you look at the pieces. As you do this, you are using different starting points, broadening your perspective, and trying on a different frames. This is good for mental flexibility, and it nurtures an important intercultural competency: the gift of looking at the world from another's set of starting points.

This inner practice may seem a stretch at first, but it is something that all of us do. It is even embedded in our language: "I'm going to look at that from another angle," we say, or, "Perhaps next week this will appear less important to me." Shifting frames means to make this effort intentionally, changing time, space, or approach to see what is revealed. Though it is an inner practice, it has applications in many interpersonal and intergroup situations.

People in cross-cultural marriages have constant opportunities to shift frames. Indeed, successful cross-cultural marriages depend on both partners' abilities and willingness to do this. What seems normal and "just common sense" to one is abnormal, not common, and nonsensical to the other. To build a strong marriage, each person needs to maintain flexible boundaries, learn to shift perspectives, and be able to shift frames of understanding. This need operates in cross-cultural friendships and business partnerships too.

> The story of Natasha and Muriel is one of different starting points that nearly led to a parting of ways. In Natasha's Russian upbringing, family and friends were tight-knit, with many mutual obligations, expectations, and porous boundaries. Her starting point was communitarian, focused on the group more

than on individual desires or needs. Natasha approached friendship with commitment and passion, taking its obligations and fruits seriously. Muriel's starting point for friendship was more individualistic, as she had been raised in the Northeastern United States. She tended to focus on autonomy and privacy, taking a more casual approach to their time together. She also enjoyed the friendship for its playfulness and richness.

The friendship developed for several months. Natasha and Muriel shared confidences, a variety of activities, and a few family occasions. Their sons became friends as they played on the same sports teams and spent leisure time together. Once, when Muriel was out of town, Natasha took both boys to their hockey game, where she sat next to Sandy, the caregiver for Muriel's son. Natasha talked with Sandy freely, sharing stories and ideas. During the conversation Natasha remarked that she was frustrated that Muriel had not played a more active role in resolving a miscommunication between Natasha and Evelyn, a mutual friend. When Muriel returned home, Sandy told Muriel that she had been uncomfortable hearing about this concern from Natasha.

Muriel was unhappy to hear of Sandy's discomfort and of Natasha's comments to Sandy criticizing Muriel's role in resolving the miscommunication with Evelyn. She wanted to let Natasha know how she felt, but she also wanted to understand how Natasha had made sense of this situation. Muriel used the practice of shifting frames, paying attention to her own ways of seeing the situation.

Muriel identified a breach of her boundaries in Natasha's actions. Natasha had spoken to her son's caregiver about something personal between Natasha and Muriel, and this violated Muriel's idea of privacy. But privacy is a frame that looks different in individualist and communitarian contexts. To Muriel it looked like a solid line drawn around two people who share confidences. Standing back, she imagined what it would be like to draw the boundary differently—what would it be like if the line were dotted or if it were stretchy, sometimes accommodating two people and sometimes a dozen? Muriel played this out in her mind—a different frame for privacy might change ideas of what is and what is not a violation or a breach of privacy.

Muriel also played with her frames for understanding. When she first learned of Natasha's actions, she had thought about them in a linear way, like this: Natasha and Muriel were friends. Natasha talked about private matters in the friendship to Sandy. Therefore Natasha's loyalty to her friendship with Muriel came into question. But then Muriel tried changing her way of seeing this situation, instead imagining Natasha, Sandy, and herself as part of a circle of relations. This opened up several possibilities—Natasha may have been trying to give Muriel an indirect, face-saving message by talking with Sandy. Natasha may have been trying to work out her feelings about Muriel's behavior without confronting Muriel directly.

Muriel did this frame shifting internally, before she ever spoke about the incident to Natasha. The inner practice of shifting frames gave her some suppleness about the issue, replacing more rigid perceptions that were fixed and blaming. It helped her entertain different frames for understanding so that she could approach the situation with more heart, whether or not she ever shared her analysis or frame shifting with Natasha directly.

The practice of frame shifting is easier as we cultivate a spirit of inquiry, because this spirit orients us toward generosity and learning.

Continuing Inquiry. *Continuing inquiry* means putting ourselves into culturally unfamiliar situations, carrying a spirit of inquiry and discovery with us and tracking and integrating what we learn. Bringing all of these elements together is important. It is not enough just to be in culturally unfamiliar circumstances, because it is quite possible to carry our own *culture bubble* with us in such situations, almost never stepping outside to genuinely encounter others and their ways of being in the world. It is possible to be in the vicinity of events without engaging them. The classic example of this may be seen in the person who has traveled to Cairo or Beijing, staying in American hotels and eating nothing but hamburgers. Cultural differences may be felt as they are brushed against, but it is never really necessary to take them on board, to engage them. A commitment to continuing inquiry asks us to do something else, engaging, reflecting, and integrating our learning about cultural differences.

To live from a spirit of inquiry is to step outside the comfort of our culture bubbles, asking, exploring, unearthing, and connecting ways of knowing and being in unfamiliar contexts. It is to suspend judgment about approaches different from our own, maintaining instead a childlike curiosity about others in context—the ways they see and how their worlds make sense. It is to step out of the givens we take for granted, to relate to those with whom we do not always know the rules, to go toward difference rather than insulating ourselves from it. For many of us this goes against our inclination, which is to surround ourselves with those we perceive to be like us.

I recently heard of an interaction that reminded me how difficult it can be to stay committed to this spirit of inquiry.

At a conflict resolution conference in the United States, an American professor, Leona, encountered a Japanese colleague, Yoshi. Like Leona, Yoshi is a university professor, and she respects his work in their field. He asked Leona to sit down with him for fifteen minutes and compare notes on their recent research. Though she was tired, Leona welcomed the opportunity to talk with Yoshi. As they were about to find a place to sit, they encountered another American colleague, one quite well known in their field. I'll call this colleague Sam.

Sam has written one of the best-known books about conflict resolution. Yoshi was familiar with Sam's work, but had never met him. Immediately after Leona introduced the two of them, Yoshi asked Sam whether he would sit down with him then for fifteen minutes and compare recent research and activities. Sam agreed, unaware of the preexisting plan, so the arrangement made between Yoshi and Leona moments before was displaced. As Leona was about to leave them to talk, Yoshi turned to her. "You'll come back in fifteen minutes," he said in a declarative tone. She declined as politely as possible and left the area.

Reflecting on these events, Leona quickly understood that Yoshi's hierarchical starting point and what is called *vertical relational primacy* (the idea that those with higher status take precedence) were operating. Her starting point was more horizontal, leading to the conclusion that first-made plans are honored even if someone with higher status presents other opportunities. Seeing this, she could understand Yoshi in context and let go of the sense of surprise and offense that initially attended the apparently blatant rejection. Still, Leona nursed a small sense of hurt at the way she had been so summarily cast aside by Yoshi.

This is where continuing inquiry came in. Using what she knew about starting points, Leona had come to a good enough understanding of her transaction with Yoshi. But practicing a spirit of inquiry meant going further than this; it meant stretching. Leona talked with a couple of others who know the Japanese cultural context better than she does, asking them for help in understanding. One of them suggested that Yoshi's relative lack of fluency in English may have led to his using an apparently declarative tone for what he may have meant to be an invitation or a request to meet later. Another guessed that there was a gendered component to this interaction, because rules about gender and status in Japan are different from those used in America. These suggestions helped Leona step further out of her frame of reference and into an exploration of Yoshi's. Although she did not ask Yoshi directly about what had happened because of concerns about face and not wanting to embarrass, she was able to find a way to put the experience in a more comfortable context for herself.

Was the onus solely on Leona to adapt, stretch, and inquire? Intercultural conflicts are best addressed when both people are willing and able to do so. Yet this is not always what happens. In some instances, one of the parties may not even be aware that there is a problem. Leona's attempts to make meaning of the story are related here because I heard the story from

her perspective. Any ideas about Yoshi's understandings or perceptions are conjectures, because no one spoke with him about
it directly.

Whether Leona's ongoing inquiry led to valid conclusions or
wrong guesses, it took her attention from judgment to a place of
acceptance. She realized that Yoshi's behavior had to be understood in a cultural context, just as her behavior made sense
according to her groups' norms and shared understandings.

Was it possible that Yoshi was just rude or inconsiderate?
Rudeness and lack of consideration exist across cultures just as
they exist within cultures. The difficulty is that rudeness is
much harder to assess and the margin of error is much greater
across unfamiliar cultural boundaries. Sustaining a commitment to continuing inquiry means withholding this judgment
at least until the picture is clear. And the picture is opaque
when we have only a thin understanding of the cultural dynamics in a situation.

Opportunities like this one come to us frequently, especially
when we are committed to noticing them. As we put ourselves into
unfamiliar situations, we expand our capacity for continuing
inquiry. Spend a day in an unfamiliar part of town, seek out someone different from you at a gathering, put yourself in situations
where you experience music, art, and rituals with those from other
cultural contexts. Find ways to stretch.

As you notice overlaps in your circles and those of people you
meet, you are drawing on connected ways of knowing. Connected
ways of knowing are what they sound like: they direct our attention
to what is shared instead of what separates us. These ways of knowing may be counterintuitive, because we are programmed to attend
to what is different, to what stands out. Yoshi's behavior in changing plans without consulting Leona was different from her cultural
expectations. What they shared was the desire to learn from and
talk with others whose work they respected.

There are almost certainly other layers to Leona's interaction with
Yoshi that could be explored. This is also part of continuing

inquiry. Drawing on a spirit of inquiry and the other practices outlined earlier, the project of developing awareness is ongoing. There is much we can do by ourselves to cultivate the flexibility and creativity so essential to bridging cultural differences. To move forward in relationships and joint projects, another set of practices is needed, practices that operate at the interpersonal and intergroup levels. These practices are described in Chapters Eight and Nine.

CHAPTER EIGHT

Out of the Fire

Interpersonal Practices to Help Bridge Differences

Rupert Ross, a white Canadian prosecutor, tells the story of his first trip to Hollow Water.[1] In this Aboriginal community on the shores of Lake Winnipeg in Manitoba, Canada, a team helps victims and abusers heal from sexual abuse in a process called *family group conferencing.* This process involves offenders, victims, family members, teachers, court officials, health and community workers, and community members in addressing issues related to sexual abuse, alcoholism, and other related matters. The focus is healing and reconciliation rather than punishment or retribution.

A number of cases were to be addressed on the morning Ross arrived, and members of the healing team were there in a circle—nurses, child protection workers, addiction counselors, Aboriginal and non-Aboriginal community members. Ross wondered where the schedule was, which cases were to be dealt with first, and how matters would proceed. He was surprised when, before any business was conducted or cases were introduced, the first question posed to team members was, "How do you feel this morning?"

Ross recounts how the people in the circle then spoke about the things they were carrying with them that morning—worry about a daughter away on a school trip where one of the students had taken a drug overdose, delight at the experience of seeing the sun glint on a spider's web in the early morning, and pleasure at the way kids in the community were moving away from drinking and gas sniffing. As he listened to everyone speak about what they belonged to that morning, Ross had one of the most significant cross-cultural realizations of his life. He saw how the team members' practice of caring for each other and having the space to express connections to others and the outside world enlivened the team because it was centered in relationship.

This realization came as Ross saw that his expectations, derived from experiences of meetings elsewhere, mirrored quite different cultural understandings. He was familiar with meetings focused on agenda items and getting down to business, meetings where efficiency, speed, and substantive problem solving were the focus. In Hollow Water the first principle governing the team's work was that "[i]t is . . . possible to understand something only if we can understand how it is connected to everything else."

As the team members listened to the descriptions of the place each person had occupied that morning, they related to each other in their wholeness and their changes. This prevented conflicts that might otherwise have occurred, conflicts arising, for example, from misinterpretations of another's bad mood or short temper. Ross speculated that this practice not only brought everyone onto the same page but increased productivity. He observed that it worked well because it helped the workers release anxiety, receive support from others, put their issues in perspective, and feel inspired by the sparks brought to the group.

As thought provoking as this experience was for Ross, he could not necessarily have imported it into meetings he attended later in other cultural settings. The question about feelings worked at Hollow Water because all the group members shared the value of holistic approaches in which the emotional and spiritual parts of life are seen as bound up with everything else. Successful use of this approach outside Hollow Water would turn on its fit with the norms, expectations, and values of those involved. Even if this approach could be adapted in another cultural setting, it would require leadership and the skills to know what to do and how to be with the feelings presented.

This example illustrates the challenge in presenting any set of practices for bridging conflict: everything takes place in cultural contexts. No strategies are universally applicable because every strategy issues from a set of cultural assumptions and understandings. Similarly, conflicts take different courses and unfold in a variety of ways depending on the cultures of those involved. The strategies presented in this chapter arise from a variety of groups in diverse settings. They are not prescriptions but guides. They are offered as both preventative and responsive resources, helping to counteract the potential of conflict to blow us off course and de-center us.

The best preparation for bridging intercultural conflicts is ongoing conflict fluency and cultural fluency. A repertoire of practices that can be drawn upon in a variety of contexts is also helpful. Sometimes the practices offered here will need to be translated or adapted; at other times they may provide the seed of an idea that leads to developing a new practice that fits organically into a specific cultural context.

Building on the personal practices described in Chapter Seven, the practices described in this chapter are primarily for addressing interpersonal conflicts involving cultural differences. Although many of these practices may start ripples that affect larger groups, the focus is on their effectiveness in shifting negative spirals in relationships between individuals and within small groups of ten or less.

Interpersonal Practices

There are many ways to address communication and conflict between people. Intercultural scholars have developed strategies for communicating across cultures and ways of building cultural competence.[2] I offer, as a companion to these strategies, a set of interpersonal practices that corresponds to the four ways of knowing underused in many approaches to bridging cultural differences: intuitive and imaginative, emotional, somatic, and spiritual. These interpersonal practices are summarized here:

Ways of Knowing	*Related Interpersonal Practices*
Intuitive and imaginative	Dancing on a dime
	Noticing magic
Emotional	Exchanging three minutes of passion
	Enacting rituals
Somatic	Using metaphors
	Embracing paradox
Connected	Partnering
	Sharing songs

Practices That Draw on Intuitive and Imaginative Intelligence

As Rupert Ross observed after witnessing the staff practices at Hollow Water, unfamiliar cultural contexts are powerful teachers. In our diverse communities and organizations, we have increasing opportunities to take advantage of the richness our diversity brings. When a variety of ways of knowing and being are brought together in a diverse group, more creative and productive outputs are possible.

It is also true, however, that multicultural groups are more vulnerable than more homogeneous groups to conflict and miscommunication. Getting along across cultures is often not intuitive. Running into the unexpected, even the most culturally savvy among us refer to our own set of starting points, and miscommunications compound. From miscommunications and different ways of making sense of the world, conflicts arise. If we are to use our intuition and imagination to bridge these conflicts, we need interpersonal practices that work with the surprises and possibilities that arise in diverse contexts.

Two conflict bridging practices that draw on intuitive and imaginative ways of knowing are dancing on a dime and noticing magic.

Dancing on a Dime. *Dancing on a dime* is a pivotal practice for successfully bridging cultural differences. To dance on a dime is to be graceful and flexible while responding to the movements and behaviors of others and to changing conditions all around. It is to have plans and agendas but to be willing to let go of them when the relationship or situation requires it. To dance on a dime is to devote time to building a foundation of relationship that can sustain itself through change, unexpected events, and surprising reactions. It is to be committed to the process of relating, marrying consistency with flexibility and creativity with constancy.

The paradoxes inherent in this practice mean that it is harder to do than it looks. Yet we have all tasted this experience. Recall a time when you were working with a group or were a member of a group and things weren't working. Perhaps a conflict was escalating, or things were going sideways that were meant to go straight ahead. Sometimes this momentum continues, and meetings or gatherings get off track or end with damaged relationships. But sometimes someone steps into place at just the right moment and intercepts the pattern gone awry. The interception or shift may be dramatic or it may be subtle. Either way it works. This is dancing on a dime.

A simple example comes from a dinner party for a foreign guest. The hostess was serving lamb. After clearing the appetizer plates, she brought out a small bowl of mint sauce for use as a garnish. It was placed near the guest so that he could have first and easy access to it. But the guest's access was too easy. He picked up the small spoon on the saucer under the bowl of mint sauce, and began to eat the sauce, thinking it his portion. Foreseeing his embarrassment, she quickly returned to the kitchen and prepared small bowls of mint sauce for everyone at the table, complete with their own small spoons. Then she served the lamb.

Anyone who has traveled abroad or entertained sojourners has similar stories to tell. When we are in unfamiliar settings, the rules are opaque. Even for the culturally fluent, hidden pieces of knowledge and starting points may lead to unanticipated places. And some of the errors are more difficult to address than helping oneself to mint sauce.

A more momentous story about dancing on a dime is told by Nobel Peace laureate Jimmy Carter about his historic meetings at Camp David in 1978 with President Anwar Sadat of Egypt and Prime Minister Menachem Begin of Israel. At pivotal points in the negotiations, Carter stepped in to prevent impasse, drawing on his relationships with the men and his understanding of their cultures, values, and concerns. On the eleventh day of the summit President Sadat indicated he was leaving. Carter met with him alone, emphasizing that this unilateral action would harm the relationship between Egypt and the United States, and that Sadat would be damaging one of Carter's most precious possessions—his friendship with Sadat and their mutual trust. Responding to this personal and emotional appeal, and to Carter's insistent vision of a new relationship between Israel and Egypt, Sadat agreed to stay.

On the thirteenth day the Israelis expressed their view that prospects for an agreement were bleak. Carter recalls finding Begin on the front porch of his cabin, distraught and nervous

about the breakdown of the talks. He brought the prime minister pictures of Begin, Sadat, and Carter together, signed by
Sadat and personally autographed by Carter to Begin's grandchildren, by name. Carter remembers that he . . . "handed him
the photographs. He took them and thanked me. Then he
happened to look down and saw that his granddaughter's
name was on the top one. He spoke it aloud and then looked
at each photograph individually, repeating the name of the
grandchild I had written on it. His lips trembled, and tears
welled up in his eyes. . . . We were both emotional as we talked
quietly for a few minutes about grandchildren and war."[3]

In each of these cases Carter was dancing on a dime, drawing
on imagination and intuition to show a way forward even as the
negotiations seemed to be collapsing. He had prepared as thor-
oughly as possible, then he kept the positive possibilities always in
view. An important aspect of dancing on a dime is illustrated by
this story. Dancing on a dime is an alternative to giving up, walking away, losing hope. It is to tap intuition and imagination at turning points, reengaging and reenergizing processes. Dancing on a
dime relies heavily on the personal practices outlined earlier, for
it requires listening for intuition and inspiration within. It requires
discernment and courage and a tenacious refusal to walk away
while progress, however, remote, is still possible.

This practice is closely related to the other practice that draws
on intuition and imagination, noticing magic.

Noticing Magic. *Noticing magic* is to uncover the gems in intercultural situations. It is to take the time to notice, with a spirit of
inquiry, what can be learned, revealed, uncovered. It is to search
out the sparks in relationships—to name, enjoy, and remember
them. Intuition directs our attention to the sparks that can cut
through layers of enmity and distrust, sparks that hearken back to
shared values and experiences. Imagination helps us envision
magic in the future that builds on what is treasured of the past.

The story of a family conflict illustrates this practice and its
application in a context where norms about relationships and
inheritance were in the midst of change. The conflict involved
three brothers and their families, extended family members, community members, and community elders.

In Zimbabwe a father belonging to the Shona tribal group died, leaving three sons and a daughter. According to Shona tradition the eldest son inherited the property and obligations of the father. This son assumed ownership of the father's farm and expected his younger brothers to move away when they came of age. They did move away, securing jobs in the city and adopting urban lifestyles. But each of the younger brothers also came back to visit, and they began to build houses on the farm where their older brother lived. The older brother objected and tried to demolish the houses, feeling that his brothers were trying to deprive him of his inheritance. The younger brothers charged that he was trying to sever their ties with their deceased father.

Understanding this conflict requires knowing how life and death are viewed in traditional Shona society. The Shona believe that their identities are intimately connected with their pasts, that their present is derived from their past. They also believe that death is not the end of existence—those who have died continue in another plane of existence. It is critical to pay proper respect to those who have died and to recognize their ongoing relationships, because they continue to have influence over family members' lives. The Shona have very tight kinship relations, and status comes from one's place in these relations.

In these difficult circumstances the brothers asked their sister's son to serve as a traditional mediator. He was a natural choice because he cared about and understood the situation yet had no stake in the outcome. Through bringing everyone together to talk for two days—the brothers, community elders, extended family members, and all other members of the local society who had an interest in harmony—a solution was found. This solution arose from noticing the magic, or sparks, in the participants' relationships with each other. These sparks came out as they spoke of their feelings and needs, reinforced by the contributions of elders who emphasized the legacy of family harmony that would serve them well into the future.

As it turned out, the two younger brothers did not want to live on the farm, they wanted only to have places there that symbolized their belonging to the family and their connections to their father. The older brother was happy for his brothers to build on the land as long as they acknowledged his inheritance and that the land would not support all of them. Through the two days of talking together, all three brothers found ways to belong to the conversation, to the web of relations, and to the circle of their departed father's family. Belonging was restored within the immediate family group and also with extended family members, elders, and community members.

How was the magic noticed, and how did it become an asset to these people? The mediator, acting according to traditional norms, was not overtly directive. He realized that it was not his conflict and encouraged the participants to do the speaking. He gave his respectful, undivided attention, sometimes one-on-one, at other times to everyone. His intuition told him that *belonging* was a central theme, a magic hub around which other things could be worked out. He validated participants' needs to belong—the younger brothers' desires to belong to the father's memory, the older brother's desire to belong to the land, and everyone's desire to belong to each other. As the days proceeded, the mediator emphasized the central value of belonging in the things he said and let belonging inform the questions he asked of the brothers and elders.

The mediator also acknowledged that this conflict was influenced by conflicting cultural values. In traditional Shona settlements, ownership was communal and shared. Upon the death of a father the eldest son would inherit the communal home and the younger sons would be allocated new pieces of land in the same area. Only after Europeans colonized Zimbabwe was the idea of individual ownership introduced, together with a prohibition against subdivision. Nearby pieces of land were no longer available to these brothers because the adjacent land was privately owned. With this understanding of the history that gave rise to inheritance conflicts like this one, belonging became even more important to the brothers to counteract the negative effects of colonization and urbanization on their traditional ties and relations.[4]

Things are changing in Zimbabwe now. Traditional ways of solving conflicts are giving way to legal mechanisms as people group together according to economics and job pursuits instead of kinship ties. Interpersonal conflicts are less easily addressed by recourse to traditional approaches. References to customary values and relationship structures have diminished resonance. Intuition and imagination are needed for people to craft new ways forward that fit with their contemporary conditions.

Just as imagination and intuition were helpful in resolving this conflict, emotions also played a central role. The Shona mediator relied on cultural norms of communication that acknowledged feelings as intertwined with facts and equally important. The next two practices illustrate ways to welcome emotional ways of knowing into conflictual relationships.

Practices That Draw on Emotional Ways of Knowing

Emotional intelligence is central to successful relationships across difference. It is both glue and alarm—it helps us connect to each other and cues us when threads are pulled that could develop into major rents in the fabric of connection if not mended. Emotional intelligence is powerful. It encompasses our feelings, our awareness of these feelings, and our sensitivity to others' feelings. Emotions are guides to action, helping us act in accordance with what we value. As we acknowledge the importance of strong relationships across differences, our feelings give impetus to our investments of time, energy, and commitment.

Recent research shows that feelings and thoughts are intertwined, each affecting the other. So it is not helpful to try to isolate logical analysis from feelings. Rather, emotional intelligence nudges us to ask how we are situated in a relationship, how it feels, and how we want to proceed, questions that include both thinking and feeling components. Because Western societies tend to privilege the thinking function, it is particularly important to focus on including emotions as full partners in our approaches to communication and conflict.

Two practices that invoke emotional intelligence in interpersonal situations are exchanging three minutes of passion and enacting rituals.

Exchanging Three Minutes of Passion. *Exchanging three minutes of passion* is a simple practice that helps refocus, recharge, and reinvigorate feelings in the midst of a gathering, meeting, or group project. It is to take an interlude from business as usual, inviting each individual to find a partner and then to sit for a moment in silence. When each is ready, one partner begins. She or he talks without interruption for three minutes, filling in the sentence "I am passionate about . . ." again and again. The partner's job is to receive what is said, listening for changes in intensity, themes, and patterns. If the speaker pauses or is stuck, the listener may ask "What else are you passionate about?" No substantive suggestions should be made. Once the initial three minutes are over, the partners sit in silent reflection before reversing roles.

This practice can be used when energy is flagging in a group, or when people have come to an impasse in a negotiation. One way to think about this practice is this: sometimes, in our attempts to address conflict, we develop momentum that takes us further from where we want to be. Feelings of anger, frustration, fear, or resentment may intensify as we engage. These feelings may be expressed in assertive or aggressive ways, or they can turn in on themselves, as a wave does. In the latter case, a group may seem listless or tired, bogged down or disconnected. Just as a car cannot change its speed from fast forward to full stop in a second, a group needs a transition time and a way to shift. A practice like three minutes of passion helps all the participants move into a neutral gear so that they can go forward intentionally in a different direction.

Far from a diversion, this practice is an intentional shift, inviting people to speak to what they care about. As what they care about is articulated, it lives in the room. The energy that accompanies this caring lives in the room too. Following the exchange, it is possible to pose questions like these:

- How can we infuse our passions into this process in ways that might assist our negotiations?
- How can we include more of what we care about in our decision making?
- Which of the things I am passionate about can I bring more fully into this meeting?
- Do themes in the passions we expressed overlap, and if so, how can we draw on these shared concerns in moving forward?

I used this practice with staff members in an agency. They were a racially and culturally diverse group with a history of painful distrust, and several of them mentioned how much they disliked their biweekly meetings. "No one ever says anything real," they complained. "The meetings are a waste of time—everything gets done behind the scenes anyway," said others. They asked me to help them develop a more positive, open climate in the office.

As the first day we spent together proceeded, we moved between the personal and the professional, between self-exploration and bird's-eye views of the office. At one point in the early afternoon, the energy in the room flagged. Some disclosures had been made, and some personal "aha's" achieved, but there was a gap between where we were and where the group wanted to be. Group members wanted to get to the place of having an honest dialogue with each other. But skeletons from the past, instincts of self-protection, and habits of not listening were still present, blocking the path forward.

We shifted gears to share three minutes of passion. People moved into dyads, looking wary and guarded. But thirty seconds into the activity, the buzz in the room was electric. How often have you had three uninterrupted minutes to speak about what really matters to you? It is an infectious invitation; even when three minutes seems long, the experience carries surprises for the speaker. An essential part of the experience is the listener. As the listener carefully attends to the feeling tone of what is said as well as the overarching themes, the speaker has the space to continue exploring. Passion resurfaces in the room, passion that was buried beneath guardedness, fear, and resentments. From this generative place, other possibilities emerge.

The members of this group did get to talk about the differences among them, both historical and cultural. Sharing three minutes of passion was a way to create an opening for this to occur. Another practice that helped was the practice of ritual.

Enacting Rituals. *Enacting rituals* is a practice in which relationship is emphasized and in which feelings and sensations take the front seat ahead of thought and analysis.[5] In rituals we have the safety to transition from the known to the unknown, from one identity to another, from one way of understanding a situation or relationship to another. This safety emerges because rituals are times outside ordinary time, when usual patterns of communication are suspended. Rituals range from the traditional religious service to the improvised ways the events of September 11, 2001, have been memorialized. They are powerful, ancient, and constantly invented. Ritual was an important practice for the people in the organization described in the previous section.

> After they completed the three minutes of passion, there was a sense of excitement in the air. They were energized, surprised at some of what they heard, and they were curious. But they were unsure of how to proceed. Their experience of meetings and dialogues was that everyone would run for cover. So they shrank from dialogue, though they knew they had to find new ways forward if they were to create a more positive working climate.

> Building on the energy from the three minutes of passion, I asked them all to return to their seats in the circle. I suggested to them that what they had just experienced was a ritual. It was an experience in relationship, outside of ordinary time, when they were focused primarily on feeling and sensing (both their own and their partner's feelings and sensations), not thought and analysis. It helped them move from being tired and wary to being energized and curious. It heightened their awareness of positive aspects of their relationships. I asked them to brainstorm other rituals that they had experienced in their organization, hoping to connect these positive experiences to ways of moving forward.

> At first there was silence. This was a group in which rituals had fallen away: the summer baseball games had given way to individual activities years before; the birthday celebrations had stopped after one person felt offended by what others thought were humorous gifts. They did not even have a watercooler to congregate around, they told me dolefully, recognizing that watercooler visits were rituals for coming together in many offices.

Then someone had an idea. The large-scale audit project they had done the year before had been a time of coming together, she observed. It involved suspending their usual daily activities, going out of the office to audit other organizations and businesses, and coming to know each other personally. Though the activity had been stressful because of tight time-lines and other limitations beyond their control, they had come together as a team to meet the expectations of the project. They had thought and analyzed together, but they had also endured discomfort, stress, and difficult working conditions together. They had traveled on trains, buses, subways, and planes, experiencing dimensions of each other that had not been obvious in the office. As their windows into each others' identities widened, so did their empathy and appreciation for each other. Their relationships grew.

They wondered if this was a ritual. It was a time outside ordinary time; it was a time of transition from a narrow way of knowing each other to a much broader way. Because they were with each other under pressured conditions, they shared feelings. Even as they conducted the analyses they were required to do, they shared the sensations of being outsiders to the organizations they visited, resisted or welcomed. They also endured difficult, cramped physical settings and uncomfortable accommodations. As these experiences of shared feeling and sensing accrued over the course of their work outside the office, their relationships changed. The whole project was a kind of ritual, a time outside usual time, in which feelings and sensations came to the fore in ways they never did in the office.

When the project ended, everyone returned to the office and to business as usual. Some individual relationships remained stronger, but the norms of mistrust and guarded postures returned as staff turnover continued, old resentments resurfaced, and the group's manager unsuccessfully tried a litany of strategies to engage and motivate them. The audit yielded some of the positive effects of a ritual, but its positive influence had not been sustained.

This realization opened a new line of inquiry for the coworkers: what rituals could be built among them that would open up the channels that had closed again? What could they do to find ways forward with the legacy of a painful past? They brainstormed then decided on a few ideas, including adding a new interactive dimension to their Web site, reinstituting birthday celebrations, and arranging weekly listening times when managers would make themselves available to hear whatever staff wanted to say.

To build on this progress, the group drew from another practice—the use of metaphors. This practice is explored in the next section.

Practices That Draw on Somatic Intelligence

Somatic intelligence is the wisdom of the body. This wisdom is evoked through personal practices of listening (see Chapter Seven) and through symbols, rituals, and metaphors that bring people together. Symbols communicate meanings and messages about identity. They mobilize people through stirring their emotions and evoking connections to ideas and groups, and they can be used for constructive or destructive ends. The Nazi swastika, for example, was a powerful symbol. Many flags, monuments, and memorials are also powerful symbols. Sharing a meal is probably one of the most universal symbols, communicating common humanity and recognition in the joint act of breaking bread. Eating together provides physical nourishment, feeding the body while symbolizing respect and caring for self and others.

People of many cultures make use of physical metaphors to help bridge differences. Extending an olive branch and passing a peace pipe are both physical symbols that communicate peace. Rituals draw on symbolic meanings, connecting feelings to various combinations of senses—smell, taste, sight, hearing, and touch—as transitions, resolutions, and passages are marked. As people share metaphors and rituals, awareness of feelings and sensations is heightened and relationships are deepened.

A number of approaches draw on metaphors to enhance communication and deepen understanding across differences. In adventure learning, groups of coworkers or community members use physical metaphors like ropes courses to help them observe and reflect on their communication, leadership, and relationships. Ropes courses pose physical challenges that can be met only through group communication and cooperation. Interpersonal relationships, from the sublime to the most conflictual, are enhanced when individuals draw on their bodies' abilities to receive and send information. Somatic ways of knowing can be the key to the door of transformation.

Two practices that come from the awareness of the essential interconnectedness of mind, emotions, and body are using metaphors and embracing paradox.

Using Metaphors. *Using metaphors* is powerful because metaphors always have physical referents. Metaphors are images used to connect people and ideas; they communicate volumes in efficient bundles. Metaphors map meaning onto events and situations, conveying emotional and sensory information at the same time. They are windows into worlds, revealing where people stand relative to their situations. Consider this metaphor for South Africa, expressing the optimism of the writer as a participant in the transition to democracy: "South Africa has been known as the 'rainbow nation' since the early 1990s when Apartheid was dismantled and a new democratic government was put in place. The 'rainbow nation' is appropriate as it captures the many-colored people who comprise South Africa. It also provides the positive, beautiful, and unifying image that people need to hold onto: finally, after many years of darkness, a rainbow was going to appear in South Africa."[6]

This metaphor communicates colors, sensations, moods, and meanings. It reveals the author's conviction that sustained work will be needed to manifest the rainbow potential of South Africa. Rainbows, after all, are not always present. They appear only in certain weather conditions. Rainbows are beautiful because their colors complement and harmonize with each other, not because of complete unification. By identifying the rainbow with the future of South Africa, the writer communicates her value of maintaining and celebrating cultural diversity within a just system.

Contrast this metaphor for South Africa with this image from Palestine: "The mountain cannot be shaken down by the wind."[7] The writer explains that this metaphor has been used heavily by Palestinians since the late 1960s and early 1970s. It conveys the strong ties among Palestinians and the unity that makes their dream of independence as strong as a mountain. Applying this metaphor to the conflict with Israel, Palestinians are able to withstand a great deal, strengthened by the image of these policies affecting their persistence and unity as wind affects a mountain.

As you read each of these metaphors—the rainbow and the wind on the mountain—different feelings and sensations arise. These feelings relate to your views about the two situations. They also relate to your personal experience of the physical world: rainbows, mountains, and wind. Because they connect to personal experience, metaphorical images tend to be remembered better and to have stronger impacts than more abstract communication.

Once you are aware of metaphors, you will notice them everywhere. Because they are physical and sensory, metaphors speak to us in a way that cuts through abstraction, lodging with vitality and impact in our consciousness. We feel and sense them in our bodies and draw from them in composing meanings and actions. Think of a metaphor for your marriage, your work group, your family. When we invite an image or a metaphor to describe a relationship or a situation, we tap wisdom that is often outside what we consciously access. A metaphor becomes a puzzle, something to put together and explore, a pathway into feelings, thoughts, cultural frames, and habits of attention that are powerful in shaping our perceptions, actions, and relationships.

> Metaphors were useful as I worked with the staff of an office whose productivity was threatened by a series of conflicts. The morning we first met they worked in small groups to generate metaphors for the office as it currently was. They came up with a variety of metaphors, most conveying a sense of feeling stuck, bogged down, or blocked—trudging through thick mud in heavy boots, toiling in the bottom of a pit with steep sides, rowing in a boat with many oars where the rowing is not only unsynchronized but others deliberately hit you on the head with their oars at unexpected times. Though I asked the participants to report as groups on their metaphors to protect their confidentiality, individuals often took credit for their metaphors, wanting to explain the sensations and feelings conveyed in them.

Once we had the whole array displayed on a flipchart, I asked the participants to meet again in the same small groups and name metaphors for the office as they would like it to be. These metaphors had a very different feeling tone; they were positive, more serene, and energized. They included images that built on or reframed the original images, such as all rowing the boat together, and completely different images, such as sharing a multiethnic feast. Looking at both sets of images, people noticed that the second set had much more mobility and ease of movement in it; it also contained a wider array of images, suggesting space for creativity.

Over several weeks we worked with both sets of metaphors to understand what they conveyed about the existing office climate and relationships and how they could offer ways to get from there to the envisioned climate and relationships. The metaphors gave people ways to talk about their painful experiences without personalizing blame and helped them talk about moving forward in ways that included their coworkers. Although the question of how to improve things generally had stumped many in the office leading to an atmosphere of resignation, the metaphors gave people tangible scaffolding for bridging the painful past, the tender present, and the ideal future.

For example, one discussion focused on leadership, on how members of a team and their coach can move from asynchronous rowing in which rowers deliberately hit each other with their oars to a more coordinated, safe team. The metaphors themselves—and the physical reality of the metaphors—suggested what was important: respect, safety, communication, working together for shared goals, and taking individual initiative responsibly within the context of an overall plan. The metaphors also conveyed the importance of patience and planning: no team becomes successful overnight, especially when team members have acquired bad habits that have blocked progress in the past.

This example also illustrates the other practice that comes from somatic ways of knowing, embracing paradox.

Embracing Paradox. *Embracing paradox* is a useful practice because it speaks to one of the fundamental realities of intercultural work: it is not linear. Within each of us and within the cultural groups to which we belong, are contradictions, paradoxes, and apparent inconsistencies. If we are to work together, harmonizing our different ways of knowing and being in the world, we will encounter paradoxes. We can react to these paradoxes in ways that distance us from each other and from our goals. Or we can embrace them as a familiar accompaniment to creative work, stretching our comfort with ambiguity.

One of the painful past experiences in the office described in the previous example related to the personnel evaluation process. There were about fifteen people in the office working at the same level. About a third were African-American, a third were white, and a third were Latino or Latina. When a young white woman was hired for a vacant position, she was perceived by several of those who had been around for a long time as a "wonderchild," favored by the supervisor. Whether there was a coherent pattern of favoritism is not certain—what is clear is that some of the people of color perceived such a pattern. The feelings of unfairness that flowed from this perception led to a painful incident. After the new employee's first performance evaluation, a copy of this positive evaluation was somehow obtained by one of her Latina coworkers. It was posted in a public place in the office, with the following comment written on it, in bright color: "Could this have been for a person of color? Racist!"

This incident shocked the new employee, leaving her feeling violated and exposed. It divided the office, as camps arose of those who supported and those who opposed the action. When the supervisor tried to impose a sanction on the woman who had posted the evaluation, the supervisor's superior refused to back her up, worsening an already charged situation and reinforcing feelings of resignation among the staff.

Over time this history was addressed, the various camps were reintegrated into the office and some wounds were salved.

This involved some honest dialogue, one of the practices described in the next section. It also involved changes in leadership approaches and some structural changes in the ways evaluations were done and results communicated. Ultimately it involved embracing paradox. Paradoxes arose because the same person who had taken this drastic and dramatic action was also one of the people who identified most strongly with the office and its mission, which was about righting injustice. She had violated personal privacy and caused embarrassment; she was also committed to creating a more just world. Her methods were at best controversial, and at worst destructive to relationships, but she was also compassionate, vulnerable, and genuinely concerned about fairness.

As the coworkers developed more complex pictures of each other, they saw the paradoxes not only in her character but also in others' characters and their own. Seeing this, they let go of some of their judgments and fixed images and found more flexibility for keeping their relationships supple. Only then did the connections and shared goals among them become more visible. Practices that draw on connected ways of knowing reinforce this forward momentum.

Practices That Draw on Connected Ways of Knowing

C. G. Jung wrote of a collective unconscious to which we all belong and from which arises archetypal images that reflect our collectivity; others have sought religious or spiritual language to describe the humanity that connects us. Viktor Frankl said we are connected by the human choice we all have—the choice to make meaning of what happens to and around us.[8] Mary Clark wrote that we seek belonging and that this need to belong to what matters to us and to each other is the glue that keeps us relating constructively.[9] Chris Mitchell suggested that gestures or symbolic acts that communicate our common humanity are critical to addressing deep-rooted conflict.[10] The theme of belonging runs through each of these bodies of work, and it also inspires the practices of partnering and sharing songs.

Partnering. The practice of *partnering* arises from the insight that it is not possible for us to attain and maintain perfect cultural and conflict fluency. We have cultural and individual blind spots. We exercise habits of attention in ways that reveal some worlds and obscure others. Our attention goes so much more easily to those things that divide us than those that bond us. Because our vision is always limited, we are wise to seek partnering with those different from us. As we partner, we discover commonalities through the rituals, shared physical experiences, and feelings that surface.

Partnering may mean working with someone whose approach is different from our own in a training, teaching, or intervention setting. It may mean having someone act as a shadow or coach, someone who does not actively participate in the work we are doing. To partner is to recognize that other cultural perspectives complement our own and so to seek those who have a range of experiences and perspectives different from ours. Choosing a partner with whom we share similar identities is not the objective, though we may experience easy communication and rapport with such a partner.

When working with a group of people from two or more distinct cultural traditions, it is important practically and symbolically to partner. The practical benefits include having someone to plan, implement, and reflect with whose experiences give him a deeper or more intuitive understanding of one of the groups. The symbolic benefits are equally significant: even if you and your partner do not perfectly reflect or mirror the members of the groups involved, your working together across racial, ethnic, or cultural identities conveys a powerful message of collaboration.

Partnering goes some way toward preventing cultural missteps and faux pas.

Years ago I worked with a fellow Canadian to present training to an international staff working on conservation issues. As part of a demonstration of conflict styles, my cotrainer and I staged an argument with each other about the timing and format of the training in front of the group. We had planned that, following a break, we would debrief this mock conflict with a large-group discussion of the styles we had demonstrated, illustrating their limitations and possibilities.

But we aroused unexpected responses. The English participants gave us sideways glances of embarrassment—a narrowing of the eyes that spoke of reproach for letting conflict flourish so flagrantly, even if it was a role-play. The Italians expressed concern about how Tom, my cotrainer, treated me, a woman. The Americans congratulated Tom for "letting her have it," and the East Africans were concerned that our relationship had ruptured. Some of the East African participants offered to help us talk about it. Throughout the day that followed, they checked in with us about the state of our relationship, offering again to help. To them, it simply did not make sense to pretend to be in conflict or pretend to be angry. Our Canadian starting points were clearly different from many others'.

Partnering might have addressed this problem—if I had been working with someone whose cultural starting points were more different from mine, we might have better anticipated the range of responses we received. Of course partnering carries its own challenges. Intercultural teams need to work together behind the scenes to ensure that team members are all on the same page before working with others. The ways of developing cultural and conflict fluency outlined in Chapters Two, Three, Four, and Five are useful when preparing for partnering.

Partnering is strengthened as partners draw on connected ways of knowing. Questions like these are helpful in exploring this dimension:

- What values and goals do the partners share?
- What have been one or two of their most satisfying experiences as trainers, intervenors, or members of diverse teams?
- To what do they have recourse when things are going badly—where is their strength, their source, their rock?
- What do they draw upon when something unexpected happens in their work? Is it intuition, imagination, creativity, a signal from their body, a quick mental shuffle through their experience bank, a prayer, or something else?
- What is their favorite piece of art or music? How does it speak to their work; how does it speak to the ways they relate to others and the ways they approach conflict?

As questions like these are asked, common ground is uncovered, adding spark and interest to partnerships. As partnerships develop, confidence is built, and synchronicity can flourish. The practice of partnering may be enhanced by the second practice, sharing songs.

Sharing Songs. *Sharing songs* also belongs to connected ways of knowing. A beloved piece of music or art is a window into a worldview—it is a whole story of interconnected ideas, feelings, identities, and meanings. Think about what Beethoven's Fifth Symphony reveals about the man behind the music: the passion, intensity, pain, and determination of someone encountering deafness, who was at the same time called to write some of the most stirring music that has ever graced the world. Think about what I reveal about myself when I share that it is a favorite piece of music. The music we love speaks volumes about us without the clumsiness of words. Music also connects us to place, time, history, and identity. It speaks to our souls while exciting our senses. And it does so in ways that reveal and invite without the controversy so often sparked by words.

Music has long fulfilled a role in conveying histories, giving voice to feelings, and connecting fellow questers. Every year, over half a million people make a pilgrimage to Ayers Rock, a huge sandstone monolith in the Australian outback. On the way, Australian Aboriginal people inhabit what they call *the Dreaming,* a complex, intricate universe that connects them and reflects their histories via *songlines.* Diane Ackerman describes songlines as a maze of invisible roads on which pilgrims travel, connecting "knowledge, perception, moral code, and recollection."[11] The continent of Australia is replete with these crossing lines, which are both precise map coordinates and ancient, magical records of past journeys.

These Aboriginal songs seem to describe the nature of the land over which the song passes. Bruce Chatwin reports that "[c]ertain phrases, certain combinations of musical notes, are thought to describe the action of the Ancestor's *feet.* . . . An expert songman, by listening to the order of succession, would count how many times his hero crossed a river, or scaled a ridge—and be able to calculate where, and how far along, a Songline, he was."[12]

Inspired by this rich tradition of music integrally linked to history, identity, and landscape, the power of music to evoke and connect can be used in other settings.

Suppose two Canadians, one with an Indian heritage (Prem), and another with a German heritage (Henry), were in conflict. What would happen if, in addition to the words they used to attempt understanding, they had recourse to music to express their identities and ways of making meaning? It is notoriously difficult to convey worldviews to another, because so much of the meaning-making and identity material within them is invisible even to the holders of the worldviews themselves.

As part of coming to know each other better, Henry and Prem could each choose a meaningful piece of music to play for the other. For the purposes of illustration, imagine that Henry chooses a Bach prelude, and Prem chooses music composed by the prolific Indian poet and musician Rabindranath Tagore. The measured, distinct voices of a Bach prelude speak to an appreciation for distinct order, clarity, interwoven turn taking, and clean resolution of different themes. The lyrical music of Tagore conveys the sense of labyrinths within labyrinths, nuances of meaning, and spiraling patterns. The shapes of the music, and the feelings and moods evoked are different. Would listening to and reflecting on the meanings of the music to each open ways of understanding that might remain closed through days of talk?

Listen to a few of the words of "My Song" by Tagore:

This song of mine will wind its music around you,
my child, like the fond arms of love. . . .
My song will be like a pair of wings to your dreams,
it will transport your heart to the verge of the unknown. . . .
My song will sit in the pupils of your eyes,
and will carry your sight into the heart of things.[13]

As Henry and Prem listen to each other's songs, several things may happen. They may like or dislike each other's selections. They may find them discordant and unpleasant or satisfying and beautiful. Structured dialogue could assist Henry and Prem to talk about their choices and the meanings of these choices for them. As they share the contexts from which the music arises (both personal and historical), they may reveal more about their respective cultural contexts and values.

In Chapter Nine the possibilities from sharing songs will be explored further.

Of course it is not only songs that inspire, connect, and speak to our hearts across differences. For those who prefer other forms, sculpture, paintings, poetry, or experiences with nature may serve the same purposes. Many facets of the arts are windows into symbolic and spiritual ways of knowing. In my book *Bridging Troubled Waters,* I related the story of a class I taught on spirituality and conflict transformation, in which we began our class at a museum of modern art.[14] As we observed color, form, texture, and perspective in the pieces of art, we engaged each other in conversations about perception and meaning that would have taken much longer to arise in the formal classroom, if they arose at all. Somehow the art and our responses to it—emotional, sensory, spiritual—opened up whole worlds within and between us that fed our ongoing exploration throughout the semester.

The eight practices described in this chapter all share this objective—to open up worlds within and between us so that communication is enhanced. When communication becomes clearer, relationships are strengthened. It is difficult to trust someone we do not understand. When we seek to understand and be understood in context, using a range of senses to step out of narrow labels and judgments that confine, we are more likely to be able to effectively bridge intercultural conflict.

CHAPTER NINE

On the Larger Stage
Intergroup Practices to Help Bridge Differences

Have you or children you know played a game called Snakes and Ladders? The game, sometimes called Chutes and Ladders, involves moving from the bottom to the top of a board with rows of squares, aiming to reach the top corner square before any other player. Players roll dice, moving ahead on the squares by the number indicated. Their progress is interrupted and set back when they encounter a snake on their square, a snake that they follow downward, taking them a dozen or two dozen squares back toward the beginning. Young players delight when they come to a ladder that allows them to move diagonally from their square to one several rows higher. Suspense, excitement, and dread are part of the experience of traversing the board, as players hope to land on ladders and not on snakes (Figure 9.1).

Snakes and Ladders

Is Snakes and Ladders a fitting metaphor for intergroup conflict? To some extent it seems so: progress is often slow and incremental, setbacks may involve long slides into past pain and intransigence, and there are few ladders. Those involved have mixed emotions, and these emotions swing as impasses, breakthroughs, and tough slogging accompany efforts to address their differences. Both sides need to stay engaged for a successful outcome to be achieved, and just when you think you are doing well, you hit a snake.

Figure 9.1. Snakes and Ladders.

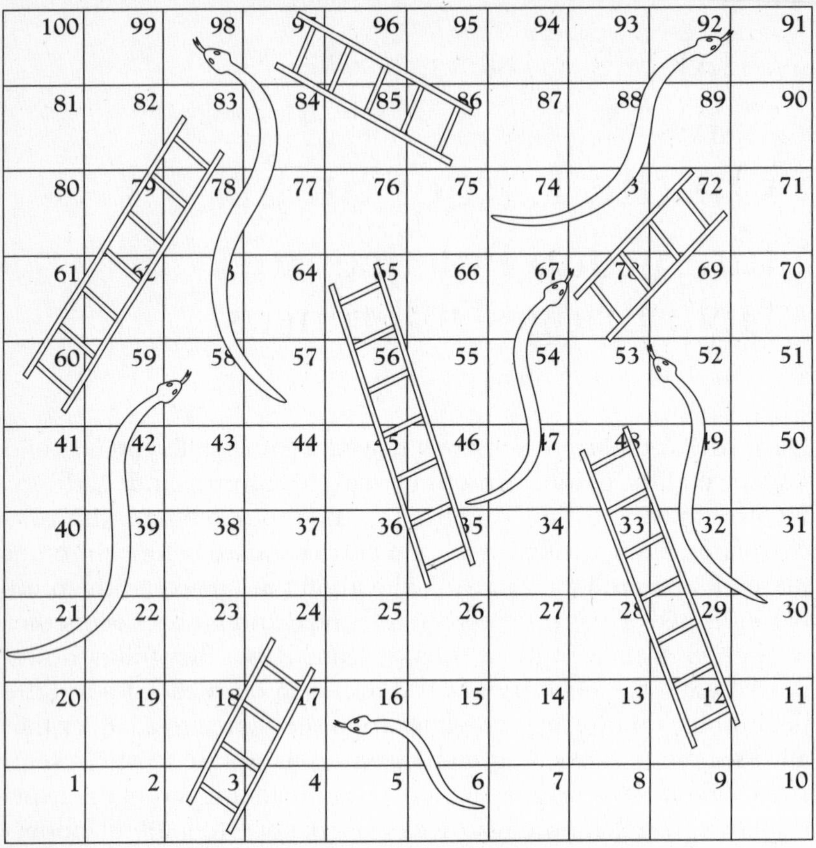

100	99	98	97	96	95	94	93	92	91
81	82	83	84	85	86	87	88	89	90
80	79	78	77	76	75	74	73	72	71
61	62	63	64	65	66	67	68	69	70
60	59	58	57	56	55	54	53	52	51
41	42	43	44	45	46	47	48	49	50
40	39	38	37	36	35	34	33	32	31
21	22	23	24	25	26	27	28	29	30
20	19	18	17	16	15	14	13	12	11
1	2	3	4	5	6	7	8	9	10

Note: Boards like this first appeared in the United States in the 1940s.

Although this metaphor shows some aspects of intergroup conflict, it is not a perfect fit. From the ways it does not fit come important insights into what is required to successfully bridge cultural differences across groups. First, Snakes and Ladders is competitive, allowing only one winner who renders every other player a loser. Addressing conflict effectively, however, means recognizing interdependence, thus opening the possibility of creative collaboration. Second, players in the game know clearly who won and who lost, and they know when it is over. Things are seldom so clear in real life, where addressing conflict is an ongoing process, with many layers, shapes, and dimensions. Third, the game rarely has long-term ramifications outside the room where it is played. Intergroup conflict can affect families, tribes, regions, nations, and ultimately the global community, sometimes for generations.

Finally—and most important—Snakes and Ladders is essentially a game of chance—the outcome is out of the players' control. Although intergroup conflicts are also influenced heavily by events and decisions outside parties' control, nevertheless, choices are always present, and resources—both internal and external—are available to support resolution and even transformation of conflicts. Intergroup conflicts are unpredictable in part because people have influence over outcomes. The ways this influence can be exercised and resources that help are the subjects of this chapter.

But before leaving the metaphor of Snakes and Ladders, we examine another of its dimensions. The game is very old, developed in India sometime between the second and twelfth centuries. Originally it was a game of morality, with the bases of the ladders located on squares representing aspects of goodness and the more numerous snakes representing forms of evil. Among the evil squares were those named Disobedience, Rage, Pride, Murder, Lust, and Drunkenness, while the good squares included Faith, Reliability, Generosity, and Knowledge.[1] Historians believe that the original game, called Moksha-Patamu, was used to teach Hindu children about actions and consequences. Good squares facilitated progress toward a better life, and evil ones led the player back, through reincarnation, to lower levels of existence. The final square symbolized Nirvana, a state of bliss and the highest attainable state in life.

The game was brought from India to England in the 1890s, first appearing in the United States in 1943. Along the way, it was changed in ways that reflected cultural understandings. In Victorian England the vices and virtues were renamed. Penitence, Thrift, and Industry became the names of ladder squares leading to Grace, Fulfillment, and Success, and Indolence, Indulgence, and Disobedience marked snake squares, from which players descended into Poverty, Illness, and Disgrace. In the U.S. version, the names for the game squares were deleted altogether, and the squares were labeled only with numbers.

This glimpse into history yields these observations:

- Cultures shape how we see things, and how we see things shapes culture in an unending, multidirectional exchange. The game of Moksha-Patamu taught children about reincarnation and life choices, and the understandings children applied in their lives affected the cultures around them. Subsequent cultures adapted the game to conform to their own values (as in the case of Victorian England) or priorities (as in the United States, where the moral agenda was removed entirely and only numbers and winning or losing remain).

- Any approach to conflict reflects a cultural ethos and cannot be directly imported without adaptation. Canadian and U.S. children playing Snakes and Ladders, or Chutes and Ladders, today would find the original labels on the squares strange indeed, accustomed as they are to more secular versions.

- The way a conflict is framed has a powerful subliminal effect. The ladders in the game suggest implicitly that progress is "a linear vector," a "hierarchy of rungs" in a ladder leading to ever higher levels of evolutionary progression. The snakes slither in and upset "all this order," attaching negativity and suspicion to the nonlinear and natural worlds.[2] Because framing is such a powerful influence on the course of conflicts, examining the implicit assumptions in how the conflict is described and understood by each party is important.

- Just as Snakes and Ladders is not a recent invention but comes from a rich cultural tradition, many conflict situations contain artifacts and emotional effects of past events, relationships, and understandings. These relics of the past need to be understood, because when unrecognized or ignored, they can cause a straightforward conflict to escalate, seemingly without warning. Not all past influences need to be excavated, but awareness that they may exist is important.

- Worldviews—our symbolic understandings of the world and our places in it—are reflected in the games we play, the songs we sing, and the books we read. Exploring common activities, songs, proverbs, and beloved stories is a way of understanding others in context. Contextual understanding helps us to counteract our tendency to judge and distance ourselves from those with whom we differ.

The history of this child's game reveals multiple layers of history, meaning, and tradition. How much more thickly are long-standing conflicts imbued with interpretations that link to cultural understandings and identities. Just as Snakes and Ladders is more than a board game with numbered squares, so intergroup conflicts have many dimensions below the surface. Effectively bridging these conflicts summons our whole selves, with spirits of inquiry and discovery, to the important quest for understanding and peaceful communities.

Intergroup Conflict

Many volumes have been written about bridging difficult conflicts. Sadly, human history provides us (or our minds tend to remember) more examples of what not to do than of what helps. We are still on the frontier of developing effective ways to know and befriend conflict and the people with whom we experience conflict. If it were not so, we would not be so advanced technologically yet so divided across hemispheres, regions, and neighborhoods. Before introducing some promising practices, a brief exploration of intergroup conflicts sets the stage.

Dynamics of Intergroup Conflict

Intergroup conflicts are those where the shared values, identities, and meanings of the members of one large group or community somehow collide with those of the members of another large group. When an important aspect of someone's identity feels threatened, conflict quickly escalates. The abortion conflict in Canada and the United States is a case in point. Prolife and prochoice advocates' identities are bound up with their causes and reinforced by religious and secular philosophies, moral codes, and particular worldviews. Resolution of this conflict cannot be accomplished as cells can be moved on a petrie dish, because the conflict is intimately bound up with people's identities. Because our identities—who we see ourselves to be—are essential to our sense of efficacy, order, and belonging, we resist resolutions of conflicts that might compromise or change them.

Identities are resistant to compromise, and so are the meanings that get attached to events and relationships. These identities and meanings are perpetuated as they are supported and reinforced by those with whom we have significant relationships. Historical events come to symbolize struggles between groups, solidifying lines between *us* and *them*. Whether related to the Hatfields and the McCoys, Palestinians and Israelis, or one of the two warring sides of a single estranged family, descendents of those present at the beginnings of these conflicts carry the meanings of past generations into their current perceptions and dealings unless something different happens to interrupt the negative patterns.

Several human tendencies work to maintain these patterns. First, we tend to gravitate to those who are like us and those who reinforce our beliefs, meanings, and identities. We tend to avoid meetings and social gatherings with those whose views are very different from our own and especially with those whose ideas contradict or threaten ours. Second, the fundamental attribution error operates, excusing our own failings as arising from anomalous situations and attributing others' missteps to flawed characters. This adds to the perception born of limited contact that there are substantial and problematic differences between us and them. Third, because of limited contact and the fundamental attribution error, we tend to simplify and streamline our views of others, resisting alternative or more complex explanations. As we continue to explain others in negative ways to ourselves and members of our group, there is a tendency to blanket the other with pejorative labels like "inferior," "stupid," and "evil."[3] Thus a negative foundation for relationship is built, robust and resistant to change, in which others are ranked below members of our own group.

The practices described in this chapter are designed to create a positive momentum to counteract these tendencies. They are directed at large-group issues; at the same time they encompass the interpersonal and personal practices of Chapters Seven and Eight, as the largest concentric circle in a pool encompasses the smaller ones. Any action engaging large groups depends on the willingness and capacity of members of the group to participate meaningfully. Meaningful participation is enhanced when we recognize the connections between our inner lives, our interpersonal relationships, and our actions on the larger stages of our communities, regions, and nations.

How does a people move from enmity to friendship? Many times, all those involved cannot and do not sit down together for extended talks. More often, members or representatives of the groups engage each other in ways that have ripples into their larger communities. Understanding the ways that relational shifts with people from the other side get translated into group understandings and buy-in is hugely important. Because the boundaries protecting identities—ways of seeing self and others within a conflict—are so thick, there are often negative consequences for even talking with the other. These complexities make it even more important for representatives of groups to work toward integrating and generalizing understandings reached in negotiations for their larger communities.

The examples used to illustrate the eight practices discussed in this chapter veer away from the political and the personalities behind today's headlines. These breaking news stories are not the focus of this book, and they deserve sustained, complex treatment in their own right. Rather, the practices and the examples used to illustrate them are drawn from more grass-roots local and regional experiences in my work as well as stories shared with me by colleagues. These examples are windows into ways to create shifts and to initiate and sustain conversations across significant differences. They are offered in a spirit of hope, humility, and urgency, with the wish that they will inspire, invite innovation, and integrate some of what has gone before.

Intergroup Practices

Resolving conflict is ultimately about change. If we stay the same, we risk continuing negative relational cycles, comforting ourselves with the rightness of our positions while facing the bitter fruit of our divisions. Change happens at multiple levels—within us, between us, and among us. To lift ourselves out of patterns of conflict that have entrenched themselves in our identities and the meanings we make of life, we must exercise effort and courage.

These intergroup practices draw on this effort and courage and on the creativity generated from multiple ways of knowing.

The eight intergroup practices are summarized in the following list:

Ways of Knowing	*Related Intergroup Practices*
Intuitive and imaginative	Discovering common futures Composing shared images
Emotional	Cultivating emotional intelligence Facilitating conversational learning
Somatic	Learning through adventure Applying participatory action research
Connected	Dialoguing Metaphor journeying

Practices That Draw on Intuitive and Imaginative Intelligence

How much we need our imaginations to envision and enliven a world different from the one with which we have surrounded ourselves. Wendell Berry captures the magnitude of the challenge we face at the beginning of his moving book *Life Is a Miracle:* "No change is foreseeable in terms of the present mechanical explanations of things. Such a change is imaginable only if we are willing to risk an unfashionable recourse to our cultural tradition. Human hope may always have resided in our ability, in time of need, to return to our cultural landmarks and reorient ourselves."[4]

Berry is writing about the importance of centering our understandings in our lived experience, focusing on how we make sense from, act on, and collaborate from what we know, rather than questing for ever more sophisticated knowledge. Drawing from our lived experience—and cultural fluency that helps us stay open to others' lived experience—we can build new understandings, imagine positive futures, and intuit ways to live into these futures.

Two practices that help us move in positive directions are discovering common futures and composing shared images.

Discovering Common Futures. *Discovering common futures* is a large-group practice of imagining alternative futures. It is an exercise in exploring ways to move toward common purposes and, in the process, redefining others and laying "the groundwork for a [new] conception of 'us.'"[5] People in conflict are painfully aware of the issues that divide them. They tend to be less aware of what connects them. Feeling estranged, they do not see invisible ties that link them. Angry or resentful, they focus on the problems that divide them rather than possibilities for joint action arising from shared commitments or values. To discover common futures is to turn the heads of those in conflict so that they can see different views of themselves, others, and their shared potential.

There are many ways to pursue common futures, including Open Space Technology, future searches, and dialogue.[6] These approaches share some commonalities—they are ways of helping groups view a range of perspectives and possibilities for creating joint futures. Each of these approaches recognizes the wisdom of participants and provides opportunities for sharing stories and developing creative, shared visions. They differ from each other in several ways, including the degree of control exercised by facilitators over topics and processes. I offer brief descriptions of them here.

- *Open Space Technology* involves eliciting topics from self-selected groups. After the groups complete their work, their information is compiled, with the assistance of computers, into a composite picture. Groups have complete control over choice of topic and how to proceed in their groups. Facilitators maintain control over how information gathered from groups is aggregated and shared.
- *Future searches* bring people together for three days, during which time preselected groups choose their own focus related to selected themes or issues, generating specific action plans. Groups have some control over choice of topic and how to proceed. Facilitators maintain overall control of topics and processes through specific techniques, including mind mapping, identifying common ground, and two-stage action planning.
- *Dialogic approaches* are the most general. They are explored in detail as a practice related to connected ways of knowing later

in this chapter. There are many types of dialogue; here, dialogic refers to approaches where facilitators maintain control over the overall process and the way topics are framed. Participants work in small and large groups with the aim of expanding their understandings of the issues and people involved in a conflict. Fundamental to dialogue is concentrated awareness, a willingness to set aside agendas and judgments, and a positive desire to see a given topic from every possible perspective.[7] It is to listen deeply, interrupting conversational patterns of rapid exchange. Both future search and Open Space Technology use some elements of dialogue in bringing people together.

All three approaches aim for participants to "experience wholeness,"[8] drawing on multiple ways of knowing and multidimensional views of issues, self, and other. Another thread that connects them is the optimism that accompanies activities like imagining ideal futures and developing relationships. Because these are positive activities, people who may have felt drained by downward spirals of conflict now tend to feel energized and hopeful.

During future search meetings, for example, which typically last three days, participants move from a focus on the past and present to ideal future scenarios and action planning. The four tenets of future search meetings require having[9]

- The "whole system" in the room
- The "whole elephant" as the context for local action
- A future focus
- A commitment to self-management

Having the whole system in the room means including a cross-section of people who loosely represent those involved. Taking the whole elephant as a context for action is a reference to the story of the six blind men and the elephant, in which each man touched the elephant in a different place and each one came up with a completely different impression of it.[10] This metaphor emphasizes the importance of understanding as many aspects of a situation as possible before acting. Employing a future focus is important because it engages people's imaginative energy in acting out new ways of being. Participants are encouraged to imagine detailed futures as they really want them to be. Having a commitment to self-management means that participants share responsibility for meeting leadership, recording, reporting, and timekeeping, rather than relying on authoritative facilitators.

None of these methodologies is culture neutral, so applications across groups require adaptation and ongoing assessment, as the following example illustrates. In Bangladesh in 1994, two U.S. consultants ran a future search conference for Bangladeshi consultants, trainers, and managers interested in learning the future search approach. The selected focus for the conference was "the future of the children of Dhaka."

The conference was enthusiastically received, and it taught the consultants some important lessons. Generally, future search facilitators encourage participants to image ideal futures, no matter how unrealistic or grandiose. But the Bangladeshi participants demurred. Instead of envisioning the end of child labor, participants chose to imagine less child labor. The consultants observed that "so great are the nation's problems that people had trouble dreaming large future dreams."[11] Although this difference was probably attributable in part to the scale of Bangladeshi problems, it may have also related to the Bangladeshis' different cultural starting points, such as fatalism rather than free will and acceptance rather than optimism.

Until an approach like future search has been experienced, it may seem idealistic and unreal. Before it was used successfully to bring management and union members together in a 3M plant, it seemed like a "pipe dream."[12] In the 3M environment, past tensions between union and management had made joint planning and action difficult. Through a future search process, members of both groups, working together, produced a vision of their workplace reconfigured around customer needs. Both groups reported lasting benefits and better relationships as a result of their involvement.

A simple adaptation of a future search process can be used to help groups in conflict discover common futures. When these two groups come together, they can be invited, first, to work on their own, answering these questions:

- How do I belong to this conversation? (Ask people to include reasons for attending besides duty or requirement: for example, they might have a commitment to honest talk, concern for others in the group, desire to make progress on issues, personal experience that motivates participation, high regard for a person or people involved in the groups, or need to talk about difficult or potent issues.)
- What assets and gifts do I bring to this conversation? (Guide participants to think of positive resources: imagination, intuition, multiple perspectives, desire for resolution, commitment to openness, attitude of learning, ability to cut through layers of information, sensitivity to feelings, awareness of interdependence, focus on the big picture, experience with other similar issues, hope, optimism, and so forth.)
- What do I need to participate fully and heartfully in this conversation? (Invite people to include requests relating to timing, pacing, listening, time structuring, ways of framing issues, balanced participation, inclusion of others, inclusion or exclusion of topics, and other boundary issues.)
- What do I imagine could happen in this conversation if my biggest dreams were realized? (Encourage participants to suspend disbelief; set aside fixed ideas they hold about themselves, their group, or the groups' joint histories; and then imagine what could be. Ideas and images shared are to be received without judgment or critique.)

Once groups have listed answers to these questions, ask them to share their results with everyone. Questions of clarification are welcomed; discussion, criticism, and negotiation are not. Only after this material has been shared do people from both groups work together to develop a shared vision for the process, answering the following simple questions:

- What do we want to do together? (The response to this question is the vision—referencing the assets, gifts, and dreams identified by each group.)
- How do we want to do it? (The response establishes steps to accomplish the vision—taking into account requests from each group to facilitate their full participation.)

- With what results? (The response describes the effects, products, and realization of the vision and how these elements relate to the dreams identified initially.)

As group members create detailed pictures of where they want to be at the end of a course or project, the images of that future begin to live in the room. They are made possible by detailed planning about how to achieve the vision. The question about results is also important: it focuses the energy of the group, anchoring it in a generative vision of the future rather than in a tired, negative view of past or present. This entire process communicates the message that ownership in the process is shared, as is responsibility for the moment-by-moment monitoring and success of the process.

This process can be adapted depending on group history, size, and cultural context. For instance, the first set of questions may be answered in writing, with the results compiled and circulated. When groups are large or when speaking in front of a large group is uncomfortable, a carousel debrief may be useful. In this process, two concentric circles of small groups rotate—one clockwise and one counterclockwise—each group on the outside of the circle visiting each group on the inside for a few minutes to share answers and ideas. In other cases, answers to these questions are fed into computers, with results posted or distributed to inform the next choice points or directions and to ultimately lead to an integrated action plan.

> This process of discovering common futures was used with two groups conflicted over gender issues in their organization. They called themselves "traditionalists" (those who saw no problems with traditional roles for men and women and did not believe that women were disadvantaged in the organization) and "agitators" (those who rejected traditional gender roles and saw women as disadvantaged in the organization). Over the course of a day, they made progress that surprised them, accustomed as they were to hearing each other out in agitated and stressful encounters.
>
> One of the turning points came when they reflected on their "biggest dreams." The members of the two groups

realized that their dreams had many common elements, including shared desires for respect, mutual acceptance of personal choices, and improved transparency of promotion and evaluation processes. This realization contradicted their habitual images of each other imbued with negative judgments like "unaware," "insensitive," "radical," and "misguided." It set the stage for constructive conversation and detailed planning to realize their dreams.

In this case, participants were asked to imagine that there was a reason to talk with the people they disagreed with, with whom they had been doing a negative dance for years. They had to exercise their imaginations to go in a different direction, to envision different outcomes and reconfigured relationships. Their intuition that progress was possible helped them frame and name their issues in new ways so others could hear them.

Ideally, the process of discovering common futures engages imagination to identify fertile avenues for exploration and intuition to discern how to pursue these avenues. Another practice that draws on intuitive and imaginative ways of knowing is composing shared pictures.

Composing Shared Images. *Composing shared images* is a way of exploring a gestalt, or whole, of an experience and expressing that whole to others. It is often used as a component of a larger process like discovering common futures. The practice of composing shared images has a powerful message embedded in it: there are many perspectives about any issue and each of these has its own integrity and its own impermanence. These perspectives are cultural and shared, personal and individual, situational and dynamic.

To experience composing images, the participants get into pairs. When there is a particular conflict dividing two groups, each pair should have one person from each group. Then choose a focus. For example, if the issue is stalled negotiations, the focus might be stuckness or impasse. Have the pairs sit silently together and bring a felt experience of the dynamic into their awareness. When was the dynamic of stuckness experienced personally? What did it feel like? What sensations did this trigger? What pictures did it conjure?

When everyone has brought these sensations and feelings into his or her awareness, one person in each pair is designated to be a photographer. The other member of the pair closes his eyes, preparing to become a camera. The photographer leads her partner to a place inside or outside until she finds an image that mirrors her felt sense of the dynamic. Perhaps it is a cactus, a dammed stream, a narrow corridor; perhaps something else. Once she has found it, she stops and, without naming the image, orients her partner, adjusting his head and stance by gentle directions so that when he opens his eyes he will be gazing in the direction of the image. The photographer then taps her partner on the shoulder.

This is the partner's cue to open his eyes and take in the image framed by the photographer. The partner acts as a camera, not turning his head or averting his gaze, simply taking in the image presented by the photographer. After a minute or two, the partner again closes his eyes, and the photographer leads him back to the place they started from. All of these steps are done in silence. Once they return, it is time to switch roles, with the partner who was led becoming the photographer and the photographer taking the role of the camera.

This experience is interesting because the image framed stands out after the darkness of closed eyes, vivid and remembered. It also expresses and evokes powerful feelings. The beauty of this exercise is that it can be done to this point without the use of language, so it is particularly useful for those who do not share fluency in a common language. When language is a barrier, the experience can be debriefed with the aid of interpreters or by asking partners to draw their images and later work together to draw a composite image that encompasses the feelings each sought to express.

When participants do have a language in common, the debriefing can draw on multiple ways of knowing, including somatic and emotional. Debriefing questions may include the following:

- What was the predominant color of the images?
- If this image were a song, how would you describe it?
- What feelings did the images evoke for you?
- Where are the feelings located in your body?

- How did the image your partner showed speak to you about this situation?
- What possibilities did the image contain or reveal for shifts or movement?
- What correspondences between your image and your partner's image did you notice?
- Which shared and different meanings did you and your partner associate with the images? How do these relate to cultural differences or similarities between the two of you?
- Given the images you and your partner chose, what is your intuition about how to move forward?
- How have the initial feelings you had about the focus of this exercise stayed constant or shifted?

As partners complete their dialogue, encourage them to share an overview of their dialogue with everyone present. Listen for patterns, convergences, departures. Use the exercise to illustrate that there are a range of feelings and interpretations in the room and that these are not fixed or immovable but change as people change perspectives. We all see images through our own perceptual, meaning-making, and cultural lenses, and these lenses are continuously influenced by context and others around us.

> Composing shared images can be a bridge across cultural differences, as it was for a group of scholars from an Eastern European university who were visiting the United States for the first time. The scholars were part of a multiyear exchange program in which the American institution was providing mentoring and the materials to start a new academic program in the Eastern European university. There had been differences between the Americans and their Eastern European colleagues over allocation and use of resources, timing and focus of visits, and selection of exchange participants. Relations needed to be rebuilt after the American project manager left his institution and a new manager took over. At about this time, a new cohort of Eastern European scholars arrived at the U.S. university.
>
> During this visit the Eastern European scholars worked with a matched group of American scholars to compose images. Their chosen theme was "windows into our worlds."

Each American and Eastern European scholar chose three images, symbolizing

- Something I love about America
- Something I love about Eastern Europe
- Something I want to know more about

Each scholar took turns being the camera and the photographer for three shots (one for each image). In one pair, the image of America for the Eastern European was a shiny red sports car, and for the American, a beautiful flowering tree. The Eastern European image selected by the American was a brilliant blue sky; her counterpart chose a nearly blooming rose to symbolize her Eastern European home. These choices led to a rich discussion for the pair, including their choices of organic metaphors for three out of the four images.

Though the theme did not address the conflictual history between the groups explicitly, the images started longer conversations about cultural differences, preferences, images, expectations, and communication. Through these conversations, curiosities and perspectives about the history of the project surfaced, and questions were answered by the American hosts in ways that were part of the fabric of conversation rather than stark, less comfortable exchanges. Composing shared images positively affected the climate of the project, injecting new energy for collaboration.

Composing images is a practice that creates new pathways for sharing information that are not verbal. It also brings the feeling dimension into a conversation, as do the practices that draw on emotional intelligence.

Practices That Draw on Emotional Intelligence

Awareness and action informed by emotional ways of knowing are essential to bridging cultural conflict. Emotions are too frequently submerged, managed, or viewed as uniformly problematic. They hide behind and fuel judgments, attributions, and accusations. They maintain stuck positions. Emotions are powerful forces for action, yet they sometimes inhibit action even when action could be beneficial.

Inviting emotions into our efforts to address differences is important and useful. To weave in emotions, we have to be aware of them and willing to receive them. Acknowledging that everyone has strong feelings is preferable to getting into a contest about whose feelings are more justified, more extreme, or more intense. Rather than running from feelings, going toward them, sharing them, and exploring their complexity can be a constructive way forward.

All the practices described in this chapter draw on emotional ways of knowing in some way. These two practices focus specifically on building capacity to weave emotions into bridging conflict: cultivating emotional intelligence and facilitating conversational learning.

Cultivating Emotional Intelligence. *Cultivating emotional intelligence* is the broadest practice presented here, with applicability at three levels: personal, interpersonal, and intergroup. Emotional intelligence encompasses awareness of feelings and the ability to act on those feelings—our own and others'. Cultivating this intelligence is important because without an ability to recognize and express genuine feelings, our relationships are limited, our decisions are difficult, and we simply find ourselves at sea, out of touch with ourselves and others.[13] Our ability to prevent, navigate, and bridge differences is also severely curtailed.

The following example of the importance of emotional intelligence is drawn from the academic environment, where intellect has long been privileged over emotions, and IQ (intelligence quotient) has traditionally not included EQ (emotional intelligence quotient). As Jeanne Segal says, "IQ without EQ can get you an A on a test but won't get you ahead in life. . . . EQ's domain is personal and interpersonal relationships; it is responsible for your self-esteem, self-awareness, social sensitivity, and social adaptability."[14]

This example shows that EQ and IQ are essential partners, even in intellectual pursuits. It is useful because it illustrates that cultural differences are not always visible. Though these two groups might look quite similar to outsiders, between them were gaping chasms related to working assumptions and ways of making meaning. Their starting points were different in important ways that played out in the tasks they tried to do. One group believed that meaningful information could be obtained in the laboratory through manipulation of variables. Another group was committed to partnering with study participants, relying on their experience as it related to real cases. Not realizing the extent of their differences, the two groups focused on the tasks at hand, not their relationships or ways of making meaning. They dismissed their feelings until the very negative feelings they wanted to study came between them in their collaboration.

> Faculty members from a psychology department and a peace studies department agreed to conduct a series of joint research projects over three years. The psychology department faculty were well-known for extensive quantitative research projects and prolific publishing. Members of the peace studies faculty had done more qualitative research and tended to use more participative approaches. Together, they wanted to investigate a shared interest—the effects of negative emotions on the styles and strategies of negotiators across cultures.
>
> What they did not realize fully at the beginning was that they themselves were working across substantially different cultures. They spoke different disciplinary languages (the interdisciplinary peace studies faculty members had training in political science, law, and international relations); they thought about research differently; they saw the subjects they were to investigate through completely different lenses. Of course they knew at the outset there would be differences emanating from their backgrounds. But none of them anticipated how difficult or divisive the differences could be.
>
> One of the first conflicts to surface was about research methodology. The psychologists wanted to investigate the effects of negative emotions on negotiations by giving culturally diverse student negotiators in simulations adverse evaluations of their performances. They planned to compound the effects of the adverse evaluations by revealing that independent raters behind one-way mirrors had rated these negotiators

poorly on attractiveness, friendliness, and composure. Then they would ask the same negotiators to role-play another negotiation simulation and measure behavioral differences to see whether the negative feedback had impaired their effectiveness. After the second negotiation, the role-players would be debriefed and told that the negative feedback was contrived.

The peace studies faculty members disagreed with this methodology. They argued for a naturalistic approach involving follow-up interviews with negotiators about the effects of negative emotions on negotiation processes. The second stage of the research would involve participants' viewing a videotape of a mediation, noticing when tactics designed to evoke negative emotions were used, and assessing the effects of these tactics on the people in the tape. Participants in the study would be drawn from a range of cultural backgrounds.

The disagreements did not stop here—they encompassed almost all areas of methodology, research design, and analysis. Conflict surfaced over everything, exhausting both groups as they waded through differences such as whether negative emotional expression was best measured in increments of two or three minutes. The conflicts became more intense, veered toward the personal, and finally reached a wall. In the end, the psychology and the peace studies faculty members conducted their research independently.

Their collaboration had been attended by a convergence of high IQs, but little EQ. EQ would have cued them to attend to the importance of building their relationships with each other, exploring their different starting points and lenses before trying to collaborate on tasks.

Here are a few things third parties can do to stimulate and welcome emotional intelligence in diverse groups:

- Start your own sentences with "I feel . . ." This can be a powerful model, depending on the cultures operating in the group.
- Use a variety of feeling words, not just a thin repertoire.

Encourage others to weave their feelings into conversations, dialogues, and problem solving.

- Name feelings explicitly or implicitly, depending on the cultural communication norms, when you see or sense them operating in a group. Observing and naming anger, frustration, appreciation, disappointment, and so forth gives others a license to clarify, challenge, or expand. When feelings cannot be named explicitly, use metaphors, stories, and rituals to inquire about, emphasize, and express them.

- Inquire further into feelings that are named, normalizing contradictions, complexities, and conflicting feelings, as is done in this statement to an upset daughter leaving for college: "I know you must feel pulled between your attachment to family and your passion to spread your wings and be independent." Recognize that different cultures— family, organizational, disciplinary, ethnic and racial—have different implicit rules about the expression of emotion. Adapt to them, and push the envelope when there is an opening.

- Find ways to talk about feelings that don't sound too "sweet." People for whom feelings are murky, dangerous, or embarrassing may need invitations to "express concerns" rather than "share feelings"; to "expand on where your group is with that" rather than "express how you feel." Depending on the group you are dealing with, you might want to invite emotional expression in more than one way in order to include people with different feeling vocabularies.

- Use activities that highlight positive emotions, like the three minutes of passion exercise described in Chapter Eight, attending to cultural norms about expression and face.

- Ask questions that have a feeling component embedded in them, such as, "What is that like for you?" and, "Can you trace how others' sense of this has changed over time?"

- Don't shrink from the expression of sadness, anger, or other strong emotions in conversation or dialogue. If these elicit discomfort for you or others, find ways to stay with the feelings, while recognizing that they are not the whole picture. Sometimes silence is the most valuable resource for this—allowing a feeling to simply *be* in a group without explaining, exploring, or analyzing it.

Once a group develops comfort with emotional ways of knowing and being, group members are better able to collaborate on research and any number of other goals. As they collaborate, the other practice in this section will help them stay in touch and learn together.

Facilitating Conversational Learning. *Facilitating conversational learning* in diverse groups means paying attention to the spaces where conversations take place and making intentional choices about them. These choices are important in preventing and bridging conflicts, because so many pitfalls, clashes, and unintended miscommunications occur across linguistic and cultural boundaries. Learning comes from conversations when participants give themselves to the process, listening deeply and welcoming feelings— their own and others'. Conversations need safe, receptive spaces to flourish. Participants in learning conversations

- Bring a spirit of inquiry.
- Combine passion with discipline.
- Are candid and respectful.
- Welcome diverse multiple perspectives.
- Ground their conversation in lived experience and stories.
- Listen reflectively to others.
- Acknowledge both cognitive and emotional components of what is said.
- View differences and conflicts as learning opportunities.[15]

Conversational learning can be encouraged and invited through the ways conversational space is set up and unfolded. Facilitators of learning conversations bring a spirit of humility and cultural fluency to their work. Rather than setting themselves above participants, they draw on their own lived experience to communicate common cause with others; give implicit permission for revealing complexities, dilemmas, and vulnerabilities; and model the inclusion of emotions in conversations. Mindful of the importance of safe conversational space, they help groups develop the capacity to talk about difficult topics in ways that communicate respect for different ideas and starting points.

Effective facilitators of learning conversations are also aware of their own cultural starting points. As Ann Baker points out, cultures give messages about space that shape our ideas of what is natural, appropriate, and normal in conversation. Westerners tend to focus on objects within a space, while those from other cultures focus more on the spaces in between. Paying attention in their way, Westerners tend to fill up conversational space with more objects, or words, and to regard silence or inaction as empty. Viewed from other cultural starting points, however, silence may be an open space for people to move into, a clean space cleared of the negative positions and hurt that have come before.[16]

A comfortable balance of silence and talk is only one of the cultural dimensions of conversation. Cultural starting points also influence many other factors, including whether participants come to conversations with ideas of absolute truth or multiple realities, rushed or relaxed attitudes to time and turn taking, primary identification as individuals or group members, and a focus on pragmatic specifics or broad-brush generalizations. Awareness of diverse starting points is essential for the culturally fluent facilitator, who can influence pacing, setting, sequencing, and other aspects of conversation to accommodate a broad range of communication styles and preferences.

As facilitators bring cultural fluency and conflict fluency to their work, the conversational process resembles a circle of inclusion rather than isolated clusters with the facilitator stretched among them. Progress in learning conversations can be subtle yet significant, as was the case in a class on cultural dimensions of conflict.

A graduate class in an American university was focused on the ways racial and cultural identities play out in conflict. Of the twenty-five students, five were black, three Asian, four Hispanic, and thirteen white. About half were women. Class members ranged in age from twenty-five to sixty-nine. The professor was a white woman. The participants were from many countries and had diverse backgrounds, and it was early in the semester. The discussion of cultural and racial identities was not abstract or theoretical for them. It evoked lived experiences of exclusion, pain, insult, and injustice for many of the students of color. Some of the white students carried resentment about perceived preferential treatment given to people of color. They all walked in a thicket charged with tensions, unhealed angst, and apprehension carried forward from the wider world.

The dialogue described here took place after the class members had collaboratively developed an intention for their work together that emphasized respect, people speaking from their own experience, and candor. Lori, a white student, used a racial pejorative as she was summarizing something she had read. She was challenged by Lavinia, a black student, who suggested her use of the term was provocative and unnecessary. The ensuing conversation centered on language and labeling, exploring questions like these:

- Do offensive terms reinjure even when they are quoted?
- Who gets to decide which terms are offensive and which are not?
- What is the effect when members of a group use terms in reference to themselves that would be offensive if outsiders used them?
- How should a group respond when there is disagreement about which language can be used and by whom?
- How can conversational freedom be balanced with boundaries that promote respectful language?

Even as the conversation broadened to include several class members and perspectives, it got more heated. Lavinia got increasingly angry as Lori defended her action, insisting that she had intended no injury in her reference to someone else's use of a pejorative term. Others contributed their views, some preferring an atmosphere where participants are relatively unfettered in their choice of words as long as their respectful intention is clear and others wanting more limits. After a time there was silence. Resisting the urge to break it, the professor sat with the silence as did the participants.

Seconds passed, then minutes. Then Lavinia spoke. The emotion in her voice was strong as she related the first time she heard the pejorative label when she was a young girl. She related the story of how she had been jeered on the way to class that day by a passing motorist for no apparent reason. She said she was tired. Finally, Lavinia faced Lori with an unwavering look that did not capitulate, yet was clean of the judgment and blame that characterized their earlier exchanges.

More minutes passed. Someone suggested a break. As people got up, Lori and Lavinia talked together. Lori later reflected that she was better able to listen when Lavinia told her story than when she was blaming and demanding that Lori change. Lavinia's story was simply her experience—it provided a window through which others could see Lavinia as she made sense of the world and as the world made sense of her. In the story there was no controversy. Choices became clearer— choices Lavinia had made about the world in response to her experience, and choices the world made about Lavinia without any input or action from her.

Lori and Lavinia still disagreed about acceptable limits on language. They disagreed on the extent to which history should dictate present comfort with particular words. Yet they became constructive participants in ongoing conversations, supported by the safe space in the group to express feelings honestly, referencing their own experience. As each had stopped trying to change the other, empathy and compassion came into the space once occupied by anger. With a spirit of inquiry, they checked in with each other from time to time about particular words and their effect. During the semester, Lavinia heard more of Lori's experiences that had led to her fierce attachment to values of free expression.

The group had passed an important milestone, recognizing that conversation was less about changing each other than hearing each other into speech. What contributed to this realization? Lavinia's story, with its genuine emotion, marked a shift. The questions the group was considering became contextualized and connected to real events, feelings, and people. Group members learned more about each other, as other stories were shared in the wake of Lavinia's. They realized through this conversation and the conflicts within it that respect meant different things to different members of the group. Rather than encouraging them to agree on one meaning of respect, the professor helped them make room for multiple understandings. Rather than making inflexible rules about language, they recommitted to a spirit of inquiry and to considering others' feelings when choosing words.

Although this conflict in the classroom centered mainly around Lavinia and Lori, it was also about the groups to which they belonged. Group stories play out in interpersonal transactions, and these transactions ripple onto the larger stage of group relations. This group experience changed the way Lavinia and Lori perceived each other and interrupted some of their negative images of each other's group. Over the course of the semester they developed more complex understandings of race and its dynamics through listening with a spirit of inquiry and choosing openness even when their reflexes screamed to shut down, defend, and deflect.

Many other aspects of the group experience contributed to these outcomes. Envisioning conversations as spaces for learning is a powerful frame, a frame that rests on trust. Facilitators of learning conversations trust the groups with whom they work and the inherent wisdom of the participants. They trust lived experience when it is expressed with genuineness. They cultivate comfort with silence and work to include multiple starting points in the substance and process of conversations. They strive for balance, recognizing that drawing on many ways of knowing brings wisdom, strength, and resilience to conversations.

Practices That Draw on Somatic Intelligence

Bridging conflict involves change and learning. An important question follows from this: what conditions most support learning and change across groups? The visionary psychologist Carl Rogers described significant learning in this way: "*It has a quality of personal involvement*—the whole person in both his feeling and cognitive aspects being *in* the learning event. *It is self-initiated*. Even when the impetus or stimulus comes from the outside, the sense of discovery, of reaching out, of grasping and comprehending, comes from within. *It is pervasive*. It makes a difference in the behavior, attitudes, perhaps even the personality of the learner. . . . The locus of evaluation . . . resides definitely in the learner. *Its essence is meaning.*"[17]

Meaningful personal involvement is accentuated and apt to be remembered when it has a physical component. In each of the two practices presented here, this physical component is present. Outdoor adventure learning builds on the capacities of our bodies to teach us about ourselves, our interdependence, and our limits. Participatory action research involves researchers and participants in a seamless, circle of engaged collaboration, jointly making decisions and taking active steps to ameliorate conflicts and injustices. Learning through adventure and applying participatory action research are explored here.

Learning Through Adventure. *Learning through adventure* is as it sounds—groups share physical excursions that engage, stimulate, and challenge, and then the group members reflect on their experiences. These adventures are rich with learning because they connect physical, feeling, thinking, and intuiting selves; physical experiences are among the most vivid ways to learn. Bring to mind a time you were burned, stepped into icy water, or first tasted a delicious or repugnant food to bring back a whole set of impressions. When physical experiences and challenges are shared, deep bonds may form between participants.

These experiences are particularly compelling for multicultural groups. We all have physical bodies, and using them as we collaborate on an external goal like climbing a mountain, crossing a stream, or dogsledding across the Arctic is a powerful way to learn about working together—and the differences and similarities that surface in the process. These experiences evoke a range of emotions, from fear to excitement to awe, and because the emotions are linked to a physical challenge, they are not easy to push aside like a passing feeling or sensation in a meeting. They also teach high levels of responsibility, both personal and interpersonal. When survival, or at least making it to camp for the next meal, is at stake, responsibility looms large.

One of the things adventure learning teaches is that it is often impossible to skirt unpleasant or undesirable things—whether muddy stretches of trail, stinging cold rivers, or negative emotions like fear or anger in conflict. The way out of these situations, in many instances, is through. Laura Evans, author of *The Climb of My Life,* puts it like this: "The only way to get stronger in the face of fear is to move through that fear. . . . Fear of anything—of heights, of dying, of failure—is what will hold you back. You've got to admit it, deal with it, and transcend it."[18] Laura Evans did this herself, recovering from treatment for advanced breast cancer to lead a team of seventeen breast cancer survivors to the top of Argentina's Aconcagua mountain, the highest peak in the Western Hemisphere, at 22,841 feet.[19]

Does adventure learning work well in different cultural contexts? Alvin Ng, a business studies lecturer in Wellington, New Zealand, wanted to find out. Knowing that adventure learning had been used successfully in the United States, Britain, and Australia to help diverse teams work effectively together, Ng wondered whether teams in societies with communitarian, or collectivist, starting points would experience the same kinds of results. He studied 350 people who had been through adventure learning programs in Singapore. His findings were that participants with collectivist starting points experience smaller, though still positive changes in attitude through their participation. Why the smaller increase? Ng believes that it is because collectivist starting points set a higher "group attitudinal base, which in turn, naturally limited the amount of possible improvements when compared against similar results from the West."[20]

Adventure learning has been used with superb results with groups of managers from many regions of the world.

> A colleague took a group of managers from one organization but from different countries on a weeklong trek. Some were from the United States, others from Asia and South Asia. As they walked, they talked about both big-picture and particular aspects of their work. They also reflected on many other aspects of their lives, broadening the depth and complexity of their understandings of each other and their passions. Connections were made among people, new ideas were born, and conflicts resolved as they shared the physical challenges of washed-out bridges, incessant rain, heavy packs, and magnificent vistas.

Reflection was a daily ritual—evening campfires were times for looking back over the day and naming insights, feelings, observations, and curiosities. Nothing was hurried—there were no phones, e-mails, or errands to attend to. In the rhythm of the natural world, their rhythms changed too, and they experienced the profound impact of moments spent in deep listening with no other agenda. Not only did they gain personally from the respite from daily routine afforded by this adventure, but their attitudes improved and their optimism about being able to work out future differences increased.

On the forest trail, communication differences caused this diverse group of managers less anxiety than they had aroused in other settings. The managers could maintain a spirit of inquiry more easily than they could when a deadline was in danger of being missed back at the office. In this environment, differences were explored more fully and resolutions achieved more completely because the resources of others in the group were available to support and assist. The managers learned about each other's "soft spots," "Achilles' heels," and "painful scars"—both their physical and psychic manifestations—through physical challenges and dialogues. This learning changed them and how they saw each other and their respective divisions and departments and increased their commitment to the team.

Another somatic practice that supports reflection and change is participatory action research.

Applying Participatory Action Research. *Participatory action research* (PAR) was developed by social psychologist Kurt Lewin to bring people with shared values about social justice together to understand group and intergroup dynamics.[21] PAR is useful in building cultural understanding because it brings outsiders and insiders into partnership, with a focus on change and action. By working together, group members and external partners develop fuller pictures of conflict issues and divergent worldviews as a basis for effective intervention. As a team, they engage in a cyclical process of formulating questions, deciding on approaches, gathering data, acting on findings, and reflecting in ways that lead to new questions and action for change.

In PAR it is recognized that social research involves more variables than can be controlled and that researchers always affect their subjects and the variables studied as they study them. It is significant that this family of approaches evolved and developed concurrently across global cultural contexts. Brazilian Paulo Freire's dialogic approach draws on colearning and critical reflection to inform action, while African and Latin American scholars use related approaches to bring about social change.[22]

PAR is a somatic practice because it mobilizes joint action to address concerns or vexing intercultural problems. It actively connects group members to external resources while communicating inherent respect for everyone involved. In place of a fly-in expert coming to study a particular cultural group, PAR involves on-the-ground joint exploration, action planning, and intervention. It has been used in many multicultural settings, in countries including Canada, Australia, and Finland, to improve community health and education, develop information systems, and address schisms between and within groups.[23]

PAR aims to produce knowledge that is directly useful and is often applied in contexts where there has been a history of oppression and prejudice. Because the experience of those involved is valued, PAR raises awareness of options that empower those whose stories have been devalued by others.[24] At the center of PAR is this commitment: to include in the project ongoing questions of equity, justice, and voice for the voiceless. PAR also welcomes the whole circle of experience, not limiting responses to particular forms or prescriptions.

PAR can help prevent conflict when it is employed in the early stages of group projects. Suppose a multicultural team has been assembled to work on the allocation of offices in a large, new building about to reach completion. As everyone knows, this is one of the most contentious tasks any team can face, because office location is not just a physical question but has deep status dimensions and symbolic implications. Wisely, team members begin their work together by investigating the dynamics of healthy diverse teams, grounding the inquiry in their lived experiences. Here are some of the questions generated by the participants:

- What factors create synergy from diversity?
- When a diverse mix of people work together, what resources are needed to help them form a functional team and maintain a sense of unity?
- What are some successful approaches to leadership in diverse teams?
- How can conflict in diverse teams be managed to create opportunities for learning?
- When people with different starting points come together, what structure and opportunities help them develop good communication and shared identities?

To deepen this inquiry, participants first look backward, describing their experiences in somatic terms. What did other well-functioning teams look like, feel like, move like; how were they shaped, and how did the shape evolve? How did they include others in their decision making? Imagining the team as an organism, what nourishment was needed to keep it functioning well? What supports? What opportunities?

These past experiences become somatic anchors, holding the felt reality of synergy and healthy functioning in participants' awareness. From this base, they develop thoughtful approaches to their work that reflect a variety of starting points. As they move forward the PAR process supports them in continuing critical examination of procedures and initiatives. It also focuses the group on the need to gather input from everyone affected as part of the decision-making process. This consultative approach is also a component of practices that draw on connected ways of knowing.

Practices That Draw on Connected Ways of Knowing

Connected ways of knowing ask everyone—facilitators, group members, critics, supporters, and observers to recognize one fundamental reality—that no one operates outside of relationship. Everything we do has effects on those around us, effects both visible and unseen, contemporary and emergent. This is why cultural conflicts need to be addressed constructively: they affect not only the parties involved in them but unforeseen others in unanticipated, potentially devastating ways. Recognizing this, we cannot take refuge in imagined invisibility or insignificance nor shrink from responsibility for the effects of our actions and contributions. It is our privilege and sacred opportunity to collaborate with others to prevent and bridge conflicts, leading us to more insights than we could ever generate individually.

Why is it a sacred opportunity? The word *sacred* relates to our everyday lives, as Mother Teresa knew when she said, "We do not do great things, we do only small things with great love."[25] Whether we are religious or secular, Eastern or Western, we share needs for belonging to each other, to the world, and to core meanings in ourselves that make our lives vital and reveal mystery as the ever-unfolding unknown. To seek answers to questions about our places, paths, and purposes is to live the sacred into being. For most of us most of the time, the answers do not come in thunderbolts or through years of devotion to an ascetic spiritual practice. They come in our relationships and conversations with others—others who are different from us culturally, religiously, racially, by sexual orientation—any number of ways. Talking and being with others is a sacred opportunity because through others come glimpses of genius, of that which is precious, and of the ways we belong to Gibran's image of "life's longing for itself."[26]

Two practices that bring diverse groups together, drawing on connected ways of knowing, are dialoguing and metaphor journeying.

Dialoguing. *Dialoguing* is a family of practices that draws on many ways of knowing. Effective dialogue captures our imagination of what is possible and engages collective intuition. Dialogue lets us into others' worlds in new ways; at its best it is genuine, moving, and life changing. Because of its transformative potential, dialoguing is one of the most important tools for addressing intergroup conflicts. It offers a clear, constructive alternative to confrontation and unproductive patterns of interaction, a very useful thing in the face of distress, anxiety, and conflict escalation.

Many great teachers, leaders, and thinkers have contributed to our understanding of dialogue and its relationship to connected ways of knowing. David Bohm wrote of it as a process through which a group "becomes open to the flow of a larger intelligence."[27] Dialogue makes it possible for a group to access a deeper "pool of common meaning," one beyond the reach of individuals. As groups give themselves to dialogue, "the whole organizes the parts, rather than trying to pull the parts into a whole." This image from Peter Senge's work expresses what happens: "If collective thinking is an ongoing stream, 'thoughts' are like leaves floating on the surface that wash up on the banks. We gather in the leaves, which we experience as 'thoughts.' We misperceive the thoughts as our own, because we fail to see the stream of collective thinking from which they arise."[28]

As I have studied dialogues about abortion, the ordination of homosexuals in churches, and race, I have seen that careful structuring of and preparation for the dialogue are very important. This is critical for dialogue across cultures, where miscommunication is likely to occur—having a clear and reliable structure gives everyone involved a touchstone to rely upon. Clear goals, careful framing, skilled facilitation, and cultural and conflict fluency of leaders and participants are important elements in effective dialogues across differences.

There are many ways to write about and experience dialogue. For our purposes, a *dialogue* is a focused conversation about an issue or situation with agreed process boundaries to which people bring a spirit of inquiry. Process boundaries are set in advance and typically include commitments to speak personally, not on behalf of any group, and to engage with others without an agenda to persuade or convince. Bringing a spirit of inquiry means that participants come with curiosity, suspending judgment as much as possible about others and their values, aims, and attributes. The goal of dialogue is understanding, not agreement. In the quest for understanding, relationships are built and strengthened, and a number of outcomes may follow, including joint action.

As dialogue shows participants to each other in context, they learn about how they make meaning and who they see themselves to be. Dialogue allows a peek into another's logic, stories, and precious values. It asks participants to suspend judgment and any desire to win others over to a particular point of view. It need not dampen advocacy or passion for outcomes; it can proceed parallel to advocacy. Extensive preparation, careful structuring, and well-trained facilitators are essential to effective dialogue. If people involved in conflicts sit down to talk with each other without these resources, they may reproduce the very dance that has escalated the conflict. Dialogue is about having a different conversation.

Dialogue asks honesty and genuineness of participants. It goes where they can go rather than where the ruts in the road of past histories might lead them. Where can talk go after painful history has rutted the roads? Talk can reveal and liberate when grounded in personal stories. Prolife and prochoice advocates, for example, know a great deal about each other's positions; they know less about the personal routes by which their counterparts came to their views. Talking about these life events and how meaning was made of them gives a human face to "the other" that was missing in the bare caricature that stood in for the other previously.[29]

During a series of dialogues about abortion, participants were invited not only to share life stories but also to talk with each other about their heroes and heroines. These figures were often not controversial and were sometimes shared. Nelson Mandela, Martin Luther King Jr., Mahatma Gandhi, and Jane Goodall were named as heroes by participants on both sides in dialogues I observed. Other participants chose family members or people in their communities, explaining what it was about them that they admired. This question took participants directly into connected ways of knowing because it tapped their deep values and their ideas about what is meaningful. As they shared heroes, they came to see each other in the broader context of what each cared about.

Dialogue can be a vehicle for linking practices from all four ways of knowing—imaginative and intuitive, emotional, somatic, and connected. Besides naming heroes, participants can explore aspects of their worldviews by sharing songs, stories, or art in structured ways. In this example, I suggest a way that songs could be used as part of a dialogue about a contentious plan to build a temple in a neighborhood.

In this process, equal numbers of people from the two communities involved meet in small groups with a local pair of facilitators trained in dialogue facilitation. Participants are also matched for status, gender, and generation—for example, a senior figure from one community and her or his counterpart from the other community would be in the same small group whenever possible. They agree not to try to convince or persuade but to listen to each other with a spirit of inquiry. They arrive at the meeting knowing that it will not achieve closure about whether the temple will be built or its scale. Participants are asked in advance to bring a short piece of music that speaks to them and has some relation to an aspect of their ethnic or cultural heritage.

> Prem and Henry are of Indian and German origins, respectively. Both now live in Canada. Prem is part of an Indo-Canadian group that strongly wants to build a temple conveniently located for community members. Henry belongs to a group of mainly European-Canadians who strongly oppose the temple because they are concerned about noise, traffic, and scale. Prem and Henry are in the same small group. Prem brings a tape of Tagore's music (described in an example in Chapter Eight) and plays it for the group. Henry brings a Bach prelude, played on a harpsichord. The other four members of the group also bring music that speaks to them. After each piece of music is played, the person who selected it briefly addresses these points, prompted by the facilitator:
>
> • What is important for people to know about this composer and her or his context (time period, historical events, life events, motivation for writing the music)?
> • What about this music speaks to me?
> • How does this music speak to the kind of community I want to live in?
>
> Others in the group may ask questions about the music or what the speaker has said. These questions should not contain veiled judgments (asking, for example, "Why is the music so jumbled?") but should be questions of genuine curiosity. Questions may be answered by anyone in the group who is familiar with the music played, not only the person who selected it.

As contemplated in this scenario, music may be a window into who we are and what we gravitate toward. As participants in the groups listen to each piece with genuine curiosity, they learn more about the others in context. As they address the ways the music speaks to the kind of community they want to live in, they articulate and hear a set of visions for their community, visions that improve the foundation for working through the substantive questions that divide them. Although this example is imagined, it points the way to the integration of music into a dialogue process.

Sharing music is meant to be just one part of a larger dialogue. Its aims are to humanize and give texture to those involved, building a relational, experiential foundation from which participants can work together to address the substantive issues dividing them. So often people plunge into the substance of issues and aim for agreement but instead find themselves caught by unforeseen cultural missteps or completely different ways of seeing communities and people's places in them. Dialogue cautions that we may have to start slowly to get anywhere, that it is important to build a relational foundation even as we are tackling the substance of a negotiation, especially across cultures.

What if those involved in the conflict don't like music and can't relate to this part of the process? A careful assessment to discern openness and interests should be done up front by the convenors of the dialogue. If participants can't or don't want to share music, there are other ways to open up their understandings of each other. As already suggested, sharing heroes and personal life stories related to the theme of the dialogue broadens people's identities and gives insight into meaning-making. Other ways to bring people together before, after, or during dialogue include sharing a meal; sharing refreshments from a common bowl; going on an excursion; and sharing poetry, books, favorite literary passages, art, proverbs, or cartoons.

Another way into diverse worldviews is through metaphor journeying.

Metaphor Journeying. *Metaphor journeying* is a specific way to use metaphors either as a part of dialogue or in other conflict bridging processes. As discussed in Chapter One, metaphors are literal images that structure human thought processes.[30] Metaphors are embedded in language, framing the way we see conflicts without explicit acknowledgment. When we describe our experience of an intergroup conflict as "fighting a losing battle" or "one side gaining ground," we are using a metaphor that orients our thinking about the conflict in a particular way.

Metaphors are windows into worlds—the parallel, continuously evolving and intertwining worlds in which we live. They are compact, densely packed seeds containing the imprint of our worldviews—what we value, how we order our values, and who we believe ourselves to be relative to others and the world. Because metaphors contain our ideas about relationships and connections to others and to the big picture, they are useful tools for bringing connected ways of knowing into processes. Using metaphors to bridge cultural differences taps imagination and intuition; it also enhances our awareness of cultural and worldview dimensions—our own and others'.

An example of the usefulness of metaphors comes from a conflict over a scholarship.

> The members of a large Canadian organization working for intercultural understanding were in conflict about whether to devote surplus money from a fundraising appeal to an antiracism campaign or a scholarship for a minority student. Some members of the organization (Group A) felt that a scholarship would at least provide tangible assistance while the antiracism campaign might actually generate negative responses and uncertain gains. Others (Group B) wanted to highlight the ongoing racism in their community, countering the image of multicultural harmony that implied ongoing attention to racism was unnecessary.

> To help themselves gain insight into their conflict and resolve it, the organization members shared metaphors for their ideas. Group A chose the image of stars in the sky, with one star shining more brightly than the others. They saw this bright star as the scholarship student—someone who would be a visible leader, giving hope and opening doors for others. The scholarship would be a symbol that magnified the resources of the group. Group B chose the metaphor of a thin layer of ice covering a rutted road like a sheath. Unless the ice is broken, drivers cannot avoid falling into the ruts, and road crews cannot know where to make repairs. The first priority is therefore

to break the ice and make the unevenness of the road apparent so that work can begin. This image spoke to Group B of the racism that lies just under the surface of community policies, structures, and communication patterns, racism that must be continually recognized, named, and addressed.

The metaphors might have been new sites of conflict for group members. Group B was quick to point out that a bright star will not help when you are stuck in a rutted road. Group A countered that a star's impact lasts millions of years and affects as many people while roads can be repaired in the normal course of business. Suspending judgments, members of Groups A and B decided to try introducing the elements of time and perspective into their exploration. They stepped back, envisioning overarching metaphors for contemporary conditions in Canada, conditions their organization was trying to address. One of the groups developed the metaphor of shifting sands. The other group came up with the image of porous clay.[31]

Together the group members journeyed through each metaphor in turn. The shifting sands metaphor symbolized Canada as a nation in flux. While early immigration policies were blatantly racist, contemporary official policies guarantee equality. Even as Canada continues to be a country of many immigrants, newcomers still encounter discriminatory treatment based on skin color and country of origin. Canadians have an image of themselves as tolerant and welcoming, yet visible differences still attract discriminatory responses. All of these conditions are in flux, changing as the mix of people coming into the country changes, political winds shift, and conditions within Canada evolve.

Porous clay is able to absorb many materials without losing its integrity or function. It symbolizes the welcome absorption of those who bring to Canada traditions and wisdom from around the world. Many microscopic creatures inhabit clay, complementing its ability to nourish life; so immigrant groups can retain their distinctiveness without threatening the whole. At the same time, the image of porous clay revealed another side of the Canadian picture: official policies trickle down from the surface but may not reach all the levels of the clay. So official policies do not necessarily guarantee that rights and dignity will be respected.

From their journeys into porous clay and shifting sands, group members directed their attention back to the decision facing them. How could the money be spent in a way that helped the shifting sands move in positive directions? How could the money be used to encourage the distribution of water and nutrients to all strata of the porous soil? This way of framing questions turned the groups' attention to something they agreed on: that the money would be best used as a catalyst to build positive momentum. They agreed that their overarching goal was choosing the option that would give the most leverage.

Building on the generative atmosphere created by their metaphorical journey, organization members came to a decision. The money would be used to fund a scholarship competition for undergraduate students. Applicants would write papers on racism and ways to counteract racism in Canadian society. Scholarships would be awarded at events attended by public officials and community members, raising awareness about racism. Papers would be published in journals and periodicals, further leveraging the investment. Journeying through new metaphors helped organization members make a decision that fit with their vision and reflected their shared values.

Metaphors are rich vehicles for exploration precisely because they have the capacity to reveal values and meaning. If someone says he is coming out of a long, dark tunnel into light in his life, the sensory and feeling components of his experience are highlighted. This metaphor may also reveal an individualist starting point, because it carries with it a sense of isolated bleakness. Offering such a metaphor conveys far more than saying, "I have had a difficult period in my life."

Since metaphors are so expressive, both reflecting what is and suggesting possibilities that can be created, they are useful tools for bridging cultural conflicts. Metaphors assist with analytical exploration; they can also be used to help people move from one place or set of understandings to another. This is metaphor journeying. The following example illustrates how it was used by a facilitator in a large workplace where people had experienced difficult and divisive conflicts over work allocation and remuneration. Because of the large size of the workplace, staff members met initially in groups of thirty.

> The people came into the room with minimal small talk and sat, watchful, in their chairs. There were boundaries between them, boundaries born of painful incidents, inflexible structures that had pitted them against each other, and individual hurts played out in the workplace. They said that one of the most painful things about their workplace was silence. New ideas were met with silence. Directives were met with silence. It was a silence of resignation, apprehension, and despair, not of harmony and peace. The room lit up the most when individuals talked of changing jobs and leaving the large organization.

> Breaking this silence was something they wanted to do, but the frozen atmosphere was habitual by the time the facilitator, Eve, came on the scene. What could be done to begin to broach the differences that divided them? Eve knew from talking with them before the meeting that there were racial, gender, generational, and other differences among them. There was bitterness and resentment about preferential treatment doled out according to gender. There was resistance to talk. One way to work in this place was to begin with silence.

> She asked them to form groups of three. Each person was directed to draw a picture of their workplace in silence. The picture did not have to be literal; it could be symbolic, using images from nature or items from the workplace. No words were to be written on the pictures. Everyone had four minutes to draw an image. When the participants were through, she asked them to pass their images clockwise, to the next person in each circle of three.

> As they passed their pictures, she instructed them to imagine themselves taking on a new role. Instead of staff in the

workplace, they were to be consultants, brought in to help the staff move through the difficulties they were having. Many of these staff members were very experienced. Eve asked them to bring their experience to bear as though they were outsiders invited in, looking for the first time at the images of the workplace before them. Their job was simple: add to or modify the drawing in front of them in a way that indicated how they would help shift or change things in the office.

After they had spent four minutes doing this, Eve asked each person to pass the drawing he or she had just worked on to the person in the circle who had not seen it yet. Again staff were to act as consultants, adding to or modifying the picture in a way that would turn the tide toward amelioration or improvement. Finally, each picture was passed back to its originator. This was the first point at which they could talk. And talk they did—they engaged with each other's pictures, describing, inquiring, interpreting, explaining. A warm buzz filled the room.

The pictures were revealing and surprising. One of the original drawings was of a group of sharks swimming in shallow water. There were a few smaller fish around who were at risk, and the sharks looked menacing and hungry. The first consultant who received this drawing left the sharks and fish as they were but drew a jellyfish at the periphery of the scene. What kind of help could a jellyfish symbolize? The participant explained that the jellyfish was there to protect the others from pernicious outside influences that could hurt them. This brought the larger context of the organization and the marketplace in which they worked into focus, helping them sort out what was theirs and what was attributable to outside influences beyond their control. The discussion of these contextual factors lessened the potency of the tension within the group and built empathy among the members.

The second participant in this group, faced with this image of small fish, sharks, and jellyfish, saw the sharks as dolphins. So she drew more detail on the picture, emphasizing the dolphin fins and putting pleasant expressions on their formerly downturned mouths. She saw the potential for these creatures to be sharks and deliberately worked with them to bring out their dolphinlike qualities. In the debriefing discussion afterward, she explained what she had done. She wanted to create momentum toward positive images and a sense of community. She would do this as a consultant, she explained, by a series of strategic interventions in which staff experienced the benefits of cooperation and felt each other's compassion. Some of the other practices in this chapter, such as adventure learning, were among the tools she would use.

The next step in this exercise was to have each group develop and present three strategies for change that could be implemented in the office, based on insights coming out of each group's drawings. These strategies were to be things within their control, things they could effect in the following four weeks, and things that would not be prohibitively expensive or impractical. The groups then worked together to select several of these strategies, including reinstituting an old practice of having coffee together on Fridays, bringing food to staff meetings, and working together at a charitable organization nearby.

This was the beginning of a much longer intervention, made smooth by the use of metaphors. Metaphoric images made it possible for the issues, communication gaps, and deep differences to be expressed without being individually named or attributed. The metaphors facilitated discussion because the issues, communication problems, and differences did not have to be personalized. Creativity, feelings, and imaginings were summoned by the metaphors. They brought out things that were not in the conscious awareness of the staff. And the drawings made connections among the staff explicit, inventing new connections by the time they had come full circle. The participants had gone on a metaphor journey together and emerged with new ideas and energy and renewed hope about the possibility of deepening their connections.

Metaphor journeying, along with the seven other intergroup practices presented in this chapter, is a relational tool. It helps people explore relationships between and within groups, connecting them to ideas, meanings, and identities. It makes relationships more explicit by giving them a form that can be unpacked and touched even as interpersonal and intergroup dealings have become tainted or tense. The activity of drawing pictures itself communicates the message, "we are in this picture together." Realizing the potential of diverse people belonging to shared pictures is the heart of the work of bridging cultural conflicts.

PART THREE

Standing in Between
Third Parties and
Cultural Conflict

CHAPTER TEN

Third-Party Roles in Cultural Conflict

Walking one snowy day in some open fields I noticed an approaching storm. Before I knew it I was surrounded by swirling snow. Aside from the reassuring contact between my boots and the ground, I could hardly tell which way was up. Familiar markers were missing. Images of a warm fireplace and steaming drink felt more like a cruel fantasy than a reality within reach. Cultural conflict can be like that. When we are enveloped in it, it is difficult to see ways out. Perspective is diminished, accustomed markers are not visible, and the usual rules do not apply. It is then that a third party is welcome, reaching out with heart and hand to help us get oriented and find a generative, safe place to be.

A Montenegrin proverb says that the peacemaker gets two-thirds of the blows.[1] Those who stand in between others are vulnerable to the elements of conflict, just as the parties themselves are. Third parties are the bridge walked on by both sides;[2] they are the boundary between two perspectives and the moat separating the occupants of the castle from the invading force. Third-party roles vary across cultures in the ways they are played and interpreted. They also shift over time as cultural winds change and relationships within cultures evolve.

In our postcolonial world, third parties from outside a cultural setting have no guaranteed acceptability. Cultural norms and expectations affect the selection criteria for third parties, and in many settings, insiders with established relationships with those in conflict may be preferred to outsiders with expertise in conflict resolution processes. Because third parties' credibility is tied to identity as well as capacity, good intentions and expertise in mediation may not be enough to qualify someone as a third party, sometimes called an *intervenor.*

In this chapter we consider how cultural fluency and conflict fluency inform third-party roles. Because third parties are only as effective as the relationships that link them to people in conflict, we examine a range of relational, symbolic tools that third parties can use to augment the capacities and practices presented earlier in the book. Finally, we explore how third parties can build trust and credibility across cultural boundaries.

Relational Resources for Third Parties

Conflict is relational—it engages or repels us, drawing us closer to or further from others. Those who intervene in conflicts become part of a relational system, whether or not they have a stake in the outcome. Mediators, facilitators, and arbitrators have a duty to recognize their part in the relational dance so that their choices are intentional, made with the greatest degree of awareness possible. Though not formally called mediators or facilitators, we all play a helping role in conflicts, often many times a week.

Most often, no formal label is assigned to the person in the middle, the intervenor. The parent helping two children work out a difficulty between them, the manager smoothing resentment in a team, and the neighbor in the middle explaining the neighbors on either side to each other—all these people intervene in conflict as part of their roles and relationships. As they seek to bridge differences between others, their personal conflict fluency will impede or improve their efforts. Those with minimal conflict fluency may seek to mute emotional intensity or restrain expression, unaware that their attempts to manage communication between others stem from their own discomfort with conflict. Those who are fluent with conflict do not back away prematurely but offer a repertoire of ways to engage and learn from it even as they are helping others bridge conflict.

Conflict resolution training and academic programs are taken by thousands of people in many parts of the world. Some of them become mediators or other formal third parties; all of them develop conflict fluency to enhance their life skills and relationships in families, workplaces, and communities. But when conflict is not seen for its cultural underpinnings, then the approaches studied and taught may have limited applicability beyond the academic or community contexts in which they are presented. If our work as intervenors is to have wide practical usefulness, it is important that we understand the interrelationship of cultural fluency and conflict fluency, and it is essential that this confluence infuse teaching and training about conflict intervention.

Culturally fluent people in the middle of conflict know that there is no formula for bridging conflicts, that one size does not fit all. They seek the *cultural common sense* of each person or group involved to inform an approach that will work. Remembering that identity and conflict are often connected, they guard against putting others in situations where their identities may be threatened or feel subject to negotiation. They question their assumptions about how conflict should be named, framed, and tamed, recognizing that assumptions are culturally bound and may not reveal a full range of choices.

The culturally fluent conflict intervenor does not separate dynamics of culture from issues of conflict but focuses on their interrelatedness. She is also mindful of the bigger picture in which conflict and culture intertwine. This bigger picture is made up of what are sometimes called *worldviews*. Everyone exists within his or her own worldview—an invisible, metaphorical sphere that shapes deeper levels of identity, meaning-making, and purpose (see Figure 10.1). Cultural influences and personal habits of attention interact within worldviews, shaping what is seen and not seen, what is valued and disregarded, what is expected and out of bounds, and influencing the whole realm of conflict behaviors and attitudes, including naming, framing, blaming, and taming.

Multiple cultural influences form our worldviews.[3] Mary Clark identifies three domains of culture that our worldviews include: social and moral guidelines, practical knowledge, and transcendent explanations.[4] Practical knowledge refers to shared physical requirements—housing, clothing, and food. Social and moral guidelines relate to shared structures of relationships, including family, kinship, political, and economic patterns. Transcendent explanations refer to the belief system and myths of a society or

Figure 10.1. Worldview, Cultural Identity, and Individual Habits of Attention.

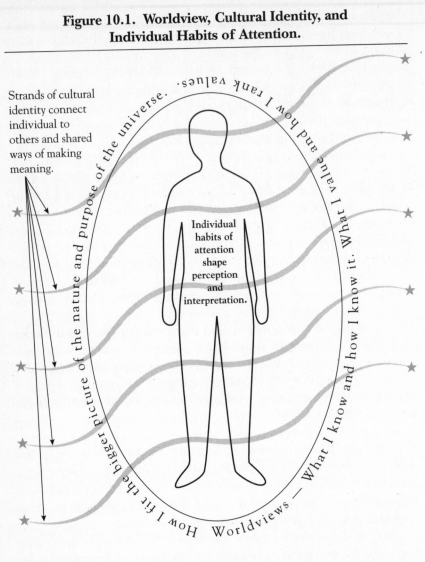

group. These lie deep within the human psyche and are the source of our capacity for coherent, meaningful existence. The importance for conflict intervenors of understanding worldviews is fourfold:

- Since worldviews encompass multiple dimensions of culture, they remind us that cultural fluency is multifaceted and multi-layered and developing it is an ongoing process.

- Because worldviews encompass our Essence—the deepest ways we know and identify ourselves and others—they remind us that spiritual, imaginative, emotional, and somatic channels are involved in our processes of meaning-making. Bridging cultural conflict necessarily calls on us to engage our whole selves.
- Since worldviews are largely unconscious, they remind us that intervention in cultural conflicts requires the use of symbolic tools that reach the unconscious level where we compose our identities and make meaning of ourselves in relation to the world and other people (described in the next section of this chapter).
- Because worldviews shape meanings and identity as expressed by language and behavior, they remind us that there are no culture-neutral ways to think of or respond to conflict. Cultural fluency is thus integral to bridging conflict.

Sometimes worldview spheres bump into each other, creating friction and even explosions; sometimes they coexist peacefully. Culturally fluent people learn to see worldviews as psychics see auras, recognizing that when deep differences divide, superficial approaches will not work. When worldviews clash, with all their submerged potency, relational and symbolic tools are most likely to make a difference.

Relational and Symbolic Tools

Because conflict happens in relationship, it is important to use tools that put relationship front and center in conflict. Because so much of our worldview is submerged, symbolic approaches are needed to engage us where we compose our identities and make meaning. These approaches begin with real people with particular worldviews inside problems, recognizing that all attempts to address conflict need to fit the people and contexts involved. Conflicts unfold as real people transition through problems in ways that make sense to them, drawing on their relational foundation to keep them on course. As they proceed, they attend to the quality of their relationships even as they engage challenges. Conflicts evolve and shift over time; at their center remain relationships.

These relationships may be battered and tattered by lack of attention, undervaluing, or negative projections, or they may be deepened by engagement on many levels—imaginative and intuitive, somatic, emotional, and spiritual. Both possibilities exist.

What would intervenor virtuosity in a relational approach to conflict look like? Virtuosity in bridging cultural conflict is surely a function of the capacity to engage in full and vital relationships. This does not mean smoothing over differences or assuming cultural similarities but recognizing cultural differences for the rich sources of learning they can be. If bridging conflict includes healing relationships as well as resolving issues, then relational and symbolic tools are essential.

Symbolic tools work at the level of relationship because they engage many levels simultaneously, touching those unconscious parts of the self where identities breathe and meaning is made. Because long-standing conflicts become part of identities, problem solving about issues is insufficient. Strategies aimed solely at improving communication are ultimately doomed to fail because they do not address the reason for the miscommunication—different conceptions of identity, negative projections of identity on the other, and dissimilar ways of making meaning. Symbolic tools penetrate the boundaries of worldviews, giving people glimpses into who others may be apart from enemy images, accumulated grievances, and unforgiven wrongs.

Symbolic, relational tools are stories, myths, rituals, and metaphors.[5] Used with intention and awareness, each of these tools conveys the cultural logic of participants in a way that much communication about conflicts may not. Humans have always gravitated to stories that explain themselves to others. Every culture has myths that speak to people's origins, identities, and ideas about human nature. Rituals also occur across cultures, smoothing and marking transitions and emphasizing relationship. Metaphors are embedded in all three of the other tools—animating stories, connecting one realm to another in myths, and lending meaning to rituals.

Stories

Stories contain people in context. They are not controversial but are full of feelings, imaginings, intuitions, and implicit decisions positioning self and other. Stories invite others into worldviews and different cultural ways of seeing. These ways of seeing need not be adopted or taken on board; it is enough that they be understood or received in a spirit of inquiry. Thinking of bridging conflict as an exercise in story cocreation opens up many interesting possibilities.

The groundwork for story cocreation begins with the mutual sharing of stories. When stories are told, choices are made—choices in how characters are portrayed, motivations explained, and closure achieved. Meanings are made public and explicit, and values communicated. Adroit participants in conversations listen for places where meanings become visible, standing out in descriptions of experiences and the interpretations or meanings assigned to them. Putting themselves inside these frames, listeners look at the world through the speaker's eyes, if only for a moment. The effort to do this may be substantial because of built-in resistance born of defensiveness and negative images of others. Yet, when done genuinely, mutual listening to stories encourages emotional intimacy that can help shift even the most stuck conflict dynamics.[6]

As acknowledgment and a deepening sense of each other in the context of cultures and worldviews develops, people find that cocreation of stories becomes possible. Cocreating stories means to find ways of understanding the past, navigating the present, and planning the future that resonate with everyone involved in a conflict. It involves uncovering and acknowledging the cultural frameworks that support our own stories and building more expansive stories from this awareness.

An example of this is related in my earlier book, *Bridging Troubled Waters,* when I describe a conflict in a racially diverse group of students over whether it is possible for third parties to be neutral. As they shared their experiences of intervening in conflict, they heard recurrent themes about privilege, power, and standpoint. Exploring these themes, the students developed a richer language for exploring impartiality and neutrality. Over time they cocreated thicker stories about the ways intervenors stand between those in conflict, recognizing how identity, nonverbal behavior, and cultural assumptions shape dynamics and perceptions of fairness and balance.[7] Students who had argued that neutrality is possible in intercultural conflicts emerged with a deeper appreciation of the ways in which worldviews act as multidimensional filters, making a middle place in conflict difficult to find and maintain. They also learned how stereotypes and assumptions associated with identity can limit the effectiveness of even a highly trained intervenor.

Cocreating stories is a symbolic, relational tool that works at three levels:

- At the personal level, stories can be retold and recast with the assistance of a guide, coach, or friend in ways that make embedded limiting assumptions visible and open to change.
- At the interpersonal level, parties can review and examine stories about their relationship from each person's perspective, with a view to finding a shared story that honors important elements of each set of cultural understandings.
- At the intergroup level, stories each group tells and retells about itself and the other group can be shared as windows into perspectives, values, and worldviews. These stories can form the basis of new, shared stories, cocreated about past events that affected both groups and about visions for the future.

Rituals

Rituals help people recognize the ties that connect them as they experience changes in roles, relationships, and identities. Rituals are times outside of ordinary time; they focus us on our relationships as they connect past, present, and future. Rituals provide containers for feelings, offering ways to acknowledge and share them even as losses, celebrations, or transitions are marked. Rituals connect people across differences, answering an instinctive need to come together when something momentous or profoundly changing happens, whether sad or happy. "The weight of this sad time we must obey, / Speak what we feel, not what we ought to say"[8] is the permission rituals give, liberating participants from everyday patterns of interaction. Marriages, funerals, ordinations, processions, observances of occasions—all of these are rituals that in some way address identity and cultural meanings.[9]

The use of rituals to bridge conflicts occurs in many cultural traditions. Rituals reflect cultural lenses, smoothing and marking transitions in ways that make sense to group members. Rituals are used to smooth transitions in conflict, marking the shift from enemy to friend (as in the signing of a peace treaty), combatant to citizen (as in a transition from civil conflict to democracy), or adversary to family member (as in the marriage of a man and woman from previously feuding clans or families).

Rituals employ symbolic communication to mark or emphasize a set of relationships. When the Centre for Common Ground brought people from both sides of the civil war in Angola together all across the country to simultaneously sing a peace song, a powerful ritual was invoked. Symbolically and literally in the words of the song, the message was sung into being: We are one people. We leave those things behind that divided us. We are hungry for peace.[10]

Rituals assist people in bridging cultural conflict in these ways:

- At the personal level, they help people realize and mark new identities, transitioning for example from refugee to citizen or oppressed to enfranchised individual. Because rituals give implicit permission for feelings, people can acknowledge the losses and gains that accompany transitions in conflicts involving changes in identity and role.

- At the interpersonal level, rituals provide ways for people to come together across differences. Large-scale events like the memorials following the attacks on the World Trade Center and Pentagon and the crash of a hijacked airliner in Pennsylvania on September 11, 2001, and the Bali nightclub bombing on October 12, 2002, draw circles of connection around those who might previously have felt distant or separate. There are many accounts of people of different cultures bonding as they participate in interreligious or secular observances of tragic events.

- At the intergroup level, symbolic acknowledgment of identity change brings people together who were on opposite sides of issues. In many conflicts, including those over abortion and the ordination of homosexuals in churches, participants in dialogue report experiencing dialogue as a ritual. Through talking together in a ways that invite emotional expression and stepping out of usual roles and relationships, a culture of common ground comes into existence alongside the cultures of each group.

Myths

Myths are stories cultural groups tell about themselves and also about others. They may speak to earlier events in history (as creation myths do), attributes of place (as myths of the Western frontier in American history do), or beliefs about people (as the heroic characteristics some ascribe to Christopher Columbus do). These symbolic tales provide windows into worldviews because they highlight relationships and belief systems. Uncovering myths reveals embedded values, ways of being, and ways of seeing. As these values and perceptual filters are uncovered, choice points can be examined and ways forward that respect divergent views of the past devised.

In the absence of shared experiences, one group may create myths about another group. In South Africa during apartheid, cultural groups developed myths about each other emanating from limited contact and stereotypes perpetuated by a system that kept them apart. As contact between groups increased and the structure of separation was dismantled, values that had been projected from one group to another could be examined for their fit or lack of fit through dialogue and shared experience. Exploring myths is also fruitful for the misconceptions it reveals about our own groups and who we see ourselves to be.

At Disneyland, the myth of the American West is communicated in a constructed environment, Frontierland. Visiting it, the assumptions and values that Disney creative designers held about the Western frontier become evident. These interpretations are not necessarily faithful to the views of history held by indigenous people, contemporary scholars, or the early settlers themselves, yet around them has grown an aura of truth. At Frontierland the dominant theme is rugged individualism and individual initiative: the Lone Ranger is the archetypal character. Contemporary historians suggest that that the American West was settled as a result of a "large scale federal presence in the form of troops, infrastructural improvements (roads), and economic incentives such as land grants."[11] In this contemporary view, women had important roles (roles nearly absent from the myths except for symbolic, stereotypical depictions) as did indigenous peoples.

Exploring myths is an important part of inviting multiple voices into the way history is told. In countless conflict situations, myth-making obscures the importance of those who were less powerful or off the radar screen of those telling and retelling the story. Revisiting myths and unpacking the assumptions embedded within them is a powerful way to reimagine history and envision a new future that does not perpetuate myths that exclude and deny the importance of multiple voices.

Of course some myths are more controversial and more connected to threatened identities than others. Extensive groundwork would be needed before exploring myths with groups representing historically divided peoples. It is too easy to dismiss the stories of others as myths while embracing our own as truth. Still, exploring myths is useful in a number of settings where cultural stories have grown up around long-unquestioned assumptions:

- At the personal level, family myths help us understand our identity and ways of making meaning. Excavating family and personal myths can reveal choice points, ways identities were shaped, and cultural influences that were previously obscured. It can also reveal values, cherished parts of identity, and things that family members want to continue to celebrate.
- At the interpersonal level, myths about relationships and roles can be uncovered as they reflect cultural understandings. Myths about past sacrifice (for example, the myth spoken by the parent who tells his child, "When I was your age, I walked five miles to school every day in snow up to my knees") open conversations into past experiences and changing cultural conditions and expectations, whatever degree of truth they represent.
- At the intergroup level, myths about cultural groups can be explored for what they reveal and what they hide. "Men don't cry," "women are sensitive," and the other gender myths found in many cultures are just one example of the many kinds of assumptions that can be aired and challenged to stimulate change.

Metaphors

Metaphors are relational and symbolic tools useful across cultural contexts. They are ways of mapping one set of ideas with another. For example, thoughts about love and conflict are often paired with understandings of journeys and physical movements. We speak of falling in love and out of love, embarking on a relationship, leaping into marriage. We speak of moving through conflict, negotiating rocky terrain, and winning the war of words. As these metaphors are invoked, whole worlds of associations come with them. Some things are possible and other things are precluded because metaphors not only associate clusters of ideas but screen out other kinds of associations. Journey metaphors, for example, have ideas of action and momentum built into them, taking attention away from the value of not making a specific effort or of simply observing what is happening without moving toward a set goal. Similarly, viewing conflict through a set of negative journey metaphors that invoke competition, obstacles, and struggle takes attention away from the possibilities of addressing differences together in ways both seamless and harmonious.

Metaphors can convey the nuances, scope, and limitations of third-party roles across cultural settings. In a recent class, a diverse group of mediators chose the fish tank as a metaphor for their roles. They explained that the fish tank conveys the idea that mediation always happens within a particular setting, responding to and reflecting the conditions in that setting. Within the tank, larger fish sometimes pursue and hurt smaller ones. Other fish in the tank may try to intervene, but often they are unable to prevent damage. The snails in the tank symbolize elders; as the snails clean the tank of algae, so elders clear relational systems through listening and offering advice to those whose vision is limited.

As this metaphor communicates, this diverse group of mediators all saw third-party roles as naturally falling to elders in the community who know the parties and their histories. These mediators were from Zimbabwe, Oman, Guatemala, and Somalia—a wide range of settings—yet, they all found meaning in the metaphor of the fish tank. This metaphor was useful when these mediators later met with some American counterparts. Through dialogue about the metaphor, questions were generated, such as, "Can outsiders usefully enter the tank to help with conflict and leave again?" "What happens if the outsider upsets some of the relationships among residents of the tank—who will fix the damage left in the outsider's wake?"

This use of metaphor illustrates its evocative potential to engage people in reflection on third-party roles. Metaphors are also useful tools for third parties both as windows into participants' worldviews and as nonthreatening ways to direct attention to change. They open the possibility of pairing new kinds of associations with old ideas, creating new vistas and options for future relationships.

- At the personal level, metaphors help us see how we are constructing understandings of ourselves and what avenues of action are open to us. Changing metaphors reveals new choices, as discussed in the practice of shapeshifting in Chapter Seven.
- At the interpersonal level, metaphors provide ways to convey sensed and felt meanings about events and situations to others. When choices of metaphors are explicit, new metaphors can be developed that more closely mirror shared experience or that draw on imagination to see ways of moving forward. When third parties are working across cultures, careful explanations of metaphors—showing how they work and giving specific examples—is important to their effective use.
- At the intergroup level, metaphors help groups uncover a sense of the whole, or the gestalt, shared by group members. Metaphor journeying, a practice described in Chapter Nine, helps groups move forward once group metaphors have been revealed.

Each of these tools—story, ritual, myth, and metaphor—gives us glimpses of worldviews and the choices they contain. Used with attention to cultural starting points for communication (high- or low-context), and relationship orientation (individualist or communitarian), they significantly expand intervenors' resources for creating understanding that can lead to deep and lasting change.

Effectiveness and Credibility of Third Parties

In addition to these relational and symbolic tools, what else is needed by those who aspire to help individuals and groups bridge differences across cultures? As outlined in Chapters Two, Three, Four, and Five, the capacities of conflict fluency, cultural fluency, and mindful awareness are important aspects of effectiveness. Dynamic engagement, the approach to working through conflict presented in Chapter Six, emphasizes the importance of recognizing that appropriate ways to engage conflict differ across cultural contexts. Applying this approach and other naturalistic ways of intervening in conflict helps intervenors to build an experience bank of ways through differences.

Chapters Seven through Nine present practices that support the use of multiple ways of knowing—intuitive and imaginative, emotional, somatic, and spiritual—to bridge intercultural conflicts. These practices and capacities inform the relational and symbolic tools presented earlier in this chapter. One more resource remains. I call it *relational adeptness*. It is characterized by *collaboration, genuineness, creativity, reflectiveness, sensitivity, humility,* and *congruence*. When the capacities, practices, and tools described in this book are married with caring, relational adeptness results. Relational adeptness has two components: effectiveness and credibility.

Effectiveness

What does being effective as an intervenor in cultural conflict look like? To be effective is to

- Partner *collaboratively* with those involved in the conflict, acknowledging their experience and sense-making capacities, sharing your experiences and awareness, and making decisions that respect cultural needs, perspectives, and ways of making meaning.
- Engage *genuinely* with others, using yourself as a bridge rather than imaging yourself as a distant deus ex machina,[12] descending from on high to bring instant resolutions to conflicts.
- *Creatively* envision multiple ways forward in any situation, drawing on intuition and imagination—shared and individual. Partner when possible with intervenors who bring different cultural understandings and symbolize different identities. It can be difficult, but the learning is worth it.
- *Reflectively* observe and evaluate processes as you engage in conversation with people involved in the conflict, uninvolved colleagues, and cultural informants. Practice moving from the immediate moment to the metalevel and back, holding both levels of attention almost simultaneously. Engage participants

in reflecting with you—invite and revel in their wisdom and insights.

- *Sensitively* employ cultural fluency and conflict fluency to assess your role in relational dynamics during and after each interaction. Ask yourself what worked well, what could have been done differently, what the climate was like and how a more constructive climate might have been achieved, and whether people's cultural common sense was respected. Were bridges built between different ways of making meaning, and was a range of ways of knowing welcomed and employed by you and others?

- *Humbly* remember that you will never comprehensively understand a particular cultural group or an individual from that group. Check with cultural informants to help you anticipate cultural faux pas, understand unstated values and assumptions held by those in conflict, and reveal places where you are uncertain or need more information.

- Check that your behaviors, stated intentions, and values match *congruently*. If you profess cultural sensitivity but demonstrate disregard for differences, your effectiveness will be limited.

Effectiveness is impaired when intervenors

- Fly in and fly out of cultural contexts without sufficient attention to forming relationships or exploring how culture relates to third-party roles, setting, timing, and other variables, seeking to help in ways that are culturally bound and leaving it to recipients of the help to adapt it to their cultural contexts.

- Pack their schedules with doing at the expense of being. Listening, reflecting, and discerning are essential parts of effectiveness that require receptivity and stillness from intervenors.

- Focus on outcome at the expense of process, or process at the expense of outcome. Balance is essential.

- View culture as a compartmentalized unit that can be checked off like a discrete skill or topic, unconnected to other parts of conflict and conflict resolution.

- Use artificial methods for teaching others how to intervene in conflict or those in conflict how to move constructively forward. Role-plays and cultural simulations have their places, but working with them is often less powerful than working with real situations that carry emotional currency and cultural vibrancy.

- Privilege one set of cultural starting points as normal, arraying all others as alternatives that are sometimes drawn upon for variety or novelty.
- Develop a repertoire of cultural generalizations that are applied wholesale to any member of a cultural group.
- Imagine that culture is static, fully knowable, or reducible to a chart or a diagram. Imagine that culture exists without people and human choices, feelings, meanings, and actions.
- Get so overwhelmed by the complexity of culture that they decide to do what they do, and let others figure out the cultural dimension.
- Are deceived by the apparent similarity of cultures with a common language, assuming, for example, that Americans, Australians, Canadians, and the British or that the Portuguese and Brazilians are more culturally alike than they are. Each of these groups uses its primary language somewhat differently, and outsiders who assume cultural similarity may make themselves blind to cultural differences.
- Stop exploring. Cultural fluency and conflict fluency are ongoing processes, not destinations.

Credibility

According to a founder of the field of intercultural communication, George Renwick, there are five sources of credibility for those doing intercultural work: inherent, conferred, expert, congruent, and contribution.[13] Although these sources of credibility are understood and assessed differently across cultural contexts, each is an important component. The sources of credibility are interconnected—it is not enough to have one or two of them and ignore the others. What do these five kinds of credibility look like for intervenors in conflicts across cultures?

- *Inherent* credibility speaks to attributes like gender, generation, and nationality. These are out of our control yet relevant to others' perceptions of our acceptability as intervenors. We ignore them at our peril. In cultural contexts where men, elders, or members of particular ethnic groups are preferred intervenors, others (like women, younger people, and members of different ethnic groups) need to collaboratively engage the issue of inherent credibility with those involved. An assumption that your values about equity or other forms of credibility take precedence has the potential to limit credibility and effectiveness.

- *Conferred* credibility arises from educational credentials, association with respected mentors or people of high status, and recognition by respected bodies. The value attributed to such sources of credibility varies across cultural groups. In high-context settings, people tend to put more emphasis on introductions by high-status individuals and on relationship building than they do on professional accomplishments and task achievement.
- *Expert* credibility grows out of linguistic fluency, conflict fluency, and cultural fluency. It means to have a broad repertoire of tools and a set of practices that supports effectiveness at the personal, interpersonal, and intergroup levels. Many third parties concentrate on this kind of credibility but take their tools for bridging conflict from a particular cultural context, without considering applicability across cultural boundaries. It is important for intervenors to develop cultural fluency and conflict fluency as integral parts of their expertise.
- *Congruent* credibility is achieved when the intervenor's values fit with those of the people in conflict and when the intervenor's professed philosophy and behaviors match. This kind of credibility is very important, as the phrase "actions speak louder than words" conveys, though intervenors in cultures where expert credibility is elevated above the other types sometimes erroneously discount it.
- *Contribution* credibility is tied to actual results. Do the contributions of the intervenor make a difference to the groups or individuals in conflict? Do they build the capacity of those in conflict to work together effectively in the future? Evaluation, collaborative reflection, and follow-up over time are important for assessing contribution credibility.

Together, credibility and effectiveness constitute relational adeptness. When effective third parties realize their part in a relational system, they attend to quality relationships and ongoing cultural fluency as a part of their work. When credible third parties invite contributions with creativity and humility, the resources of groups are engaged to contribute to generative solutions. With relationships at the center, boundaries between us and them, between third party and parties, become more fluid, letting more of our human gifts into the aperture through which shared pictures are viewed.

PART FOUR

The Way Forward

CHAPTER ELEVEN

Stepping into Shared Pictures

Realizing our potential to belong to shared pictures is the heart of the work of bridging cultural conflicts. This work is accomplished within, between, and among us. We are always moving, either stepping toward this potential or away from it. It begins inside us as we welcome those parts of us that digress from our comfortable inner habits of perception and meaning-making, inquiring beyond the worlds we know. It continues as we dialogue with the conflicts within us, conflicts born of different cultural identities with contradictory messages about how to be and what to do. Gradually we come to be at home with the unique cultural mix that is always in flux inside us, a mélange of messages from family, race, ethnicity, gender, class, generation, age, place, time in history, sexual orientation, able-bodiedness or disability, discipline, workplace—the list is long and ever-changing.

Our choices to step toward or away from belonging to shared pictures continue in everyday moments. We make respectful, generous choices in responding to others, whether a voice on the phone that tiptoes uncertainly with English, or a family member or student whose ways of making sense of the world are divergent from our own. As managers, we relate to diverse employees not by pretending blindness to difference but by welcoming multiple ways of approaching problems. As community members, we make space for the voice that is not included in the fast-paced forum we attend.

Ultimately, individual choices become reflected in larger societal and governmental choices. These choices play out on the world stage, where pictures of enmity and evil are advanced about a changing parade of others, fueling fear and separation. Compassionate and generous choices create positive momentum, as United Nations programs to ameliorate child poverty and disease illustrate. Yet those who offer alternative pictures of connection and responsible, mutual relationships among world citizens are too often dismissed, termed romantic or unrealistic. And so the world continues, spinning toward a more technologically advanced, yet humanly bereft, state. Even in the virtual worlds where we increasingly work and play, we are challenged to continue cultivating cultural fluency with insatiable curiosity about people in all of their humanness.

As we develop cultural fluency we encounter new complications. It is not easy to move forward, true to deeply held values, while also remaining open to others. Gathering resources to transcend the differences that so clearly mark the canyons that divide us requires energy, discernment, and attention. With all our good intentions and small successes along the way, conflict still reaches out to enmesh us and others dear to us. It touches us at our centers, challenging the ways we make meaning and compose our ongoing identities. In the end, it is the heart that leads, showing ways to resolution.

Following the Heart's Lead

In Graham Greene's *Monsignor Quixote*,[1] an old, demented priest performs a pantomimed communion in a Mass from an altar where he no longer has real authority. As the priest makes the motion of offering a mimed wafer to an imagined communicant, a real communicant offers his tongue. He is Sando Panza, the former Communist mayor who opposed Monsignor Quixote at every turn. This act carries symbolic power because there is not even a wafer between Quixote's finger and the tongue that had previously argued against the priest's perspectives. In this act is an acknowledgment of shared humanity, a gesture of compassion and reconciliation.

The novel traces the journey of the priest and the ex-mayor through Spain, a journey both real and symbolic, in which faith and skepticism play out in braided opposition. Ultimately, the power of beliefs and dreams is clear, even in the midst of uncertainty, relentless opposition, and worldview differences. Even though following dreams may exact a high cost, it is a better alternative than giving in to despair and resignation. And so we continue, engaging the differences that inhabit our everyday lives. We do this by building capacities for conflict fluency and cultural fluency—increasingly coming to understand conflict dynamics, following conflicts' cultural topography the way a mountaineer finds passes that connect one range to the next.

As we become fluent with conflict, recognizing its potential to enhance learning and precipitate positive change, we see that the workings of culture are omnipresent. Culture is there under the surface, like the rules of grammar and diction within a text, giving form, shape, and meaning to interactions. Conflict and culture dynamically influence each other in inseparable ways, and cultural fluency makes starting points and currencies visible and expands possibilities when options seem limited. Conflict fluency, comfort with conflict even as it evokes strong emotions and knocks on the door of what we hold precious, enables cultural awareness and the creativity born of multiple perspectives to be ready resources when differences arise.

When faced with conflict, we practice mindful awareness in both our actions and the spirits with which we infuse them. It is not enough to have good skills if they are not exercised with spirits of generosity, openness, and inquiry. Dynamic engagement means to engage multiple parts of ourselves and others in devising new ways forward. It is to make mindful, culturally appropriate choices, eschewing prescriptions and formulas in favor of collaboration and creativity. A range of practices at the personal, interpersonal, and intergroup levels prepares us for challenges and gives us inspiration for engaging differences when we are in the thick of them.

Developing capacities and incorporating creative practices is an inside job—we begin with ourselves. As we increase our awareness and broaden our repertoire of choices in conflict, we have more to offer others. Mindful that cultural differences are intricately and deeply bound up with naming, framing, blaming, and taming conflict, we seek to make cultural lenses—our own and others'—a visible part of the learning conflict offers.

Continuing Questions

As we find ourselves in new situations, we inevitably encounter challenges and questions. Some of the questions have no easy answers but tap on our shoulders insistently, wanting to ride along on our journeys of contention and our times of connection. They are both big-picture and particular, paradoxical and simple. They have international and local applications. New relations to these questions continue to be born as our creativity tugs in two directions at once. Creativity advances our capacities to grow, connect, and advance while it also adds to our ways to deter, destroy, and damage those we disagree with. The capacities and practices in this book will help us address these challenges as they run through the personal to the local and global levels.

The challenges stretch us. They ask us to delve into our intuitions, imaginations, and reservoirs of hope. They ask us to work locally and interpersonally, with an eye on the global stage at the same time. The following challenges present themselves.

Choosing to Honor All Experience

How can we make choices and judgments in ways that acknowledge multiple starting points yet remain grounded in our lived experience and respect deep-seated values? Our experience as it informs our identities and the ways we make meaning is a vital touchstone. Dialogues help us articulate our experience and listen to others' experience in context in ways that replace enemy images with complex and caring faces. As we engage others with a commitment to honor all experience—theirs and ours—a third culture may emerge where our differences are not the only focus of attention. When we work from this third culture, we can make more inclusive choices and informed judgments.

- *At the local level,* a culture of common ground emerges in dialogues about a range of divisive issues from abortion to tobacco. People who participate in dialogues report that they maintain their commitment to advocacy but also develop caring relationships with their adversaries. As they come to belong to each other and to the quest for peaceful engagement across differences, they become part of a culture of common ground.

- *At the global level,* peace and reconciliation processes seek to contain stories of grief, loss, and anger as people address justice and their collective need to move on. These processes have mainly taken place within countries (the Truth and Reconciliation Commission in South Africa is the best known example), but there are moves to implement such processes between countries and also between regions in partitioned countries as part of peace-building efforts. Even in situations of ongoing active conflict, dialogue is promoted by interfaith and intercommunal organizations.

Choosing to Listen

Given that cultural ways of being are intertwined with power and privilege, how can we counteract cultural influences that disempower and silence the voices of those outside dominant groups? Deep, respectful, and proactive listening is part of the answer, as is collaborative work to change organizational and community structures that exclude.

- *At the local level,* many organizations are now having *listening days,* when leaders make themselves available to listen to whatever group members want to say. As feedback gathered at listening days informs policy decisions and structural change, leaders demonstrate conflict fluency. Conflict fluency means not only addressing conflicts well but also preventing them through designing inclusive and responsive systems.
- *At the global level,* technology now offers the possibility of interactive communication across national, ethnic, and class lines. As this technology becomes more widely available, it is increasingly being used to facilitate dialogue and provide direct channels for diverse groups' input into decision making by organizations like Dialogue by Design.[2]

Choosing Shared Standards

Given that we can never fully transcend our cultural lenses, how can we meet at the difficult crossroads of defining and taking action on human rights, social and economic development, war crimes, and justice? How can we work to develop legal and ethical standards that reflect broad consensus and at the same time allow for different starting points or ways of seeing the world? Culturally fluent approaches to these difficult issues include engaging in learning conversations and shared experiences that deepen relationships across difference. In conflict fluent approaches, powerful parties resist the temptation to impose their values and participate in processes that genuinely invite and incorporate a wide range of views. These processes do not ask any party to abandon precious values, but they delve into common ground that supports joint action.

- *At the local level,* this means going outside assumptions about local or indigenous approaches and getting actual information about how these approaches work and how they might be incorporated into shared standards. For example, when a health care program is being designed, information could be gathered about the healing wisdom and practices employed in local ethnocultural communities. When Sikhs' religious practice of wearing turbans becomes an issue in relation to such things as the regulation hats worn by members of police forces or the helmets worn by bicycle riders, an approach fluent both with culture and conflict recognizes the importance of religious practices, requirements of the police force, and safety. Such an approach would take cultural practices, institutional interests, and religious requirements into account while including multiple voices in conversations about the practical dimensions of the issue and in the eventual decision.
- *At the global level,* this means respecting cultural understandings by inviting diverse groups to develop criteria for shared standards and to have input into the standards themselves. The International Criminal Court, which will begin operations

in 2003, is an example of a global initiative to address serious infractions, including war crimes, crimes against humanity, and genocide. The United States originally signed the treaty creating the court but later rescinded its signature, citing a concern to safeguard sovereignty and prevent prosecutions of U.S. service personnel serving in foreign jurisdictions. Conflicts such as these between the United States and other signatories over global initiatives underline the complexity and political dimensions that make choosing shared standards challenging.

Choosing Ways Forward

How do we collectively decide what growth and advancement mean, and how growth, advancement, and development should be handled locally and globally? Culturally fluent ways of involving local and global communities in policy and planning decisions are urgently needed. Cultural fluency and conflict fluency in public processes means designing mechanisms that accommodate diverse starting points rather than privileging dominant approaches to communication and conflict—both prevention and resolution.

- *At the local level,* this means establishing outreach to communities speaking languages other than English, and using respectful ways of gathering and taking into account diverse ideas about the ways human problems should be managed.
- *At the global level,* this challenge is especially pertinent as world attention is turned to combating terrorism. Partnership ultimately leads to greater security than isolation, as history makes clear. Cultural fluency and conflict fluency are needed as partners work together in the quest for global safety and security. The Mayor of Hiroshima, Tadatoshi Akiba, has challenged the United States to work in partnership with others even in the midst of threats, saying, "The United States government has no right to force 'Pax Americana' on us, or to unilaterally determine the fate of the world."[3] These strong words contain

an urgent invitation to dialogue and collaboration in determining ways forward.

Choosing to Care

As we seek to express our cultural identities and group aspirations, how can we maintain awareness of interdependence, attending to those whose cultures or ways of life may be hurt by our efforts? It is challenging to galvanize a group toward a goal while also considering those outside the group who may be hurt by our efforts. This is especially challenging when our group is powerful—then choosing to remember other voices requires commitment to an ethic of care that extends beyond our immediate boundaries, personal and national.

- *At the local level,* choosing to care looks like listening to students in classes or staff in organizations whose views are outside the mainstream, and finding ways to incorporate not only their ideas but their ways of expressing them and relating to others. This means slowing down processes rather than assuming that everyone shares the values of efficiency and speed. It means sitting with resistance, drawing on cultural fluency and conflict fluency to realize that each divergent point of view may contain nuggets important to overall solutions.
- *At the global level,* choosing to care means recognizing the truism that we are only as strong as the weakest of our links. Power is always relative, and small problems ignored may become large conflicts. Cultural fluency means not only understanding our differences but drawing our circles to include constructive engagement with differences and diverse people in our shared pictures.

Choosing Authenticity

How can we help ourselves and others with whom we work to engage differences constructively yet not use culture as a crutch or a stick? What can be done when cultural identities are used to press unfair advantage, silence or shame others, or manipulate situations? There is no blanket solution to this issue, but it must be engaged as our families and communities become more diverse and histories of oppression and victimization play out.

- *At the local level,* this challenge means building trust and relationship in communities as ways of inoculating against manipulative tactics. When manipulative tactics involving culture seem to be part of the picture, genuine inquiry gives people a chance to explain themselves in context. Motivations are not monolithic, and there is often more than one explanation for human behavior. If cultural differences play out in ways that break faith or undermine trust, relationships can take years to rebuild. Cultural fluency means recognizing and working with authentic differences and acting directly or indirectly to counteract the manipulation of difference for personal or political ends.
- *At the global level,* this means genuinely searching for ways to respect cultural differences and challenging traditions that exclude or hurt particular groups. It means recognizing that change is constant and not all cultural traditions should be maintained. Activism and advocacy in cross-cultural partnerships are doing a great deal to advance the situation of women and children around the world. A delicate balance must be sought in which grass-roots and local voices steer initiatives of change in collaboration with global partners. For example, Sudanese women have worked with European partners to find places for themselves at the table of peace negotiations for the future of Sudan, even though a cultural tradition precluded women's involvement.

Of course, not everyone will choose authenticity or an ethic of care in relating to others. Not everyone will agree on what authenticity or an ethic of care means—caring, as well as conflict, looks different across cultural contexts. It is in engaging these challenges that answers will be found. Answers will be uncovered through hard work, the use of multiple ways of knowing, and an absolute commitment to respect for every human being. Answers will emerge, even as the world is in a state of constant change and

cultural boundaries are drawn and redrawn. With mindful awareness, we continue to explore new ways to move forward together,
accessing energy and resilience for the journey.

Belonging to Shared Pictures

As we continue, we draw on multiple resources. The capacities and
practices in this book are like the ropes and crampons that help
climbers achieve height, in partnership with others, so they can get
the full view. But as climbers also know, sometimes sudden storms
roll in during the final ascent, and the much-anticipated view is
completely obscured. Inevitably, questions arise for which we cannot find answers in any book. Conflicts surface that take our breath
away for a moment, and our attention away for longer, pushing us
from equilibrium and testing our resolve to be open and curious.

In these moments, our capacities for cultural fluency and conflict fluency, deepened by mindful awareness and enlivened by a
spirit of creativity, sustain us. Our lived experience of sustaining
connections across differences reminds us that it is possible, again
and again, to live transformation into being. We know it because
we have embodied it. We know it because our very cells rebelled,
straining to keep us defended, but we made a different choice. We
made the choice to walk out of the crowd of people who stood
pointing fingers at the others, made the choice to be uncomfortable, to ask with the curiosity of a child who the other might be.

We did this not out of a sense of self-righteousness but out of
our humanity, listening to the inklings that quietly affirmed that
in all of their strangeness, others were also like us. Still, we remembered that this shared humanity exists alongside real and deep
differences, differences that fuel conflict and limit resolution
to something other than "seeing it my way." We are at once different from others and the same. We belong, in the course of our
lives, to many pictures—to a very large one that encompasses us
all and to many smaller ones that separate us, giving our lives purpose, meaning, flavor, and vibrant color.

Even as conflicts on the world stage threaten to engulf us, we
live our day-to-day lives. We contribute more than we know to the
climate of the relational worlds we inhabit—making them warmer
or colder by our daily choices of openness or insularity. As we, with

others, live answers into being to the questions that vex us, we nurture our hearts to sustain us. Within our hearts beat the messages of culture, the genius of our individual natures, and our longing to belong to all of it—conflicts, challenges, exquisite beauty, love.

In the end, bridging cultural conflict is an art—it is to dance on shifting sands in scenes with others painted by brushes largely out of our control. It is to engage issues of belonging, connecting, and healing, moving out of static pictures and into the wider world where cultures change and identities are constantly becoming. As we reject the negative notion that histories of civilizations divide us hopelessly and inexorably, we breathe heart and life back into synergy, hope, and courage. With commitment and passion, we touch across the boundaries that divide us, and are changed in the process.

NOTES

Chapter One

1. Barber, B. R., and Schulz, A. *Jihad Vs. McWorld: How Globalism and Tribalism Are Reshaping the World.* New York: Ballantine Books, 1996; Friedman, T. L. *The Lexus and the Olive Tree: Understanding Globalization.* New York: Farrar, Straus & Giroux, 2000.
2. Huntington, S. P. *The Clash of Civilizations and the Remaking of World Order.* New York: Simon & Schuster, 1997.
3. Serrano, R. A. "Response to Terror: Hate Crime: Assaults Against Muslims, Arabs Escalating." *Los Angeles Times,* Sept. 28, 2001, sec. A1, p. 19.
4. Clark, M. *In Search of Human Nature.* London: Routledge, 2002, p. 190.
5. Zheng Wang, George Mason University, Institute for Conflict Analysis and Resolution, personal communication, 2002.
6. Cortez, C. *The Children Are Watching: How the Media Teach About Diversity.* New York: Teachers College Press, 2000, p. 90.
7. Bennett, M. "Towards Ethnorelativism: A Developmental Model of Intercultural Sensitivity." In R. M. Paige (ed.), *Education for the Intercultural Experience.* Yarmouth, Me.: Intercultural Press, 1993, p. 11.

Chapter Two

1. Saxe, J. G. *The Blind Men and the Elephant: The Poetical Works of John Godfrey Saxe.* Boston: Houghton Mifflin, 1882, p. 111.
2. The first four traps are described by Morris, C. A. "Conflict and Culture." Paper presented at *Preventing and Resolving Disputes in a University Setting,* July 6–10, 1998, University of Victoria, British Columbia.

3. Bennett, M. "Towards Ethnorelativism: A Developmental Model of Intercultural Sensitivity." In R. M. Paige (ed.), *Education for the Intercultural Experience.* Yarmouth, Me.: Intercultural Press, 1993, p. 19.

4. Kaufmann, A. "The Pro-Choice/Pro-Life Conflict: An Exploratory Study to Understand the Nature of the Conflict and to Develop Constructive Conflict Intervention Designs." Unpublished doctoral dissertation, George Mason University, Institute for Conflict Analysis and Resolution, 1999, p. 171.

5. Hall, E. T. *Beyond Culture.* New York: Doubleday, 1976, p. 14.

6. Novinger, T. *Intercultural Communication: A Practical Guide.* Austin: University of Texas Press, 2001, p. 14.

7. Hall, E. T. *The Dance of Life: The Other Dimension of Time.* New York: Doubleday, 1983, p. 46.

8. Hall, *The Dance of Life,* pp. 47, 52.

9. Moran, R. T., and Abbott, J. *NAFTA: Managing the Cultural Differences.* Houston, Tex.: Gulf, 1994, pp. 1–2.

10. Moran and Abbott, *NAFTA,* pp. 1–2.

11. Hovey, G. "Carter, in Low-Key Greeting to Mexican President, Views Friendship." *New York Times,* Feb. 15, 1977, p. 6.

12. Novinger, *Intercultural Communication,* p. 47.

13. Novinger, *Intercultural Communication,* p. 46.

14. Carbaugh, D. "Competence as Cultural Pragmatics: Reflections on Some Soviet and American Encounters." In R. L. Wiseman and J. Koester (eds.), *Intercultural Communication Competence.* Thousand Oaks, Calif.: Sage, 1993, pp. 168–169.

15. Tannen, D. *You Just Don't Understand: Men and Women in Conversation.* New York: Ballantine Books, 1990, p. 202.

16. Ross, R. *Dancing with a Ghost.* Markham, Ont.: Octopus, 1992, p. 21.

17. Novinger, *Intercultural Communication,* p. 36.

18. Abu-Nimer, M. "Conflict Resolution Training in the Middle East: Lessons to Be Learned." *International Negotiation,* 1998, *3,* 109.

Chapter Three

1. Hall, E. T. *Beyond Culture.* New York: Doubleday, 1976.

2. Novinger, T. *Intercultural Communication: A Practical Guide.* Austin: University of Texas Press, 2001, pp. 58–59.

3. Novinger, *Intercultural Communication,* p. 117.

4. Tannen, D. *You Just Don't Understand: Men and Women in Conversation.* New York: Ballantine Books, 1990, p. 225.

5. Wasilewski, J. H. "Effective Coping and Adaptation in Multiple Cultural Environments in the United States by Native, Hispanic, Black,

and Asian Americans." Unpublished dissertation, University of Southern California, Los Angeles, 1982, explores the use of biographies to reveal cultural starting points.

6. Hampden-Turner, C., and Trompenaars, F. *Building Cross-Cultural Competence: How to Create Wealth from Conflicting Values.* New Haven, Conn.: Yale University Press, 2000, pp. 123–126.

7. Hampden-Turner and Trompenaars, *Building Cross-Cultural Competence,* p. 142.

8. D'Estrée, T. P. "Resolving the Hopi-Navajo Land Dispute: Official and Unofficial Interventions." In M. H. Ross and J. Rothman (eds.), *Theory and Practice in Ethnic Conflict Management.* New York: St. Martin's Press, 1999, p. 121.

9. Fadiman, A. *The Spirit Catches You and You Fall Down: A Hmong Child, Her American Doctors and the Collision of Two Cultures.* New York: Farrar, Straus & Giroux, 1997.

10. Fadiman, *The Spirit Catches You,* p. 257.

11. Treviño, E. B. *My Heart Lies South: The Story of My Mexican Marriage.* New York: Crowell, 1972. Quoted in Novinger, *Intercultural Communication,* p. 100.

12. Novinger, *Intercultural Communication,* p. 88.

13. Augsburger, D. W. *Conflict Mediation Across Cultures: Pathways and Patterns.* Louisville, Ky.: Westminster John Knox Press, 1992, p. 84.

14. Augsburger, *Conflict Mediation Across Cultures,* pp. 137–142.

15. Novinger, *Intercultural Communication,* p. 84.

16. Mastretta, A. *Mal de Amores* [Lovesick]. Mexico, D.F.: Alfaguara, 1997, p. 272. Quoted in and translated by Novinger, *Intercultural Communication,* pp. 110–111.

17. Conze, E. A. *Buddhism: Its Essence and Development.* New York: HarperCollins, 1951, p. 49.

18. Belbutowski, P. M. "Strategic Implications of Cultures in Conflict." *Parameters,* Spring 1996, pp. 32–42.

19. Novinger, *Intercultural Communication,* p. 114.

Chapter Four

1. Arai, T. [Untitled.] Unpublished paper, George Mason University, Institute for Conflict Analysis and Resolution, 2002.

2. Inspired by conversations with Pushpa Iyer, George Mason University, Institute for Conflict Analysis and Resolution, 2002.

3. Venashri Pillay, George Mason University, Institute for Conflict Analysis and Resolution, personal communication, 2002.

4. Pillay, personal communication.

5. Jung, C. G. *Collected Works of C. G. Jung,* Vol. 6: *Psychological Types*

(Bollingen Series XX.1). Princeton, N.J.: Princeton University Press, 1971, pp. 150–165.

6. Myers, I. B., with Myers, P. B. *Gifts Differing.* Palo Alto, Calif.: Consulting Psychologists Press, 1980, pp. 1–5.

7. Palmer, H. *The Enneagram: Understanding Yourself and Others in Your Life.* San Francisco: HarperSanFrancisco, 1990.

8. Dator, J. A. *Cultural Approaches to Conflict Resolution.* Honolulu: University of Hawaii, Hawaii Research Center for Future Studies, 1991. Videotape.

9. Yeats, W. B. "The Circus Animals' Desertion." In R. J. Finneran (ed.), *The Collected Poems of W. B. Yeats.* New York: Macmillan, 1989, p. 348.

10. The Hutterite religious group was founded in the sixteenth century by religious refugees from Switzerland, German, Italy, and Austria. Many settled in Canada in 1918. For more information, see [http://www.hutterites.org].

11. Buber, M. *Between Man and Man.* New York: Macmillan, 1965, pp. 1–2.

12. Magidoff, R. *Yehudi Menuhin.* London: Robert Hale, 1955, p. 231. Quoted in Ferrucci, P. *Inevitable Grace: Breakthroughs in the Lives of Great Men and Women: Guides to Your Self-Realization.* New York: Tarcher/Putnam, 1990, p. 144.

Chapter Five

1. Different scholars refer to these levels using different terms. See Schirch, L. "Ritual Peacebuilding: Creating Contexts Conducive to Conflict Transformation." Unpublished doctoral dissertation, George Mason University, Institute for Conflict Analysis and Resolution, 1999. Schirch uses the terms *material, relational,* and *symbolic* to delineate levels of conflict (p. 14). See also Stone, D., Patton, B., and Heen, S. *Difficult Conversations: How to Discuss What Matters Most.* New York: Penguin Books, 1999. Stone, Patton, and Heen use the terms *what happened, feelings,* and *identity* to refer to conversational dimensions of conflict (pp. 7–8).

2. Adler, P. S. "Pig Wars: Mediating Forest Management Conflicts in Hawaii." *Negotiation Journal,* July 1995, p. 209.

3. Shook, V., and Kwan, L. L. "Ho'oponopono: Straightening Family Relationships in Hawaii." In K. Avruch, P. Black, and J. Scimecca (eds.), *Conflict Resolution: Cross-Cultural Perspectives.* Westport, Conn.: Greenwood Press, 1991, p. 167.

4 Shook and Kwan, "Ho'oponopono," p. 216.

5. Carroll, R. *Cultural Misunderstandings*. Chicago: University of Chicago Press, 1988, p. 23.

6. Carroll, *Cultural Misunderstandings*, p. 25.

7. Dator, J. A. *Cultural Approaches to Conflict Resolution*. Honolulu: University of Hawaii, Hawaii Research Center for Future Studies, 1991. Videotape.

8. Hampden-Turner, C., and Trompenaars, F. *Building Cross-Cultural Competence: How to Create Wealth from Conflicting Values*. New Haven, Conn.: Yale University Press, 2000, p. 45.

9. Hampden-Turner and Trompenaars, *Building Cross-Cultural Competence*, p. 45.

10. White, G. M. "Rhetoric, Reality, and Resolving Conflicts: Disentangling in a Solomon Islands Society." In K. Avruch, P. Black, and J. Scimecca (eds.), *Conflict Resolution: Cross-Cultural Perspectives*. Westport, Conn.: Greenwood Press, 1991.

11. Abu-Nimer, M. "Conflict Resolution Training in the Middle East: Lessons to Be Learned." *International Negotiation*, 1998, *3*, 99–116.

12. Abu-Nimer, M. "Conflict Resolution in an Islamic Context." *Peace and Change*, Jan. 1996, *21*(1), 22–40.

13. Augsburger, D. W. *Conflict Mediation Across Cultures: Pathways and Patterns*. Louisville, Ky.: Westminster John Knox Press, 1992, pp. 137–142.

14. Cockburn, C. *The Space Between Us: Negotiating Gender and National Identities in Conflict*. New York: Zed Books, 1998, p. 87.

15. Lederach, J. P. *Preparing for Peace: Conflict Transformation Across Cultures*. Syracuse, N.Y.: Syracuse University Press, 1995, pp. 19–22.

16. Loy, D. R. "How to Reform a Serial Killer: The Buddhist Approach to Restorative Justice." *Journal of Buddhist Ethics*, 2000, *7*, 145–168.

17. Taylor, D., and Nwosu, P. "Afrocentric Empiricism: A Model for Communication Research in Africa." In V. H. Milhouse, M. K. Asente, and P. O. Nwosu (eds.), *Transcultural Realities: Interdisciplinary Perspectives on Cross-Cultural Relations*. Thousand Oaks, Calif.: Sage, 2001, pp. 299–311.

18. In Canada the federal government issues an identity card, a proof of status, to all First Nations persons. For some years this status could be lost by women who married outside First Nations communities. The law has now been changed and First Nations status has been restored to women who had lost their rights through marriage.

Chapter Six

1. This extended example is drawn from Slaney, K. "Cultural Conflict Experience in Treaty Settlement Negotiations with Two Far North

Iwi (New Zealand)." Unpublished paper, University of Victoria, Institute for Dispute Resolution, 2002, pp. 2–3, 5.

2. Zander, R. S., and Zander, B. *The Art of Possibility: Transforming Professional and Personal Life.* Boston: Harvard Business School Press, 2000, p. 27.
3. Zander and Zander, *The Art of Possibility,* p. 33.
4. LeBaron, M., and Carstarphen, N. "Negotiating Intractable Conflict: The Common Ground Dialogue Process and Abortion." *Negotiation Journal,* 1997, *13*(4), 341–361.

Chapter Seven

1. Venashri Pillay, George Mason University, Institute for Conflict Analysis and Resolution, personal communication, 2002.
2. Richards, M. C. "Separating and Connecting: The Vessel and the Fire." In M. J. Ryan (ed.), *The Fabric of the Future: Women Visionaries Illuminate the Path to Tomorrow.* Berkeley, Calif.: Conari Press, 1998, p. 234.
3. Palmer, H. *The Enneagram: Understanding Yourself and Others in Your Life.* San Francisco: HarperSanFrancisco, 1990.
4. *Skraps* is *sparks* spelled backward. Skraps are things that carry a negative charge. This word comes from a workshop conducted by Ramsey, S., and Smith, J. *Accessing Creative Potential.* Sponsored by the Crestone Institute, Washington, D.C., June 2000.
5. Hyde, L. *Trickster Makes This World.* New York: North Point Press, 1998, p. 9.
6. Basso, E. "The Trickster's Scattered Self." In C. L. Briggs (ed.), *Disorderly Discourse: Narrative, Conflict and Inequality.* New York: Oxford University Press, 1996, p. 56.
7. Hyde, *Trickster Makes This World,* p. 7n.
8. Clay, J. S. *The Politics of Olympus.* Princeton, N.J.: Princeton University Press, 1989, p. 98. Quoted in Hyde, *Trickster Makes This World,* p. 258.
9. Goleman, D. *Emotional Intelligence: Why It Can Matter More Than IQ.* New York: Bantam Books, 1995, p. 36.
10. Pillay, personal communication, 2002.
11. Maslow, A. *Religions, Values and Peak Experiences.* New York: Viking Penguin, 1970, p. x.

Chapter Eight

1. Ross, R. *Returning to the Teachings: Exploring Aboriginal Justice.* Toronto: Penguin Books, 1996, pp. 140–142.
2. Hammer, M., and Bennett, M. *Intercultural Development Inventory.*

[http://www.intercultural.org/idi/idi.html]. 1998; Martin, J. "Intercultural Communication Competence: A Review." In R. L. Wiseman and J. Koester (eds.), *Intercultural Communication Competence*. Thousand Oaks, Calif.: Sage, 1993, pp. 16–29.

3. Carter, J. *Keeping Faith*. New York: Bantam Books, 1982, pp. 392, 399.
4. Muvingi, I. "Family Inheritance Conflict." Unpublished paper, George Mason University, Institute for Conflict Analysis and Resolution, 2002.
5. Schirch, L. "Ritual Peacebuilding: Creating Context Conducive to Conflict Transformation?" Unpublished doctoral dissertation, George Mason Unviversity, Institute for Conflict Analysis and Resolution, 1999.
6. Pillay, V. "South Africa: The Rainbow Nation." Unpublished paper, George Mason University, Institute for Conflict Analysis and Resolution, 2002, p. 1.
7. Sharquieh, I. "The Mountain Cannot Be Shaken Down by the Wind." Unpublished paper, George Mason University, Institute for Conflict Analysis and Resolution, 2002, p. 1.
8. Frankl, V. E. *Man's Search for Meaning*. New York: Pocket Books, 1984.
9. Clark, M. *Ariadne's Thread: The Search for New Modes of Thinking*. New York: St. Martin's Press, 1989, pp. 303, 313.
10. Mitchell, C. *Gestures of Conciliation: Factors Contributing to Successful Olive Branches*. New York: St. Martin's Press, 2000, p. 34.
11. Ackerman, D. *Deep Play*. New York: Vintage Books, 1999, p. 50.
12. Chatwin, B. *The Songlines*. New York: Penguin Books, 1987, p. 108. Quoted in Ackerman, *Deep Play*, pp. 50–51.
13. Tagore, R. "My Song." [http://www.eng.fju.edu.tw/worldlit/india/india_poetry.htm], accessed Oct. 2002.
14. LeBaron, M. *Bridging Troubled Waters: Conflict Resolution from the Heart*. San Francisco: Jossey-Bass, 2002, pp. 23–24.

Chapter Nine

1. "The Online Guide to Traditional Games." [http://boardgames.about.com/gi/dynamic/offsite.htm], accessed Oct. 2002.
2. Davis, E. "Snakes and Ladders." *Gnosis*, Fall 1994, p. 40.
3. Gergen, K. J., McNamee, S., and Barrett, F. J. "Toward Transformative Dialogue." *International Journal of Public Administration*, July 2001, p. 679.
4. Berry, W. *Life Is a Miracle: An Essay Against Modern Superstition*. Washington, D.C.: Counterpoint, 2000, p. 3.

5. Gergen, McNamee, and Barrett, "Toward Transformative Dialogue."

6. Weisbord, M., and Janoff, S. *Future Search: An Action Guide to Finding Common Ground in Organizations and Communities.* San Francisco, Calif.: Berrett-Koehler, 2000, pp. 1–15. See also Owen, H. *Riding the Tiger: Doing Business in a Transforming World.* Potomac, Md.: Abbott, 1991.

7. Grudin, R. *On Dialogue: An Essay in Free Thought.* New York: Houghton Mifflin, 1996, p. 6.

8. Weisbord and Janoff, *Future Search,* p. 13.

9. Weisbord and Janoff, *Future Search,* p. 18.

10. Saxe, J. G. *The Blind Men and the Elephant: The Poetical Works of John Godfrey Saxe.* Boston: Houghton Mifflin, 1882, p. 111.

11. Weisbord and Janoff, *Future Search,* p. 37.

12. Weisbord and Janoff, *Future Search,* p. 42.

13. Segal, J. *Raising Your Emotional Intelligence: A Practical Guide.* New York: Holt, 1997, p. 8.

14. Segal, *Raising Your Emotional Intelligence,* p. 10.

15. Baker, A. C. "Receptive Spaces for Conversational Learning." In A. C. Baker, P. J. Jensen, and D. A. Kolb (eds.), *Conversational Learning: An Experiential Approach to Knowledge Creation.* Westport, Conn.: Quorum Books, 2002, pp. 102–103, 109.

16. Baker, "Receptive Spaces for Conversational Learning," p. 104.

17. Rogers, C. *Freedom to Learn.* Columbus, Ohio: Merrill, 1969.

18. Evans, L. *The Climb of My Life.* San Francisco: HarperSanFrancisco, 1996. Quoted in Graham, J. *Outdoor Leadership: Technique, Common Sense and Self Confidence.* Seattle, Wash.: The Mountaineers, 1997, p. 105.

19. See Expedition Inspiration. [http://www.expeditioninspiration.org], accessed Oct. 2002.

20. Ng, A. *Adventure Learning: Collectivism and Consequent Impact.* [http://masseynews.massey.ac.nz/2000/publications/massey_news/may/may_22/stories/adventure_learning.htm]. 2000.

21. Minkler, M. "Using Participatory Action Research to Build Healthy Communities." *Public Health Reports,* Mar.–June 2000, p. 191. Refers to Lewin, K. "Action Research and Minority Problems." *Journal of Social Issues,* 1946, *2,* 34–36.

22. Minkler, "Using Participatory Action Research." Refers to Hall, B. L. "Participatory Research, Popular Knowledge and Power: A Personal Reflection." *Convergence,* 1981, *14,* 6–17; Fals-Borda, O. "The Application of Participatory Action Research in Latin America." *International Sociology,* 1987, *2,* 329–347.

23. Chataway, C. J. "An Examination of the Constraints on Mutual Inquiry in a Participatory Action Research Project." *Journal of Social Issues,* 1997, *53*(4), 749–767. See also Hughes, I., Goo-

lagong, P., Khavarpour, F., and Russell, C. "Koori Action Research in Community Health." Paper presented to the second Healing Our Spirit Worldwide Conference, Sydney, Nov. 14, 1994; Palmu, M. "Action Research in Finland." In I. Hughes (ed.), *Action Research Electronic Reader* [http://www.behs.cchs.usyd.edu.au/arow/reader/palmu.htm]. 1998.

24. Gatenby, B., and Humphries, M. "Feminist Participatory Action Research: Methodological and Ethical Issues." *Women's International Studies Forum,* 2000, *23*(1), 89.

25. Bender, S. *Everyday Sacred.* San Francisco: HarperSanFrancisco, p. vii.

26. Gibran, K. *The Prophet.* New York: Knopf, 1976.

27. Bohm, D. *On Dialogue.* London: Routledge, 1996. Quoted in Senge, P. *The Fifth Discipline.* New York: Doubleday, 1990, pp. 238–242.

28. Senge, *The Fifth Discipline,* pp. 238–242.

29. For more about abortion dialogues, see LeBaron, M., and Carstarphen, N. "Finding Common Ground on Abortion." In L. Susskind, S. McKearnan, and J. Thomas-Larmer (eds.), *Consensus Building Handbook: A Comprehensive Guide to Reaching Agreement.* Thousand Oaks, Calif.: Sage, 1999.

30. Lakoff, G., and Johnson, M. *Metaphors We Live By.* Chicago: University of Chicago Press, 1980, p. 6.

31. The metaphors of shifting sands and porous clay were elaborated by Karen Bhangoo, George Mason University, Institute for Conflict Analysis and Resolution, in unpublished papers and personal conversations, 2002.

Chapter Ten

1. Augsburger, D. W. *Conflict Mediation Across Cultures: Pathways and Patterns.* Louisville, Ky.: Westminster John Knox Press, 1992, p. 187.

2. Song, C. S. "New Frontiers of Theology in Asia." *South East Asia Journal of Theology,* 1979, *20*(1), 13–33. Quoted in Augsburger, *Conflict Mediation Across Cultures,* p. 187.

3. Worldviews are broader than cultural influences. They encompass cosmology (understandings about the nature and purpose of the universe), axiology (what is valued and how values are ordered), ontology (ways of relating or categorizing ideas), and epistemology (how we know and how we come to distinguish true knowledge from false knowledge).

4. Clark, M. *In Search of Human Nature.* London: Routledge, 2002, p. 190.

5. Schirch, L. "Ritual Peacebuilding: Creating Context Conducive to Conflict Transformation?" Unpublished doctoral dissertation,

George Mason Unviversity, Institute for Conflict Analysis and Resolution, 1999.

6. Volkan, V. "The Tree Model: A Comprehensive Psychopolitical Approach to Unofficial Diplomacy and the Reduction of Ethnic Tension." *Mind and Human Interaction*, 2000, *10*(3), 164.

7. LeBaron, M. *Bridging Troubled Waters: Conflict Resolution from the Heart.* San Francisco: Jossey-Bass, 2002, p. 246.

8. Shakespeare, W. *King Lear* (V, iii, 324–325). In G. B. Evans (ed.), *The Riverside Shakespeare.* Boston: Houghton Mifflin, 1974. Driver, T. *The Magic of Ritual.* San Francisco: HarperSanFrancisco, 1991, p. 5, quotes these lines in relation to ritual.

9. Schirch, L. "Ritual Peacebuilding: Creating Contexts Conducive to Conflict Transformation." Unpublished doctoral dissertation, George Mason University, Institute for Conflict Analysis and Resolution, 1999. Schirch explores rituals as symbolic tools for transforming conflicts.

10. "A Paz é Que O Povo Chama" (a song dedicated to the future of Angola) is performed on the videocassette *Making the Peace Song.* (*Africa: Search for Common Ground,* Program 6: *South Africa/Angola.*) Cape Town: Common Ground Productions and Ubuntu TV and Film, n.d.

11. Francaviglia, R. "Walt Disney's Frontierland as an Allegorical Map of the American West." *Western Historical Quarterly,* Summer 1999, *30*(2), 181–182. Quoted in Slatta, R. W. "Taking Our Myths Seriously: The Western Forum." *Journal of the West,* Summer 2001, *40*(3), 3.

12. The original deus ex machina was a device used in some ancient Greek plays; problems apparently unresolvable by humans were resolved at the play's end by a god from Mount Olympus. The god was brought in from on high by a machine, a crane. The term is now used to refer to contrived resolutions in plays, novels, and films.

13. Renwick, G. "Theory Does Improve Training." In J. Bennett, M. Bennett, and D. Landis (eds.), *Handbook of Intercultural Training* (3rd ed.). Thousand Oaks, Calif.: Sage, forthcoming.

Chapter Eleven

1. Greene, G. *Monsignor Quixote.* New York: Simon & Schuster, 1982, p. 216.

2. See [http://www.dialoguebydesign.com]. This UK-based organization specializes in developing Web-based consultations and participative processes.

3. Struck, D. "Letter from Japan: The View from the Other Ground Zero." *Washington Post,* Oct. 28, 2002, p. C1.

RESOURCES

Public Conversations Project
46 Kondazian St.
Watertown, MA 02472-2832
Phone: 617-923-1216
Fax: 617-923-2757
E-mail: info@publicconversations.org
Web site: www.publicconversations.org

Search for Common Ground
1601 Connecticut Ave. NW
Suite 200
Washington, DC 20009
Phone: 202-265-4300
Fax: 202-232-6718
Web site: www.sfcg.org

Initiatives of Change
1156 15th St. NW
Washington, DC 20005
Phone: 202-872-9077
Fax: 202-872-9137
E-mail: info@us.initiativesofchange.org
Web site: www.us.initiativesofchange.org

Study Circles
PO Box 203
697 Pomfret St.
Pomfret, CT 06258
Phone: 860-928-2616
Fax: 860-928-3713
E-mail: scrc@studycircles.org
Web site: www.studycircles.org

Conflict Research Consortium
University of Colorado
Campus Box 580
Boulder, CO 80309-580
E-mail: burgess@colorado.edu
Phone: 303-492-1635
Fax: 303-492-2154
Web site:
www.conflictresearch.com/crc2000/encyclopedia_of_con_res.htm

Institute for Multitrack Diplomacy
1925 North Lynn Street
12th Floor
Arlington, VA 22209
Phone: 703-528-3863
Fax: 703-528-5776
Web site: www.imtd.org

THE AUTHOR

Michelle LeBaron is professor of conflict analysis and resolution at George Mason University in Fairfax, Virginia. Michelle teaches about conflict, culture, and creativity and writes poetry by the sea. She consults with groups and organizations around the world on issues related to diversity, identity, meaning-making, and spirituality. Michelle is the author of *Bridging Troubled Waters: Conflict Resolution from the Heart* (Jossey-Bass, 2002).

INDEX